BUENOS AIRES

BUENOS AIRES

* Plaza to Suburb, 1870-1910 *

James R. Scobie

New York
Oxford University Press
1974

TO INGRID

Preface

At the outset I confess to my reason for writing a history of this particular city. I have studied Buenos Aires because its evolution symbolizes and explains much of Argentine development. During the latter part of the nineteenth century the expansion of a cereal-meat-wool-hides export economy, dependent on external supplies of capital and labor and on the rising European demand for agricultural products, stimulated astonishing demographic and physical growth of the country's major port and federal capital. The sudden economic prosperity redounded primarily to that city's benefit, not to the development of the rural or hinterland regions of Argentina. From agricultural wealth and external dependency emerged an enduring social and political structure, centered at Buenos Aires, which gave character not only to the city but also to Argentina. The city dominated the nation.[1]

In dealing with as complex and variegated a subject as Buenos Aires, it seems desirable to state what this study does not do, and why. This work does not attempt systematic statistical data analysis on any large scale. It does, however, provide data from censuses and other quantifiable sources, and the general conclusions that emerge will, I hope, lead me and others to further examination, testing, extension, and revision of hypotheses by rigorous study of segments of these data, especially from manuscript census returns.[2] This book does not have a political emphasis, nor does it have chapters that deal with city government or municipal politics. The role of this city as dual capital for province and nation until 1880, the intricacies of national politics (as yet largely unstudied for the period after 1870), and the problem of separating city from nation in the Argentine context make such a project the subject for another book, not for a summary statement. In similar fashion, this study does not examine the folklore of the city, not because sources do not exist, but because the tango, the *compadrito*, and the *arrabal* deserve separate analysis, not an acknowledgment within a socioeconomic interpretation of urban growth. Finally, a wealth of data on facets of the urban experience often presented in city biographies has been omitted. The reams researched and recorded—on urban services such as paving, parks, sewage, police, lighting, and garbage disposal; on the location, regulation, and expansion of industries; on education, public health, morality, and amusements—remain in notes, in large measure because these factors do not seem to alter significantly the patterns selected for emphasis in this study.

The Social Science Research Council, the Guggenheim Foundation, and the International Affairs Center of Indiana University provided financial support for this investigation in 1968–69. To many institutes, libraries, and archives I owe the investigator's principal debt—for the raw materials, for invaluable assistance in finding elusive bits and pieces of information, and for help in putting them in context. My deep thanks go, therefore, to the directors and staffs of the Graduate Library and Lilly Rare Books Library of Indiana University, the General Library of the University of California at Berkeley, and the Hispanic Foundation at the Library of Congress; and in Buenos Aires, to those responsible for the various subdivisions of the Biblioteca Municipal, Biblioteca del Honorable Concejo Deliberante, Biblioteca Nacional, Biblioteca del Congreso, Biblioteca de la Unión Industrial Argentina, Biblioteca del Banco Tornquist, Biblioteca del Instituto Torcuato di Tella, Biblioteca del Banco Hipotecario Nacional, Biblioteca de la Bolsa de Comercio, Biblioteca del Colegio Nacional de Buenos Aires, Biblioteca de *La Prensa*, Biblioteca del Instituto de Investigaciones Históricas Dr. Emilio Ravignani, as well as to the staffs and directors of the archives and map collections at the Museo Mitre, Municipalidad de Buenos Aires,

Dirección de Geodesia de la Provincia de Buenos Aires, Instituto Geográfico Militar, Archivo General de la Nación, and the Archivo Gráfico de la Nación. To several persons who gave generously of their ideas and helped me in specific aspects of the research and writing I owe particular gratitude: Alberto Ciria, Simon Fraser University; Jorge E. Hardoy, Centro de Estudios Urbanos y Regionales of the Instituto Torcuato di Tella; José María Peña, Museo de la Ciudad de Buenos Aires; Aurora Ravina de Luzzi, Buenos Aires; and Hobart A. Spalding, Jr., Brooklyn College. Ingrid Winther Scobie became my coauthor for many sections of this book, and to her, above all, it owes its present appearance. A number of persons, in addition to those mentioned above, have read all or portions of this study: Jeffrey Adelman, Samuel L. Baily, Raquel Ciria, Robert H. Ferrell, Marc J. and Judith Hoffnagel, John V. Lombardi, Brian Loveman, Robert E. Quirk, Ruben E. Reina, Arthur P. Schmidt, Jr., Joseph S. Tulchin, and Mary G. Winther. To them I express my profound thanks for much needed assistance. Three persons helped me enormously with the final product: John M. Hollingsworth, who designed the maps; Margaret Teng, who prepared the index; and Caroline Taylor, who edited the book for Oxford University Press with flair, graciousness, and constant good humor.

J.R.S.

Bloomington, Ind.
May 1974

Contents

List of Illustrations

List of Maps

xvii

BUENOS AIRES

* 1 *

The Setting

The Spanish fleet that tacked up the wide, brown estuary during the hot summer month of January 1536 carried with it the idea of a city. The Crown, in its eagerness to seize strategic positions on the dimly known land mass of America and to secure new riches in gold and silver, had outfitted and dispatched the largest expedition —1500 men—yet seen on the coasts of the New World. But no natural port, hills, or intersecting rivers met the eye, only the vast estuary and the plains reaching back from muddy banks. Nevertheless, the royal charge demanded establishment of a city. After considerable search, the explorers chose a site near the mouth of a meandering stream, later named the Riachuelo, and traced the outline of a plaza. History records little of this first Buenos Aires,* largely because it disappeared after only five years. The remnants of the expedition, beset by hunger and by increasingly hostile Indians, abandoned the precarious base and moved far up-river, to the security and modest prosperity of the little Spanish town at Asunción.

Only the selection of the general area and the name remained from this first foundation. Years later, in 1580, when a small expedition of sixty men, most of them Indian-Spanish mestizos,

---

* Named after an Italian patron saint popular with navigators throughout the Mediterranean, Nuestra Señora Santa María del Buen Aire.

threaded its way down the waterways from Asunción, its leader, Juan de Garay, laid out a settlement a few miles to the north of the original effort. The settlers built a fort, a pile of sun-dried mud bricks, on a slight rise just above water's edge. Today part of the foundations can be seen in the basement at the south side of the Casa Rosada, the presidential office building. In front of the fort, to the west, Garay traced the outline of a square where he planted the "tree of justice," a wooden pole that served as a symbol for punishment and authority. Across this plaza—now known as the Plaza de Mayo—land was allotted for a jail and Cabildo, or municipal council chamber. On the northwest corner of the plaza another lot went for the city's church. Today the foundations of Buenos Aires' first humble church lie under the Cathedral. The city's outline took the form of a gridwork of squares within a rectangle which extended twelve blocks north and south of the fort and ten blocks inland. Forty blocks centered on the plaza were each divided in quarters and assigned as lots to the sixty-four *vecinos*, or principal settlers. Outside this core, vecinos also received larger plots on which they could raise corn, beans, squash, and wheat, as well as forage for their horses. Beyond this bare outline the pampas stretched away endlessly—the habitat of a few nomadic Indian tribes and of increasing numbers of horses, which had been introduced at the time of the first founding of Buenos Aires.

From the start, Garay's little settlement was a commercial and administrative center. Expeditions inland from the first settlement at Buenos Aires and from Asunción had already dispelled dreams of mineral wealth. But on the vast, grassy plains the rapid multiplication of horses, cattle, and sheep introduced from Europe offered another source of wealth. At the same time, Spain needed to protect the outlying reaches of its far-flung empire from rapacious newcomers such as France, Holland, and England. The first and second settlements of Buenos Aires owed much to royal concern that the distant and sparsely inhabited regions of the Río de la Plata not fall into hostile hands, including those of Portugal, which was then expanding southward from the northeast coast of Brazil.

Commercial and administrative activities, nevertheless, had to contend with significant handicaps at Buenos Aires. By 1580 the structure of Spain's empire in the Americas had already taken shape. Centers of commercial power had developed in Lima and Mexico City and in several ports along the Caribbean coast. A southern access to the mineral wealth of Potosí in Upper Peru—later to become Bolivia—promised serious competition to these cities. Fifteen hundred miles, almost all across rugged mountain terrain, separated Potosí from Lima, while three-quarters of the 1200-mile distance from Buenos Aires to Potosí crossed relatively level ground. Getting freight from Lima to Potosí took four months, while only two months were needed to move merchandise from Buenos Aires to Potosí.[1] As a result, the merchant interests of the north used every device and influence to restrict the growth and administrative jurisdiction of Buenos Aires and to keep it a humble village of mud huts, garden plots, and localized commerce. The Crown in 1618 established a customs barrier at Córdoba, 400 miles northwest of Buenos Aires, to prevent European imports from reaching Potosí by this route. In 1622 it withdrew Buenos Aires' license to trade with Brazilian ports, which were already absorbing increasing amounts of the area's hides and tallow.

Despite restrictions on the city's commercial expansion, the Crown maintained its interest in controlling the mouth of the estuary. For the first few decades Buenos Aires remained under a royal governor at Asunción, although a cabildo in Buenos Aires took care of local municipal matters. Then, in 1618, Buenos Aires became the seat of a governorship with authority over a vast and virtually uninhabited region of coastal Argentina and present-day Uruguay, including the cities of Santa Fe and Corrientes.

In the long run, economic forces also came to the assistance of Buenos Aires. Despite the Crown's fondness for administrative centralization, the empire in America often had to rely on local resources. The outlying regions, in particular, acquired considerable self-sufficiency and autonomy. Around the Río de la Plata the pampas afforded an ideal habitat for horses, introduced at the first founding of Buenos Aires, and for cattle, brought in 1580. These herds, which just about doubled every three years, soon sustained a significant export of hides and animal fats. At the same time Potosí and its environs, the principal silver mining region of the empire, had gained enormously in wealth and population. Rational—

at least in sixteenth- and seventeenth-century mercantilist eyes
—efforts to keep bullion in Spanish hands, and flowing along the
protected and relatively short sea route from the Caribbean to
Spain, began to break down. Silver, at first in tiny trickles and
then in increasing amounts, began to move south to Buenos Aires,
where it encouraged a flourishing although illegal trade, assiduously
supported by Portuguese, French, Dutch, and English sea captains.
In return, smuggled fineries and manufactures, leather, and mules
traveled north.

Buenos Aires thus survived and grew on the basis of subsistence
agriculture, administrative functions, the trading of hides and fats,
and a steadily rising volume of contraband merchandise. The city's
population increased accordingly: from an estimated 300 persons
in 1580 to 1000 in 1620; 3500 in 1660; and 7500 in 1700.[2]

During the eighteenth century, with the marked decline in Spanish imperial fortunes, the Crown gradually increased Buenos Aires'
commercial and administrative role. Defense and financial account-
ability continued to be major preoccupations for Spain. The inland
customs barrier at Córdoba had proved ineffective and had been
moved inland, first to Salta and then to Jujuy in the extreme northwest. By mid-century the Crown began to allow the legal flow of
bullion through Buenos Aires with an eye to recapturing the "royal
fifth," or 20 per cent tax, which had been lost on smuggled silver.
Export of hides and fats and the import of manufactured goods,
purified by the payment of tariffs, received royal encouragement.
Then, in 1776, when the Crown sent a major Spanish military expedition to expel Portuguese and English merchants and military
forces from the estuary's left bank, Buenos Aires was named
Spain's fourth viceregal capital, the highest administrative title
an overseas city could attain. From the city emanated the judicial,
financial, and military controls for an area embracing present-day
Argentina, Bolivia, Paraguay, Uruguay, and the extreme north of
Chile.

With this increased political power and economic importance,
the city flourished. The population rose from 14,000 in 1750 to
25,000 in 1780 and to 40,000 by the end of the century. The demands of a viceregal court brought lawyers, bureaucrats, priests,
and military officers, and those men in turn increased the need for

more artisans, soldiers, laborers, and slaves. Merchants built splendid fortunes, of a size previously known only in Lima or Mexico City. The number of hides exported increased from an annual 150,000 in the 1750s to 700,000 in the 1790s. Royal revenues, largely collected at the customhouse in Buenos Aires, jumped tenfold, from 100,000 pesos in 1774 to one million pesos in 1780. Money poured into the construction of houses, which were still built of sun-dried bricks but now were plastered and whitewashed and enclosed spacious interior patios. The city also began to acquire some of the intellectual and social trappings that befitted viceregal status: a printing plant provided a modest supply of pamphlets and broadsides, while theatrical performances regularly entertained audiences of increasing size and sophistication.

The city's early administrative and commercial experience, and its self-reliance, encouraged by an exposed position on the Spanish empire's southern rim, made it the natural center for a movement to break away from the constraints of empire. Friction between the *criollo*, or American-born Spaniard, and the peninsular Spaniard increased notably at Buenos Aires after 1776. The criollo who possessed land and roots in the city struggled against an invasion of officials, bureaucrats, and merchants who threatened to monopolize political and economic positions of power. In 1810, when Napoleonic control of Spain temporarily broke the line of imperial authority in America, criollo citizens seized leadership at Buenos Aires and replaced the viceroy and cabildo with their own junta. Although they attempted to hold together the viceregal unit, the areas of Paraguay, Bolivia, and Uruguay eventually gained separate nationhood. The Argentine provinces remained, however, under the nominal influence of Buenos Aires. By 1816 the demand for autonomy from Spain, which had begun with the viceregal capital, evolved into a wider movement that gained the region's independence.

The breakup of the empire benefited Buenos Aires enormously. The Argentine area, oriented toward Potosí and the mining regions of Bolivia for much of the colonial period, now completed the 180 degree turn—first begun in the eighteenth century—toward the estuary of the Río de la Plata. Buenos Aires became Argentina's door to the world. Withdrawal of mercantilist restrictions permitted a sharp rise in prices of hides and fats at the port, and the introduction of new techniques in the *saladeros,* or meat-salting plants, which sprang up around Buenos Aires after 1810, contributed to even greater profits. As methods of exploitation had changed from hunting for hides to slaughtering for hides and fats and, finally, to use of the entire carcass, the value of both land and animals leaped upward. The *estanciero,* or owner of huge tracts of pampas and vast herds, assumed political and economic control of Argentina's destiny. In line with these developments, Juan Manuel de Rosas, a *porteño*—resident of Buenos Aires—as well as Argentina's wealthiest estanciero, emerged as the country's strong man from 1829 to 1852.

As time went on, commerce became even more Buenos Aires' principal function. Porteños profited from the increasing amounts of trade that passed through the city, and the interior reluctantly acquiesced. European manufactured goods, usually cheaper and of better quality than products of Argentine household industries, flooded into the port in return for rising amounts of pampas exports. Gradually the foreign imports pushed further inland, outselling the homespun of Catamarca, the brandies of Mendoza, and the furniture of Santiago del Estero.

The Argentine pampas as well as the coastal ports gained in prosperity as the nineteenth century advanced. During the 1820s, within protected inner areas extending twenty to sixty miles from Buenos Aires, sheep began to be raised along with horses and cattle. By the latter decades of the nineteenth century, the wool and skins from these flocks became the country's leading export. Indians who had roamed unchallenged over most of the pampas during the colonial period now felt competition from criollos and immigrants.

Gradually, political and military authorities at Buenos Aires extended their control west and south of the city. Expeditions, treaties, and frontier forts pushed the Indians relentlessly back, although the final expedition of decimation and conquest did not occur until 1879–80. Crop-farming in the 1860s further accentuated the pampas' importance, and the sowing of wheat, corn, flax, and alfalfa by immigrant colonists and tenant farmers provided new products and exports.

The addition of new laborers and new investment to agricultural exploitation led to no slackening, however, in the trend toward concentration of landownership. The frontier lands taken from the Indians and the grasslands that blossomed as wheat fields or alfalfa pastures for the most part did not pass into the hands of small farmer-owners or immigrant colonists, but remained parceled out in huge estates owned by several hundred families.

Political adjustments reflected the economic changes taking place on the pampas. Porteños, whose dominance over the hinterland had first been given substance by royal fiat in 1776 and had been carried forward by criollo leaders in the port in 1810, had to struggle for power over the Argentine provinces. Valiant and often violent efforts to overthrow porteño influence and to confederate provincial interests gave Argentina an initial political experience sometimes verging on anarchy. But as the country's focus of population growth and wealth shifted from the interior toward Buenos Aires, local caudillos found themselves increasingly hard pressed to assert independence from the authorities at Buenos Aires. During the 1830s and 1840s, Rosas maintained porteño dominance by using his financial resources and political cunning. The advent of the railroad, the telegraph, and the Remington rifle—each an innovation that enabled the central government to respond quickly and effectively to local uprisings—confirmed the demise of provincial autonomy in the 1860s and 1870s.

Buenos Aires in the late nineteenth century thus possessed a legacy of political domination and of commercial supremacy based on nearly three centuries of steady growth and evolution. By 1870 the exhausting conflict with Paraguay, a war which had bloodied the Río de la Plata for six years and embroiled Uruguay and Brazil as well, had drawn to a close. European immigration had begun to climb in the closing years of the war, and settlement of new arrivals at Buenos Aires set the stage for the massive influx of Europeans during the boom years from 1884 to 1889 and from 1905 to 1912.

The troublesome issue of allocating a district to the national authorities as a capital continued to simmer throughout the 1870s. Its solution, in 1880, consolidated even more political power in the city of Buenos Aires. The conflict between porteños who wished to keep the city as capital of the province and other porteños, joined by many provincials, who wanted to make Buenos Aires the permanent national capital reached its climax in the 1880 presidential election. Julio A. Roca, candidate of the nationalist forces, emerged victorious over Carlos Tejedor, Governor of the province of Buenos Aires. In June 1880 localist forces received a further defeat in a brief civil war that was fought largely on the southern outskirts of Buenos Aires. The subsequent legislation that created the Federal District—the city of Buenos Aires plus generous new areas to the west and north for future growth—definitely confirmed the city as the political center of the nation.

Agriculture on the pampas also underwent transformation. The first agricultural colonies of European immigrants in the provinces of Santa Fe and Entre Ríos had begun to supply much of the local demand for wheat, corn, and flax. Even more important, these colonists began to break up the tough sod with plows and thus facilitated the planting of alfalfa pastures. These developments supported the major technological breakthrough of the 1870s, the transportation of refrigerated meat to Europe. As early as 1866 a group of farsighted landowners in Buenos Aires had banded together as the Sociedad Rural Argentina. They began a long and often frustrating campaign in favor of wire fences, blooded stock, and improved feed. As the demand of the European market for meat made the need for these improvements evident, coastal estancieros gradually shifted from rangy native cattle to stocky Shorthorn and Angus herds. Increasingly, these landowners called on immigrant tenant farmers to cultivate the land for five or six years with cereal crops before leaving the fields sown with alfalfa. This attention to fences, breeds, and feed enabled Argentine livestock growers to capture a major share of the European market for frozen carcasses by the end of the nineteenth century and to improve their position even further with the export of the more palatable chilled beef and mutton after 1910.

Railroad building added another dimension, although at first to the benefit of Buenos Aires' principal rival, the port of Rosario, located 250 miles upstream on the Paraná River. In 1870 nearly 400 miles of Central Argentine track were completed, linking the major inland city of Córdoba with Rosario. But a potentially more important railroad system, with Buenos Aires as its hub, had already begun to take shape: in 1857, a six-mile section running due west to the town of Flores; in 1864, a twenty-mile stretch north along the estuary, which would eventually tie Rosario into the porteño network; and in 1866, a seventy-mile line to Chascomús, in the south.

In 1870 horse-drawn cars ran on streetcar rails within the city of Buenos Aires for the first time, forecasting the rapid expansion of population beyond the limited one- or two-mile radius of the "walking" city. Piped water from the river had appeared in a few homes, and debates had begun on the construction of a water and sewage system for the whole city. In response to the increasing volume of trade, engineers, merchants, and politicians developed plans to convert the shallow mudbank—which forced ocean vessels to anchor several miles offshore—into a modern port. Although in population and physical structure Buenos Aires was still a large village in 1870, it stood on the threshold of the period of its most rapid and sustained growth.

By 1910 the revolution on the pampas had reached its climax, with an increasingly intensive livestock industry closely supplemented by tenant farming and cereal crop production. An industrial base devoted primarily to processing agricultural products for export admirably supported the exploitation of the pampas. The completed deep-water port virtually eliminated competition in the import-export trade. The lines of a national railroad system radiated from Buenos Aires like the spokes of a wheel and encouraged all to buy and ship through the national capital. The city had grown from a relatively modest trade and political center of 180,000 inhabitants to a major world port and metropolis with a population of 1,300,000. The streetcar system, electrified and consolidated in the first years of the twentieth century, made it possible for built-up areas and suburbs to spread across much of the seventy-four square miles of the Federal District. Public services such as schools, potable water, sewers, paving, lighting, garbage collection, and police protection, and cultural activities represented by plays, newspapers, lectures, concerts, horse-racing, and *fútbol*—soccer—reached more and more porteños. Immigrants, most of them Italians and Spaniards at the height of their productive years, provided the basis for these changes. To them went much of the credit for the country's economic expansion, as well as for the city's demographic and physical growth. By 1910 the largest influx of these newcomers to Argentina was drawing to a close, not to be approached by the upsurge of immigration in the 1920s nor by that in the period immediately after World War II, and the "Argentinization" of their sons and daughters was well under way. The direction of Argentina's development, however, remained firmly in the hands of a "progressive" elite, men imbued with the tenets of nineteenth-century liberalism and capitalism and with an eye for material improvements. These landowners, professional men, politicians, and merchants administered the city unchallenged and, beyond that, ruled the nation.

These forty years marked the "flowering" of the city of Buenos Aires. The city's population grew at an astonishing 4 per cent per year.*[3] Technology and investment revolutionized transportation. The ecology of the city changed dramatically, yet the city's social structure showed remarkable stability and continuity. To capture some of this flavor of change and permanence, we should take a look at the complex, far-flung city of 1910 and then step back into that large village of 1870.

* The average annual growth of the city of Buenos Aires between 1869 and 1895 amounted to 44 inhabitants per 1000 population. During the next census period, from 1895 to 1914, the rate decreased slightly, to 43 per 1000.

A Study in Contrasts:
The Paris of South America
and the Gran Aldea

Visitors from Europe or the United States to Buenos Aires around
1910 invariably expressed their amazement at the enormous metropolis which sprawled back from the muddy estuary. The centennial celebrations of Argentina's first independence movement,
which reached their climax on May 25, 1910, brought many observers. The city's increasing wealth and cosmopolitan air had also
put Buenos Aires on the schedule of many touring celebrities. Demands for lectures and consultations resulted in visits ranging from
several days to two or three months for Joseph Antoine Bouvard,
the Paris city planner; Georges Clemenceau, later the Premier of
France; Enrico Ferri, the Italian criminologist and socialist leader;
Jean Jaurès, the French socialist; Rafael Altamira, the Spanish his-
torian; and such men of letters as Anatole France, Vicente Blasco
Ibáñez, Ramón del Valle Inclán, and Guglielmo Ferrero.[1] Those
who were interviewed by the press often compared the new avenues, chic shops, and ornate public buildings with those of Paris—
a recognition eagerly sought by porteños. Others left much longer
impressions of their visits in books published after their return
home.[2] From the reports of these travelers, as well as from Argentine literature, contemporary newspapers, maps, census reports,
and photographs, there emerges a composite view of a city highly
European in construction, citizenry, and culture. The metropolis

13

1. The city of Buenos Aires as seen from the northern harbor, around 1900. Compare with Illus. 15, taken in the 1870s. (Archivo General de la Nación.)

of 1910 contrasted sharply with the Buenos Aires of 1870, which was affectionately known as the *gran aldea*, or large village.

The Argentine-bound traveler in 1910 almost always approached the city from the estuary, which gave quite a different view from that seen by the rare visitor who came through the back door by way of one of the rail lines after a long dusty ride across the seemingly interminable pampas. Usually, the ship had touched at a couple of Brazilian ports. Recollections of the spectacular beauty of Rio de Janeiro, or the slightly less impressive mountains behind Santos, mingled with memories of vivid color, omnipresent blacks, and tropical vegetation. Montevideo provided a European environment, unimpressive with its low, whitewashed buildings, tiny downtown center, and village atmosphere. After a night's trip up the estuary of the Río de la Plata, the visitor rushed on deck in the early morning—only to see a few spires and towers across the endless, brown water. Not surprisingly, most were tremendously disillusioned by this first glimpse of South America's leading city and

1. Outline of the Waterfront Zone, 1910.

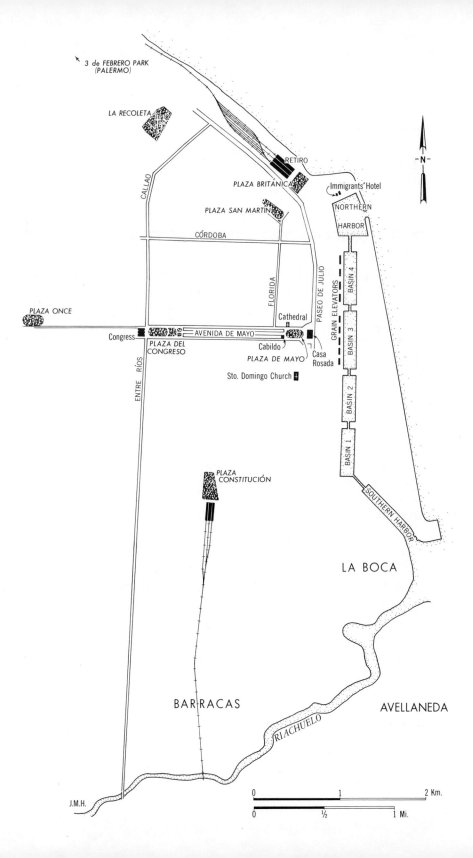

port. It seemed hard to believe that this was the home of 1,300,000 inhabitants.

The ship, which had been threading its way between a double line of buoys, now turned to enter one of the two main channels into the port. As it moved closer to shore, the visitor's feeling of disappointment gradually changed to amazement at the activity of the port and the grand expanse of city. Whether one entered the southern or the northern harbor before passing into one of the adjoining basins whose wharves lay parallel to the downtown center of the city, the same scene met the eye (see Map 1).

Far to the south, where the shoreline seemed to curve out into the river, the haze from a number of tall chimneys outlined the future industrial city of Avellaneda, already a center for processing agricultural products for export. A glimpse of the mouth of the Riachuelo, especially if one entered the southern harbor, which shared with that stream the southern access channel, revealed the masts of the coasting and fishing fleets. Here sat the squat warehouses and low houses of La Boca, which faced on the Riachuelo and the southern harbor. Low-lying land and frequent floods had caused the Genoese settlers, who had first occupied this district early in the nineteenth century, to build shacks on stilts, to raise the level of houses and sidewalks as much as six feet above street level, and generally to resort to wood construction—in contrast to the bricks, mortar, and plaster used elsewhere in the city. Splashes of color relieved the weatherbeaten boards and poverty of the area: an occasional house blazed with a front painted blue, orange, or green, and potted flowers could be glimpsed through sidewalk windows or through an open door to a patio.

Behind La Boca rose another backdrop of warehouses and scattered factory chimneys. Barracas, like its partner Avellaneda, on the other side of the Riachuelo, housed much of the city's nascent industry—sawmills, brick factories, meat-packing plants, tanneries, breweries, distilleries, and wool-washing establishments. A sizable coastal fleet based in the Riachuelo and occasional oceangoing vessels, as well as bales of wool and hides, beef on the hoof, and bags of wheat and corn flowing into Plaza Constitución—the main railroad access from the south—kept the wharves and sidings at Barracas humming. The proportion of Italian-born to total population

2. Plaza Constitución, around 1900. Compare with Illus. 14, taken in the 1870s. (Archivo General de la Nación.)

remained higher in La Boca and Barracas (Census District 4, see Map 3) than anywhere else in the city: 31 per cent, according to the 1909 municipal census, although this marked a decline from the 52 per cent reported in 1887.* Of this population only a few could not claim at least one Italian parent. La Boca in particular had conserved the atmosphere, the language, even the smells of Genoa.

To the west, beyond Barracas and La Boca, the eye did not reach. There the Riachuelo became a meandering shallow stream with seemingly endless bends and turns, of little use for navigation. Low-lying, easily flooded terrain characterized the whole south side of the city, and that situation had postponed settlement, except in La Boca and Barracas, during much of the nineteenth century. Cheap rents and inexpensive real estate encouraged occupation of these marginal lands by small factories that needed large areas of land for processing or produced unusual amounts of noise,

* These calculations are based on Census District 4, which embraced all of La Boca and approximately half of Barracas (see Table 1 in Statistical Tables, pp. 259–73).

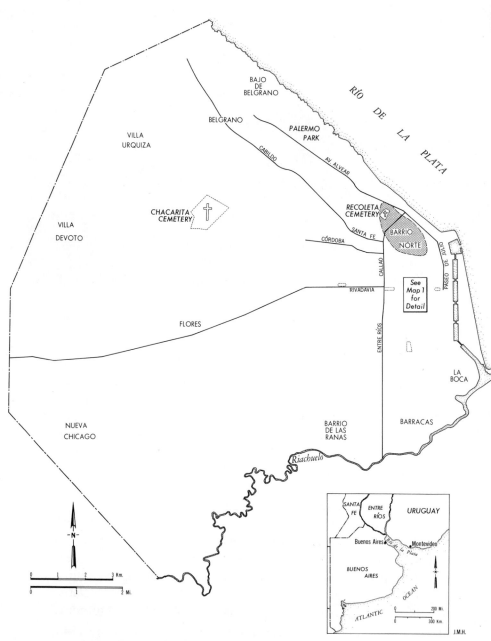

2. The Federal District of Buenos Aires, 1910.

residues, or smells. The municipal slaughterhouse had always been located on the city's south side: before 1870 it was adjacent to Plaza Constitución; then it shifted a mile to the west; and finally in 1903 it removed to the extreme southwest corner of the Federal District, to a newly developing suburb appropriately named Nueva Chicago. Just to the west of Barracas festered one of the worst urban sores, the city's garbage dump. Refuse from all over the city came by rail and cart to this enormous dump. In the adjacent Barrio de las Ranas—literally, neighborhood of the frogs—a population of 2000 men, women, and children earned their livelihood and frequently found their next meal while picking through the smoldering remains of the city's garbage (see Illus. 44, p. 212). A few enterprising people made a handy profit by fattening herds of pigs on such leftovers.

These very handicaps made the south side one of the most promising areas for workers who were anxious to buy their own land and escape the downtown tenements. After 1900 the number of houses with three rooms or less—the most characteristic residences for blue-collar and white-collar, upwardly mobile groups—began to increase in the three large districts west of Barracas and La Boca. The population in Census District 1 of Vélez Sársfield—the whole southwest corner of the Federal District, encompassing twenty-one square miles, or more than one-quarter of the city's total area—had increased from 17,000 inhabitants in 1904 to 48,000 by 1909, and by 1914 would total 103,000. Of the 7600 houses in this district in 1909, 4500 had three rooms or less; by 1914, out of a total of 13,900 houses, 9300 would fall into this classification. Nearly all of the increase between 1909 and 1914 came in houses with fewer than four rooms (see Table 2).

Despite the influx of people—in particular, less affluent families—the city's south side remained underpopulated. District 1 recorded the lowest population density of the entire city. Interspersed between the scattered nuclei of population lay numerous blocks that boasted only one or two houses, open fields of alfalfa or corn, vegetable plots, and even pastures where cattle and horses grazed. Beyond La Boca and Barracas, sewers and a municipal water supply did not exist.[3] The inhabitants resorted, as they had since colonial times, to rainwater cisterns or to shallow, often polluted wells.

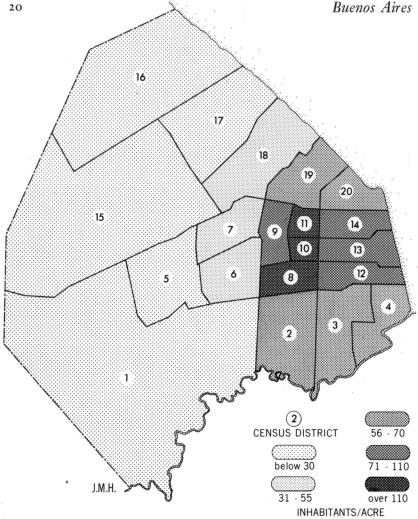

CENSUS DISTRICT   56 - 70

below 30   71 - 110

31 - 55   over 110

INHABITANTS/ACRE

J.M.H.

3. Population of the Federal District, 1909.

Privies filtered human waste back into the water table, which lay close to the surface, while garbage and trash decomposed in the streets or in vacant lots. Except for the streets of La Boca and Barracas, which were paved with small granite blocks imported from Europe or quarried in the southern part of the province of Buenos Aires, the south side had only dirt roads and no sidewalks. Simi-

3. Crowded conditions in the port of Buenos Aires, May 1912. Compare with Illus. 16 and 17. (Archivo General de la Nación.)

larly, gas lamps kept the streets of La Boca and Barracas well lighted, but outside those centers only an infrequent neighborhood claimed even a few kerosene lamps.[4] The reasons for the lack of municipal services and the low price of land lay not only with the unattractive nature of the terrain, but also with the nearly total absence of streetcar lines. By 1910 tracks had just begun to penetrate the area immediately west of La Boca and Barracas. The huge portion of the city encompassed in District 1 had only three short lines, which reached out from the suburb of Flores; these merely continued the westward thrust initiated by the tracks of the Western Railroad and did nothing to serve the southern expanse of the zone (see Map 10, p. 162).

As the traveler's gaze shifted northward from La Boca and Barracas, a long line of grain elevators virtually blocked his view of the downtown area that lay immediately in front of the ship. Ships crammed the four basins as well as the north and south harbors, while many freighters lay anchored farther out in the estuary, awaiting their turn to unload. Freight cars crowded the sidings as numerous locomotives edged their cargoes closer to the wharves that filled both sides of each ship basin. On the wharves, huge freight cranes hoisted net after net of hides or baled wool over the ships' sides, while long tubes from near-by elevators poured forth a constant stream of grain into the holds. Alongside this modern machinery labored an army of stevedores, running up and down the gangplanks like a swarm of industrious ants and carrying equally improbable burdens.

Beyond this foreground of surging activity, some returning resident might point out a few notable landmarks to the visitor. Such an orientation usually began with the pink stucco structure of the Casa Rosada, which stood on a slight rise above the port area. A few blocks to the south rose the towers of the Church of Santo Domingo, famed for the holes left by cannonballs during the British invasions of 1806–7, while just to the north one could barely discern the dome of the Cathedral. Around these landmarks centered the city's major retail and wholesale stores. A few blocks north, another cluster of taller buildings showed the location of the financial district.

Once again the eye could not reach to the western edge of the Federal District, ten miles distant, to perceive the vast extent of the city. That western area resembled in many ways the southwest corner of the city, with its pastures, small farms, widely scattered houses, and some rapidly expanding zones alongside newly laid streetcar tracks or around railroad stations. These western outskirts, however, possessed an air of prosperity and promise only rarely present among the squatter shacks and small worker houses of the southwest. By 1910 streetcars had begun to reach into the area (see Map 10, p. 162), although the long intervals between cars and the distance between lines testified to recent settlement. Paving usually graced only those streets with streetcar lines. The residents secured water and disposed of sewage and garbage as best they could. Gas lit a few streets, and scattered clusters of alcohol lamps outlined more prosperous suburbs. At the western edge of the Federal District, alcohol lighting marked the thriving area of Villa Devoto. Despite the absence of streetcars, this settlement had grown

4. An outlying district near the suburb of Flores, 1902. (Archivo General de la Nación.)

to nearly 100 city blocks because of two railroad stations, those of the Buenos Aires Pacific Railroad and the Central of Buenos Aires (see Map 8, p. 94).*

The city had initially expanded westward, following the country's first rail line, which was completed in 1857 to the town of Flores, six miles distant from the Plaza de Mayo. By 1900 the city's main east-west street, Rivadavia, along with streetcar lines and the Western Railroad, had encouraged the growth of a line of settlement—two to six blocks wide—all the way to Flores.

Flores showed signs of established prosperity. Its elevation, nearly 100 feet above sea level, and the accompanying pleasant breezes gave it an advantage over the area south of the Plaza de Mayo and had attracted some wealthy porteños to the zone by the 1870s. Summer homes and weekend retreats similar to those de-

---

* Unlike the two tracks that traversed Census District 1, which served only as shunting and connecting lines for freight cars, the Pacific and the Central of Buenos Aires carried a flow of passengers in and out of the city and made regular stops at Villa Devoto.

veloping along the estuary north of the city spread out around Flores. Increased speed and frequency of trains from downtown Buenos Aires, along with the extension of streetcars to the area, brought added wealth as well as numerous blue-collar and white-collar workers in the 1880s. Such established settlement showed up in the number of native-born in Flores. The two leading immigrant groups, Italians and Spaniards, appeared in Flores in percentages well below those nationalities' averages for the city as a whole. The native-born, many of whom were second-generation sons and daughters of immigrants, contributed almost two-thirds of Flores' nearly 50,000 inhabitants in 1909—somewhat more than the city-wide figure of 54 per cent native-born.

Flores, along with the corridor of two or three blocks on each side of Rivadavia that reached back toward Plaza Once, enjoyed sewer and water service. Electric lamps lit the sidewalks and stone-paved streets of the eighty blocks that surrounded the central plaza of Flores—a privilege otherwise reserved to the districts around the Plaza de Mayo and a tiny cluster of blocks near the municipal slaughterhouse on the city's southwest edge. The rest of Flores, except for the southern fringe, enjoyed some type of illumination by gas, alcohol, or kerosene lamps. In addition to the Western's tracks that linked Flores by train to Plaza Once, streetcar lines served the area well. At the district's outskirts one had to walk as much as eight or ten blocks, often through the mud or dust of dirt streets, to catch a car, but nearer the center of Flores transportation came to within two or three blocks of one's house, and sidewalks made the stroll easy.

Population increased as one left Flores and approached the streets of Entre Ríos-Callao, the western edge of the city in 1870. The rectangle of 500 blocks formed by Census Districts 8, 9, 10, and 11 covered three square miles and had a population of 235,900 persons, with an average density of 122 per acre. This area, immediately to the west of a similar rectangle formed by the three census districts located around the Plaza de Mayo, formed the city's most densely settled and built-up zone in 1910 (see Map 3). The highest concentrations occurred in Districts 10 and 11, ten blocks west of Entre Ríos-Callao and eight blocks north and south of Rivadavia. A cluster of 4000 Russian Jews who occupied two

5. View south along Montes de Oca, looking toward Barracas, 1905. Compare with Illus. 13, which was taken from the exact same spot in the 1870s. (Archivo General de la Nación.)

blocks in the center of District 11—one of the few clearly visible ethnic enclaves in the city—gave evidence of these crowded conditions. Despite such compact settlement, many inhabitants still lived in individual family homes, albeit in small and crowded quarters. The inhabitants who lived in *conventillos*, or tenements, in Districts 10 and 11 had totaled 21 per cent of the population in 1904, somewhat below the 27 per cent recorded in the three districts surrounding the Plaza de Mayo. For the larger area of the

four districts (8, 9, 10, and 11), conventillo inhabitants numbered
15 per cent. Aside from the Jewish enclave in District 11 and another smaller Jewish settlement in District 9, these four districts
provided an ethnic mixture quite similar to that of the city as a
whole. The percentage of native-born Argentines, 54 per cent, was
slightly under the city average. Spaniards, at 12 per cent, were
somewhat below the city average of 14 per cent, while the Italians,
at 26 per cent, remained slightly above their city-wide figure, 23
per cent.

In these districts one was never far from the rattle of wheels and
the clang of streetcar bells. The cars were no more than four blocks
from any house, and the ride to Plaza de Mayo took thirty to forty
minutes. All the houses, except for those in a small section of the
southwest corner, enjoyed municipal water and sewer service as
well as garbage collection. Asphalt covered almost all of the streets
in District 11, while paving stones provided a permanent, if somewhat rough, surface for streets in the other districts. Sidewalks,
many shaded by trees, and gas street lamps gave a further air of

6. Paseo de Julio (later Leandro Alem), looking north from the vicinity of the
Casa Rosada. (Archivo General de la Nación.)

7. Elite residential area along Avenida Alvear in Barrio Norte, around 1900. Compare with Illus. 10. (Archivo General de la Nación.)

stability and security to the zone and made it pleasant and safe to take an evening stroll.

Census Districts 12, 13, and 14, centered on the Plaza de Mayo, had constituted the built-up area of the gran aldea in 1870 and still embraced the city's core in 1910. Its population, some 193,900, occupied an area of 400 blocks, but because of land regained from the estuary by port construction the districts covered more than three square miles and had an average population density of 88 inhabitants per acre (see Map 3).

The downtown center around the Plaza de Mayo (within Districts 13 and 14) contained the government administration, financial operations, and most of the major retail and wholesale establishments of the city and the nation, as well as the educational and amusement facilities of the upper class. In addition, the wealthy still followed the Hispanic custom of building their homes near the principal plaza. Between 1870 and 1910 the focus for the upper class merely shifted from the south side to the north side of the Plaza de Mayo. The growth of the upper class, as well as changing architectural styles, encouraged this northward adjustment. By 1910 upper-class residences also reached to Plaza San Martín, ten blocks north of the Plaza de Mayo, and had begun to develop the elite area of Barrio Norte.

Recently arrived immigrants made their presence particularly felt in the downtown center, where they took over deteriorating houses formerly occupied by the wealthy. In the heart of the old colonial city, just south of the Plaza de Mayo, many formerly elite residences built around three interior patios became conventillos. Into the low-rent rooms crowded individual families or groups of single men. Manual laborers thus gained proximity to construction sites and to jobs involving carrying and lifting, in stores, on the streets, and at the docks. These downtown districts consequently provided a mixture of wealth and poverty, elegance and dirt, mansions and tenements, old established families and humble immigrants just off a transatlantic steamer, and men whose skills ranged from manipulating the destiny of a nation of eight million inhabitants to hoisting a 160-pound bag of wheat.

The Spaniards who flooded into Buenos Aires in the first decade of the twentieth century largely took over District 13. According to the 1909 census, nearly one-third of the district's 68,000 inhabitants had been born in Spain. District 12, to the south, had a population (also totaling 68,000) that was one-quarter Spanish. This pattern of dominance by recent arrivals applied also to the area north of the Plaza de Mayo, where, in District 14, with 57,500 inhabitants, the 6 per cent Frenchmen, 23 per cent Spaniards, and 3 per cent Russian Jews impressively outranked the city-wide average for these nationalities (see Table 1).

These three districts possessed all the services and conveniences that could be expected of a metropolitan center in 1910. Except for the southern half of District 12, which still depended on gas street lamps, electricity lit the streets and most of the houses. Running water, sewers, and garbage collection served all homes. Streetcar tracks covered the area with a grid, so that a passenger was never more than a block from a line. Except for a few streets around the edges that still had stone paving, all others had been smoothed and quieted either by asphalt surfacing or by small wooden blocks cut from the quebracho forests in the provinces of Santa Fe and Santiago del Estero. Sidewalks lined every street, although the narrowness of the streets, which had been laid out at the founding of the city in the sixteenth century, often resulted in a jostling and dangerous jumble of pedestrians, carts, streetcars, and carriages. Especially in the financial and commercial zones, the pedestrian's major concern was to avoid being elbowed into the path of a passing streetcar or horse-drawn vehicle. A few streets had served since colonial times to empty rainwater and wastes toward the estuary, and the height of their sidewalks, which were raised several feet above street level, added further hazards.

The view of the northern and last section of the waterfront to be seen from the ship's deck in 1910 gave evidence to the visitor of the second major thrust of porteño growth—along roads and, subsequently, along railway lines that linked Argentina's interior provinces to Buenos Aires. From the vantage point of the port, however, the northern part of the city seemed to consist largely of one- and two-story buildings and occasional church spires that dwindled away as one's gaze moved to the right. In the foreground rose an ugly gray mass of concrete, the recently completed Immigrants' Hotel, which served as home during an initial five days for arriving third-class passengers and as a center from which agricultural laborers were dispatched by rail to the wheat and corn fields of the pampas. Beyond and to the right, timbers and supports jutted out into the estuary, the skeleton of further enlargements of the port. Behind the Immigrants' Hotel lay the newly constructed railroad station of Retiro, terminal for major lines to the north and west of Argentina. The plaza in front of the station had long served as a wholesale and livestock market for the north side of the city. Now rebaptized Plaza Británica, it was dominated by a brick clock tower donated by the British residents of Buenos Aires in commemoration of the centennial of the city's first move toward independence from the Spanish Crown. Above Retiro a grassy knoll marked the edge of the Plaza San Martín, which was, until 1870, the location of the city's major military garrison and the northern limit of urban expansion. Farther to the right, where the shoreline seemed to recede sharply, the solid green of trees along the bank indicated the extent of the 3 de Febrero, or Palermo, Park.

The northern sector of the city, situated like a wedge of pie alongside the estuary, consisted of five rapidly developing Census

Districts, 16, 17, 18, 19, and 20. Like the downtown area, these districts provided contrasts, for in them beggar and patrician, recent arrival and established family, garbage collector and Senator could be found.

The apex of District 20 near the Plaza San Martín marked Barrio Norte, a retreat of the wealthy who wanted to be close to the Plaza de Mayo yet wished to display their wealth ostentatiously in mansions. But alongside the mansions sprawled some of the city's worst slums. At the very tip of District 20—between Paseo de Julio and Córdoba—a few blocks housed in compact misery Buenos Aires' major settlement of *turcos*—a term that embraced Syrians, Lebanese, or anyone from the Near East. As the visitor moved along the railroad lines northward from Retiro, he could see in one view squatter shacks near the tracks and riverbank and the elite homes located on a slight rise to the west along Avenida Alvear. Still farther to the northwest, beyond Palermo Park and between the city's two racetracks (in Census District 16), lay another slum, the Bajo, or Lowlands, de Belgrano, which rivaled the Barrio de las Ranas, on the south side, for wretchedness and disease.

The suburb of Belgrano stood on higher ground, immediately west of the Bajo. Like Flores and La Boca, Belgrano in 1870 had been a distinct settlement. By 1910 urban expansion along the streets of Santa Fe/Cabildo and the tracks of the Central Argentine railroad had engulfed the town. Again like Flores, this suburb had drawn some wealthy settlers in the 1870s, when the elite families had sought summer retreats and cooling breezes along the estuary. For a few days in June 1880, Belgrano even became Argentina's capital; it was there that the national authorities regrouped their forces during the brief civil war that preceded federalization of the city. As railroad service improved and streetcar lines stretched out across the whole of this northern sector, the modest homes of the city's rising blue-collar and white-collar group and the more substantial chalets of the professional men and merchants began to fill the landscape.

The location of Belgrano's central plaza near the edge of District 16 and adjacent to District 17 caused these two zones to have much in common (see Map 2). The large unpopulated zones in District 16 contributed to low population density for the two districts—100,700 inhabitants spread over fourteen square miles, with an average density of twelve persons per acre (see Map 3). The ethnic composition revealed a slightly higher proportion of native-born than the city-wide average (see Table 1). The 1904 census reported virtually no conventillos in these districts, while the percentage decline in the number of houses with three rooms or less spoke of the inhabitants' rising prosperity. Housing increased from 7800 units to 20,300 units in the two districts between 1904 and 1914; the percentage of one- to three-room homes decreased in the same period, from 59 per cent to 42 per cent (see Table 2).

By 1910 trains served Districts 16 and 17 with six stops (see Map 8, p. 94). A substantial streetcar system had developed around the main plaza of Belgrano, and it brought houses in that 250-block zone within a maximum walking distance of five blocks of a line (see Map 10, p. 162). At the western edge of District 17 another thrust of settlement, accompanied by streetcar tracks, had reached the zone of the Chacarita cemetery and beyond, into the western part of District 18 to the recently established and rapidly growing suburb of Villa Urquiza. Belgrano's water and sewer lines constituted a separate system served by the municipality, while Villa Urquiza boasted the only artesian water supply in the city. Paved streets provided some relief from the mud and dust of the outlying suburbs: there was paving throughout the built-up zone of Belgrano, along two streets in Villa Urquiza, and in a forty-block zone at District 17's southern edge. Street lighting also followed that pattern: there were gas lamps for Belgrano's central streets, for Villa Urquiza, and for the settlement at District 17's southern edge; alcohol lamps for recently developed clusters of population that spread out from these three centers; a few spots lit by kerosene lamps; and then the darkness of the outskirts.

As the visitor moved back toward the central city from Belgrano, he crossed the Arroyo Maldonado, a small stream which, until the formation of the Federal District in 1880, had traditionally marked the city's northern boundary. By 1910 the tracks of the Pacific Railroad ran along this former stream bed in its westward curve toward Villa Devoto. The built-up city had nearly reached this limit, a growth facilitated by excellent communications. The Pacific's station at Palermo, as well as the hub formed by several streetcar lines radiating out of Plaza Italia, five blocks to the south, permitted easy movement to and from the city's center.

These transportation facilities and the relatively low cost of land, at least in comparison with the downtown district and the centers of Flores and Belgrano, made this zone particularly attractive to modestly paid blue-collar and white-collar employees. The population of District 18 jumped from 64,000 in 1904 to 103,000 by 1909. In 1909, 60 per cent were native-born Argentines, suggesting considerable second-generation or native settlement. Of the foreign-born, only the Italians, who made up 26 per cent of the population, stood above their city-wide average. Population density totaled 60 per cent that of the downtown districts.* Despite the absence of good streetcar service at the western limits, which forced a walk of as much as ten blocks for some, the number of houses with three rooms or less declined sharply between 1904 and 1914; by the latter date, these small homes contributed only one-quarter of the total (see Table 2). Conventillos, however, hardly figured in the 1904 count; only 3 per cent of the population lived in such dwellings. By 1910 water and sewage service had just begun to enter District 18. Houses along Santa Fe, as well as three small clusters of settlement to the west of that street, used municipal water. Cobblestone or granite paving covered almost all the streets, and gas streetlights reached across the entire zone.

These patterns largely held true in the next district, 19, the last before one reached District 20, with its striking contrasts of slums and mansions. District 19 had municipal water and sewage; all the streets were paved with stone and lighted with gas. Except for the squatter settlements along the railroad tracks and near the shoreline, streetcar lines came within four or five blocks of all homes. The population density was slightly higher than in District 18, but the rate of growth had clearly slowed down—by 1909 only 4000 inhabitants had been added to a population that had numbered 71,000 in 1904. Houses with three rooms or less declined in number from 1904 until they amounted to roughly 10 per cent of the buildings registered in 1909 and in 1914. The ethnic mixture

---

* Actually, density in Census District 18 was more pronounced, because the zone included the large unoccupied area of Palermo Park and the right-of-way of the railroad lines.

showed no sharp departures from that of the city as a whole, while in the census of conventillos taken in 1904 only 9 per cent of the population lived in slum housing.

Census District 20 encompassed much of Barrio Norte, the cemetery of the upper classes at the Recoleta, and the elegant Socorro parish. It also embraced the railroad tracks, the newly expanding port area, the Immigrants' Hotel, and the squatter huts along the riverbank. As few as four mansions might occupy an entire city block, while nearly 1000 turcos crowded into several conventillos just around the corner in a block along Paseo de Julio. Such contrasts often were obscured in the statistics. Thanks to the large extensions given over to port works, to the railroad's right-of-way, and to the dispersed settlement of the wealthy, population density statistically was lower than in adjacent District 19 and registered only three-quarters that of the downtown districts. Rarely did one have to walk more than two blocks to catch a streetcar. Electric streetlights reached all blocks, sewers and water mains served all houses, and asphalt surfacing made for smooth, quiet carriage rides on most of the streets. Indeed, the only indicators in the census reports that point to unusual factors are the high proportion of turcos, Spaniards, and Frenchmen, as well as the large percentage—30 per cent—of conventillo dwellers. But the contrasts that lay below the surface made this a fascinating zone and a rival to La Boca or the downtown center for the visitors' attention.

This overview of Buenos Aires in 1910, as seen from the vantage point of a visitor well prepared by guidebooks, travelers' accounts, census reports, and maps, provides some sense of the size and complexity of the extended metropolis. That visitor, however, could appreciate little of the true character of this sprawling city as he followed his bags through the huge customhouse sheds, saw them snatched up by eager porters, and found himself rushed into a carriage and on his way to a hotel in the Avenida de Mayo.

The ride up from the wharves left him with an impression of dusty or muddy—depending on the season—vacant land behind the warehouses and grain elevators. The horses climbed briskly up the fifty-foot rise which marked the line where the riverbank had been

8. View from the Plaza de Mayo, looking west along the Avenida de Mayo, 1898.
Compare with Illus. 9. (Archivo General de la Nación.)

before port construction reclaimed nearly 150 city blocks from
the estuary. As his carriage moved around the Plaza de Mayo—approximately the same one laid out by Garay in 1580—and up the
broad Avenida de Mayo, the visitor received many fleeting impressions: of a low and columned Cabildo, the only reminder of
Spain's architectural heritage remaining on the plaza; of the pillars
and squatness of the Cathedral, which resembled the Madeleine of
Paris; of elegance along the Avenida de Mayo, with its rows of
trees and streetlights and its sidewalk cafés; of the multistory
buildings—the Gath y Chaves department store, the offices of *La
Prensa*, and the Grand Hotel—that lent further credence to comparisons with Paris. The narrow streets off the Avenida de Mayo,
still of the thirty-foot width established by Garay, seemed to over-
flow with streetcars, carriages, huge horse-drawn carts, and auto-

mobiles. Wall posters, store signs, banners, and flags dazzled the eyes, while the cries of street vendors, peddlers, and newspaper boys, and the insistent clamor of streetcar bells, car horns, and shouting cart drivers, assaulted the ears. On all sides raged the fever of a city under full construction: sidewalks torn up for gas mains or sewer connections; piles of sand and stone half blocking thoroughfares; wrecking crews opening swaths for two newly decreed diagonal avenues or widening existing streets into avenues; paving gangs replacing cobblestones with wood blocks or asphalt; and overhead the hum of a tangle of streetcar, telephone, and electrical wiring.

People surged everywhere. To the new arrival, they contrasted sharply with the black and mulatto mixtures seen in Brazil, or the Indian elements commonly associated with the rest of South America. Beggars there were, on the steps leading into churches or huddled in doorways along the avenues, pitiful wrecks often accompanied by ragged, filthy children. But a general impression emerged of well-dressed, well-nourished Europeans. If the newcomer ventured into one of the ministries or into the Congress building, he might see some black orderlies, but unless he stumbled onto one of those few remaining clusters of mulatto settlement on the south side or on the outskirts, he would think of Buenos Aires as a city where blacks did not exist. If he traveled to outlying districts, to certain of the shanty-towns, or to the slaughterhouse district at Nueva Chicago, he undoubtedly would see men and women with an Indian cast and color to their features, and even a few of predominantly Indian blood. But in the downtown area the only reminder of differing racial strains in the city, which a bare century earlier had been 25 per cent black and 60 per cent mestizo, was an occasional mulatto orderly or mestizo servant.

In dress, the tone of prosperity and well-being predominated. Except for those actually performing the rudest or dirtiest of manual labor, the universal uniform of the porteño man was a white shirt with celluloid or starched collar, a dark tie, a hat, and a suit of somber colors. In the late afternoons, the dresses of young ladies on the more elegant shopping streets added some color to the conservative tones, although the dark clothes of matrons and the invariable black of mourning dimmed even these hues. Among the

ladies who strolled down the center of the elegant street of Florida
it was difficult to distinguish a shopgirl from the granddaughter of
the President, or to determine which one among the throngs of ad-
miring men who lined the sidewalks was a bank clerk and which
the son of the Minister of War.

The Buenos Aires of 1910, especially in its downtown area, had
an air of bustle, prosperity, and modernity. Beyond the superficial
impression of progress, however, it was more difficult for the
casual observer to penetrate. Alongside the myriad levels of economic status in the burgeoning economy, he might sense the division separating the elite from the common man. He might even
guess at some of the value and traditions that underlay the veneer
of materialism and development. But he would need to live in
Buenos Aires for months or even years before he could comprehend how strong a hold the Spanish heritage had on these apparently hybrid European people.

A glance backward to the Buenos Aires of 1870 would not have
amazed an established resident of the city of 1910. In the gran aldea he could doubtless have discerned the rudimentary outline of
the later metropolis. And much in the social structure and culture
of the porteño scene of 1870 would have seemed familiar to him.
But for the uninitiated, the shock of the physical contrast between
the two cities would have been enormous.

To the person who stood at the center of Buenos Aires in 1870,
the principal sensation was of having entered a large, peaceful
town. Brisk activity took place on the waterfront and in a few adjacent commercial streets, but the rest of the city, stretched out
along quiet streets, seemed at rest within the patios and behind the
brick and stucco walls of its one-story buildings. This was Argentina's most populous city and major port, the administrative center
of the national government, and the capital of the country's largest
and wealthiest province. Nevertheless, life moved at an unhurried
pace.

An elegant Plaza de Mayo, with landscaped beds, shade trees and
marble benches, remained a dream of the future. A rickety arcade
of small shops, known as the Recova Vieja, separated, as it had
since late colonial times, the two open squares that constituted the
traditional focal point of the city (see Map 4). This arcade held a

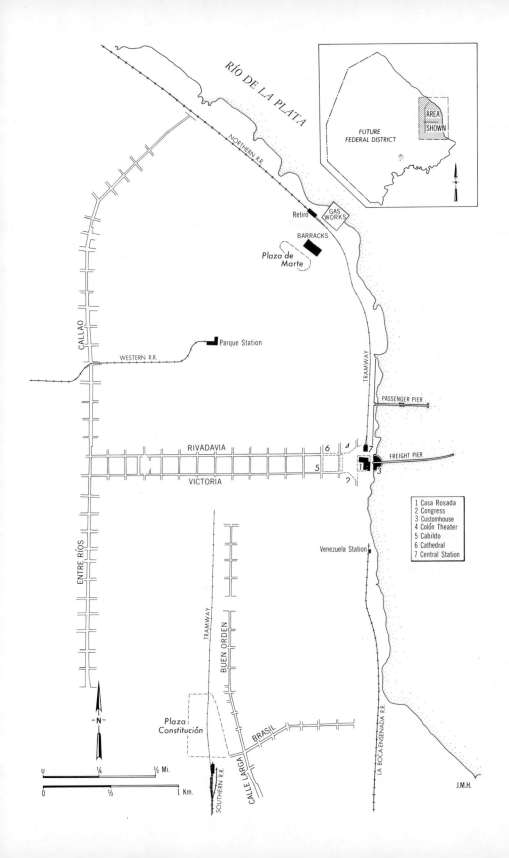

RÍO DE LA PLATA

FUTURE
FEDERAL DISTRICT

AREA
SHOWN

-N-

NORTHERN R.R.

Retiro

GAS
WORKS

BARRACKS

Plaza de
Marte

CALLAO

Parque Station

WESTERN R.R.

TRAMWAY

PASSENGER PIER

RIVADAVIA

6

7

FREIGHT PIER

5

1

3

VICTORIA

2

ENTRE RÍOS

1 Casa Rosada
2 Congress
3 Customhouse
4 Colón Theater
5 Cabildo
6 Cathedral
7 Central Station

Venezuela Station

TRAMWAY

BUEN ORDEN

Plaza
Constitución

BRASIL

LA BOCA ENSENADA R.R.

-N-

0   ¼   ½ Mi.

0   ½   1 Km.

SOUTHERN R.R.

CALLE LARGA

J.M.H.

few tailor and pastry shops and many shoe repair stalls—thirty-two shoemakers lived and worked there.

The square nearest the waterfront, then known as the Plaza 25 de Mayo, had long served as a parade ground for soldiers from the fort. In 1870 it still was little more than a muddy or dusty field, although several important buildings gave promise of its future improvement. Over the years the city's fort on the riverbank had been altered and rebuilt; now it served as offices for the President and the government ministries. The recent construction of a red sandstone wing set the tone for a new façade and would give the entire building its name, Casa Rosada. Beyond the Casa Rosada rose a new building that jutted into the river, the huge, five-story, semi-circular Customhouse. On the plaza's south side, just across from the Casa Rosada, a hall erected in the 1860s served the national Congress. Since provision had been made for only a single chamber, the Senate and the Chamber of Deputies met on alternate days. On the north side of the plaza, the recently completed Colón Theater, with a 2500-seat capacity, attracted some of Europe's best opera and repertory companies for the winter season of June, July, and August.

The square to the west, known as the Plaza Victoria, had at its center a small brick pillar commemorating Argentina's independence movement. A few benches and trees provided modest adornment. On the west side of this plaza stood the Cabildo, a two-story, columned and whitewashed edifice which housed the Supreme Court, the municipal council, and the police headquarters. At the back of the Cabildo was the city jail, which accommodated an average of 200 inmates on any given day. To the north, broad steps led up to the low-domed Cathedral; at its side were the church offices and the archbishop's residence. The numerous shops that formed the arcade separating the two plazas also extended to fill in the south side of Plaza Victoria.

Ever since the establishment of Buenos Aires in 1580, these two plazas—which together constituted the Plaza de Mayo and were united as such in 1884—had served as the place where all important actions were made or sanctified. Parades and celebrations, revolutions and executions, proclamations and demonstrations, all had given drama to this center and heart of the city.

9. Plaza 25 de Mayo, looking northwest toward the Recova Vieja and the Cathedral, around 1880. Compare with Illus. 8. (Archivo General de la Nación.)

From this core the city had grown outward. By 1870 its population of 180,000 inhabitants had pushed the edge of the built-up area into the shape of a semicircle, with a radius of slightly over a mile, centered on the plaza. The introduction of railroad lines in the 1850s and 1860s had begun to distort this regular pattern of expansion and subsequently would stimulate the growth of three prongs of settlement, west, south, and north.

To the west, the thrust along railroad tracks that followed long-established oxcart and mule trails in and out of the city had only been suggested by a narrow line of built-up blocks toward Plaza Once. This plaza, nearly two miles from the Plaza de Mayo, had long served as a major wholesale market, especially for grains, wool, and hides. Its commercial importance increased still further when it became the principal terminus for the country's first railroad, the Western, opened in 1857. This line initially ran to Flores —a town of 2300 which in 1870 still lay outside the municipal limits of Buenos Aires—and then reached out to the provincial towns of Merlo, Luján, Mercedes, and Chivilcoy and tapped the rich agricultural zone to the west of Buenos Aires.

To the south, La Boca and Barracas, although within the municipal boundaries of 1870, were still separate villages. The La Boca–Ensenada Railroad, whose Venezuela Station was five blocks south of the Plaza de Mayo, had begun in 1865 to attach those two settlements more closely to the main part of the city. The intervening marshy land, a handicap to stagecoach or cart travel, could now be crossed easily; one could take a ten-minute train ride to La Boca, or a twenty-minute ride to Barracas. Likewise, the opening of the first stretch of the Southern Railroad in 1865 linked Barracas, by a ten-minute ride, to the major rail terminus at Plaza Constitución. That plaza was the main produce and wholesale market for the city's south side.

To the north, the Northern Railroad had established its terminus in 1866 at Retiro, a mile from the Plaza de Mayo, for the start of a line which ran first along the estuary and then inland to Zárate, fifty miles distant, in the delta area of the Paraná River. This northward push, reinforced by several more railroad lines, soon became most important to the city's expansion. In 1870, however, the railroad merely served to connect several small towns, such as Belgrano, with 1200 inhabitants, San Isidro, with nearly 1000, and San Fernando, with 3200, to the city. The built-up zone of the city itself had not yet reached out beyond the area of the Retiro Station.

Each of these major railroads, west, south, and north, had by 1870 been closely linked to the city's heart at the Plaza de Mayo. The Northern Railroad had built the Central Station in the block adjacent to the north side of the Casa Rosada and connected it to the Retiro Station with a spur line. Not until 1875 did the La Boca–Ensenada Railroad receive authorization to bridge the five-block gap between its Venezuela Station and the Central Station. In a fashion similar to that of the Northern, the Southern Railroad also extended a spur from its terminus at Plaza Constitución, to bring passengers within half a mile of the Plaza de Mayo. When the Western Railroad initiated service in 1857, its cars traveled along a spur line from the Parque Station, seven blocks northwest of the Plaza de Mayo, to its main terminus at Plaza Once. The opening of the city's first two horse-drawn streetcar lines (as distinguished from railroad spur lines) in February 1870 enabled passengers of both the Western and the Southern railroads to reach the Plaza de Mayo directly and easily. During the next several decades, the city's streetcars would fill in and expand this skeleton outline provided by the railroads.

Despite the city's expansion toward Plaza Once in the west, and the future bulges north and south suggested by the railroad lines, you would have to return to the center at the Plaza de Mayo in order to understand the dynamics of what in 1870 was still a "walking," or pedestrian, city, oriented around a central plaza. From here an imaginary walk around the built-up area, although it does not parallel the overview of the 1910 metropolis, captures some of the atmosphere and intimacy of the gran aldea.

Turning south from the Plaza de Mayo, you retraced the initial growth of Garay's city, remaining, for a few blocks, in the political and intellectual center of the city. From the Cabildo, walking one block along Bolívar brought you to the famous "Square of Enlightenment," laid out in the 1820s (see Map 5). In this block stood the Church of San Ignacio, parish church of Catedral al Sud; the walled and cloistered Colegio Nacional de Buenos Aires, the country's most famous preparatory school; the legislative chambers of the province of Buenos Aires, modeled after the Parisian Chamber of Deputies; the Law School of the University of Buenos Aires, established in 1822; the national library, public health office, museum, and departments of education and topography; and the commercial tribunals. The Colegio Nacional served a particularly important role as training ground for many of Argentina's future political and intellectual leaders. Several hundred of the students lived in the homes of their parents or relatives in the city, but 190 boys, aged twelve to nineteen, and largely from the provinces, roomed and boarded at the Colegio and there formed friendships and associations that would last throughout their lives.[5]

Aside from its intellectual institutions and resources, this stretch of Bolívar witnessed a political activity second only to that of the Plaza de Mayo. While the question of a permanent national capital remained unresolved, both the authorities of the province of Buenos Aires and those of Argentina used the city as their seats of government. In the provincial legislature and law courts in this square, and in the offices of the provincial governor and his ministers, located across the street to the south, negotiations and ar-

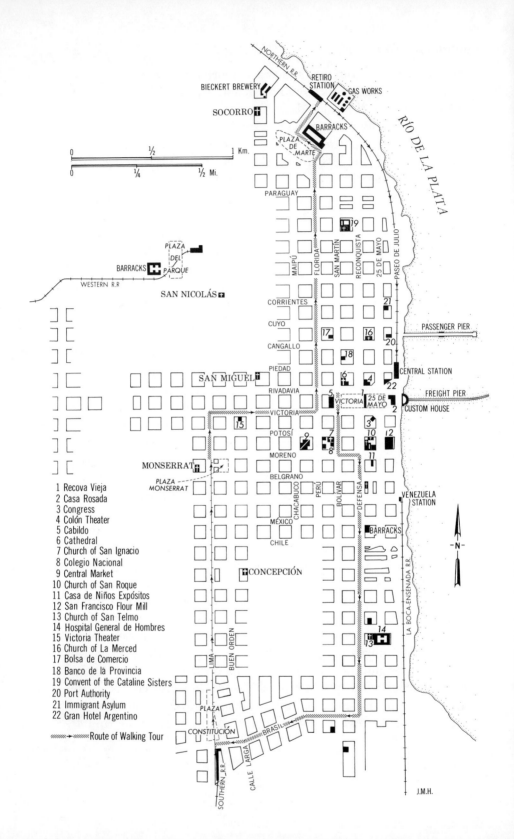

RÍO DE LA PLATA

NORTHERN R.R.

BIECKERT BREWERY
RETIRO STATION
GAS WORKS
SOCORRO
BARRACKS
PLAZA DE MARTE

PARAGUAY

PLAZA DEL PARQUE
BARRACKS
WESTERN R.R
SAN NICOLÁS

MAIPÚ
FLORIDA
SAN MARTÍN
RECONQUISTA
25 DE MAYO
PASEO DE JULIO

19

CORRIENTES
21
CUYO
PASSENGER PIER
17
16
CANGALLO
20
PIEDAD
18
CENTRAL STATION
4
SAN MIGUEL
RIVADAVIA
6
22
5
FREIGHT PIER
VICTORIA
7
25 DE MAYO
CUSTOM HOUSE
2
VICTORIA
15
1
3
POTOSÍ
9
7
10
12
MORENO
8
11
MONSERRAT
BELGRANO
PLAZA MONSERRAT
CHACABUCO
PERÚ
BOLVAR
DEFENSA
VENEZUELA STATION

1 Recova Vieja
2 Casa Rosada
3 Congress
4 Colón Theater
5 Cabildo
6 Cathedral
7 Church of San Ignacio
8 Colegio Nacional
9 Central Market
10 Church of San Roque
11 Casa de Niños Expósitos
12 San Francisco Flour Mill
13 Church of San Telmo
14 Hospital General de Hombres
15 Victoria Theater
16 Church of La Merced
17 Bolsa de Comercio
18 Banco de la Provincia
19 Convent of the Cataline Sisters
20 Port Authority
21 Immigrant Asylum
22 Gran Hotel Argentino

MÉXICO
CHILE
BARRACKS

CONCEPCIÓN

LA BOCA-ENSENADA R.R.

N

14
13

LIMA
BUEN ORDEN

PLAZA
CONSTITUCIÓN
BRASIL

SOUTHERN R.R.
CALLE LARGA

▰▰▰▰▶ Route of Walking Tour

J.M.H.

rangements were made that affected the city almost as much as did those of the national government.

Just to the west, behind this center of political and intellectual power, a very different series of sounds and smells emanated from the city's oldest food retail center, the Central Market. Walls enclosed the entire block. Around the four sides were ranged permanent stalls for the sale of vegetables, fruits, and meats, while temporary stalls filled in much of the center. During the early morning hours you could barely squeeze past the piles of cabbages, carrots, potatoes, peaches, and plums freshly gathered from outlying gardens, thread a path around the hanging quarters of beef, the braids of small intestines, the links of sausages, and the mounds of liver, kidneys, and sweetbreads at a butcher's stall, or dodge the handcarts loaded with lattice-work crates of quacking ducks and cackling chickens. By noon, however, the haggling servants and housewives had departed, leaving the vendors to clean up their stalls, sweep out the marketplace, and prepare for the next dawn's round of activities.

For two or three blocks along any of the adjacent streets in this area one could find a number of the homes of Buenos Aires' wealthy and powerful landowners, politicians, and merchants. Small shops had taken over the ground floor of the remaining residential houses that faced on the Plaza de Mayo, but the powerful still chose to live close to the plaza. On Bolívar, directly across from the Colegio Nacional, stood the house of Baldomero García, an elderly and respected judge who had served under the Rosas regime and then, during the 1850s, had supported Justo José de Urquiza and the Confederation against the province of Buenos Aires. With him and his wife lived one daughter with her husband, a lawyer from the province of Salta; two younger daughters; two young sons; and five servants. Around the corner, on Moreno, lived José Mármol, poet, journalist, and one of the country's leading intellectual figures. Since he had recently been widowed, his unmarried sister helped him raise his three boys, aged fifteen, eight, and three. His oldest daughter and her husband and their two small boys, along with five servants, also lived with him. Near the end of this block, at No. 41, was the home of the Sáenz Peñas, a family which would contribute two Argentine Presidents. Luis, a lawyer

5. Walking Tour of Buenos Aires, 1870.

10. Elite residence of the Gutiérrez family at Perú 490, in the 1850s. Compare with Illus. 7, 27, and 28. (Archivo General de la Nación.)

who would serve as President from 1892–95, headed this household, which consisted of his wife, six children, and eight servants. His oldest son, Roque, now eighteen and just finishing his studies at the Colegio Nacional, would become one of Argentina's most famous Presidents—he served from 1910 until his death in 1914.[6]

In spite of the many servants needed to make frequent trips to market, prepare food, care for children, wash and iron clothes, scrub patios, and clean rooms, the households of these powerful families remained remarkably modest. The Roman, Greek, and Arabic heritages had all fused in the Spanish culture to encourage the enclosed and guarded world of the individual home. The passerby saw no more of these elongated, rectangular houses than the brick or stucco front wall, rising from the sidewalk's edge and broken only by a sturdy paneled door and several heavily barred casement windows.

Occasionally, a glimpse through a street door left ajar to catch a breeze revealed the filigreed grillwork of an inner door that gave access to the first, or formal, patio, with its potted plants and mosaic floor tiles. Onto this patio opened the family's formal rooms: on one side, a drawing room with an antechamber, perhaps a small reception room, and a dining room; on the other, another reception room and a study or library. This patio was as far as anyone who did not belong to the family could penetrate, and even to reach this, one had to be a close friend. The first patio opened into a slightly larger second patio, which provided the center for family activities. Potted plants and trees, an ornate well or fountain, and a small sitting room provided a pleasant center for the family's activities, as well as an outlook for the individual bedrooms. From here one moved into the large open service patio at the end of the house. Fruit trees, a vegetable garden, chickens, and sometimes even a few goats occupied much of this patio. Around its edges were cubicles for servants, a storeroom for wood and charcoal, a couple of latrines, the kitchen and pantries, and, often, a separate room with a large tub for baths.

The floor plan and furnishings of such a house did not focus attention on the wealth of its inhabitants. Those with substantial fortunes usually built the patio-style dwelling on a lot twenty *varas*, or fifty-seven feet, wide, by seventy varas, or 199 feet, deep (one vara equals 2.84 feet). More common was the house ten varas wide, with a depth ranging from thirty to seventy varas. These houses excited little desire for conspicuous consumption. The rooms surrounding the second patio were modestly furnished, with heavy bedsteads and wardrobes, sturdy upholstered chairs, some family portraits, and perhaps a few bird cages. Only the drawing room gave an idea of the family's wealth. The cost of carpeting, heavy sofas, delicate French chairs, mirrors, wallpaper, chandeliers with gas jets, and the occasional piano would depend upon the family's living standard.

In the homes of well-to-do families, table service likewise varied with income. The dining room might boast Limoges porcelain, Waterford glass, ornate silver platters, Lyon tapestries, Brussels linens. But whether served in elegance or merely on simple pottery or pewter tableware, the menu remained constant. Breakfast, taken informally in the bedroom or in the second patio, consisted of coffee or tea with hot milk, or the more traditional *mate*, a strong infusion of Paraguayan tea that was sipped from a gourd through a

11. Above: the third, or service, patio of the elite residence of the Castillón family at Independencia 373, as it was in the 1870s. (Archivo General de la Nación.) Op-

silver tube. At noon the basic dish was *puchero*, a boiled dinner consisting of a wide variety of meats and vegetables, including beef, chicken, sausages, cabbages, carrots, squash, potatoes, navy

posite: the entrance to the first, or formal, patio of the elite residence of the Anchorena family at Suipacha 50, still maintained as it stood in 1870. (Photo by Ignacio Corbalán.) Compare these with Illus. 29 and 30.

beans, and onions. The colonial and rural custom of dining early in the evening died slowly. A few families had taken up the English four o'clock tea, and they pushed their evening meal ahead to eight o'clock. But most still ate between five and seven o'clock. The evening meal invariably consisted of a roast or ribs of beef, preceded by soup and followed, in the summer, by fruit. A pitcher of water, a flagon of wine, and a basket of bread joined the salt as complements to the standard fare.

The wealthy and influential families around the Plaza de Mayo enjoyed equally simple pastimes and entertainment in 1870. The *tertulia*, or gathering, still took place occasionally in the evening in the more intellectually oriented homes. Literary, philosophical, and political discussions flourished at these gatherings, which often were highlighted by someone reading a few of his poems or playing a new composition. But the literary salons which had enjoyed such vigor in the years immediately after independence seem to have vanished. Families occasionally gave a recital or dance; the home, nevertheless, had declined as a center for entertainment, although no substitute location had emerged. A few social clubs for men had developed, among them the Club del Progreso and the Club del Plata, both of which also had political overtones, and the gathering place for foreign merchants, the Club de Residentes Extranjeros. Men could also slip out in the evening for a game of cards or dice at a café around the corner. Houses of prostitution that catered to a wealthy clientele supplemented their standard offerings with elegant drawing rooms where men could converse and smoke.

Women had less opportunity for social contact than men did, although daily Mass and an occasional outing to purchase finery for themselves or furnishings for the home gave them a chance to chat with acquaintances and to see and be seen. Performances in French, Spanish, and Italian by visiting European companies of course drew many well-to-do families to the magnificent Colón Theater or to the other three theatrical houses of the city. The Colón also occasionally offered dances or social events at which ladies of the best families could be seen.

Other public spectacles and social activities remained for the most part in the domain of the common people. Cockfights drew large crowds and stimulated betting; the pits, however, were all located on the western outskirts of the city, far from the homes of the better families. Horse racing was largely a rural sport, except for an occasional race along the main street of Barracas or Belgrano. A number of British residents had begun to play soccer in the 1860s, but native Argentines gave no sign of recognizing this as Argentina's future national sport—they still considered it a game for the mentally ill. Basques had introduced some *canchas de pelota*, or handball courts, in the 1850s; but this also remained a sport of crazy foreigners.

Nevertheless, the city's affluent families participated in certain public gatherings. Each summer, just before Lent, all of Buenos Aires celebrated Carnival with great enthusiasm. The upper balconies of houses afforded perfect retreats from which proper young ladies could dash buckets of water or perfumed water bombs on passersby. More color was added to the festivities in 1869, when the masqueraders, in carriages or on foot, began the practice of parading and dancing along certain downtown streets. Another popular festival occurred in the fall of each year, when a major church bazaar took place on grassy banks overlooking the estuary near the northern cemetery of the Recoleta. Under the tents and awnings, rich and poor rubbed elbows at the stalls and booths set up to sell drink, food, and amusement for the benefit of church charities. The Buenos Aires of 1870 also still enjoyed an open access to its muddy waterfront. The wealthy, although able to clean themselves in a tub at home, continued to share with the less affluent the summer pastime of a dip in the Río de la Plata. From November to March, the shallow mudbank in front of the city, clearly divided by common understanding into different sections for men and women and for well-to-do and poor, served as a vast public bath, which refreshed even though it hardly cleansed.

As you left the environs of the "Square of Enlightenment" and moved closer to the river, you quickly became aware of Defensa, a main access route into the city from the south and so named for the defense of Buenos Aires against British invaders in 1807. Here the original outline traced by Garay in the sixteenth century thrust itself upon the pedestrian. The gridwork laid out in 1580 had provided for blocks 140 varas, or nearly 400 feet, on a side. The streets measured slightly over thirty feet in width, and sidewalks further narrowed that width by three feet on each side. As a result, the first signs of congestion appeared along heavily traveled streets like Defensa, where oxcarts laden with skins, hides, or bales of wool, wagons piled high with bags of corn and wheat, pushcarts with vegetables and fruit, peddlers and deliverymen on horseback and on foot, and a variety of carriages vied for passage.

The annoyingly narrow sidewalks, built by individual property owners to raise the pedestrian above the street's dust, mud, or occasional raging torrent, presented a variety of surfaces and heights and, not infrequently, hazards for the incautious. Hemmed in on one side by the street, the sidewalk could afford no elbow room on the other, as brick walls, plastered or whitewashed, crowded to its edge and to the very corner of each block. One further obstacle, inherited from earlier times, had disappeared by the mid-nineteenth century: property owners could no longer project the heavy iron grillwork and bars which protected their windows out over the sidewalk, to the detriment of eyes or heads of passersby.

Admittedly, paving had improved since the seventeenth century, when cartwheels and hooves had torn up the dirt streets. Cobblestones or rough paving stones now covered almost all streets within a mile of the Plaza de Mayo. But since the stones usually were set in sand and dirt, they tended to work themselves loose and leave a highly irregular and pitted road surface with gaping mudholes and stagnant pools. Along with poorly leveled streets went an inadequate drainage system. The land on which Buenos Aires was built had been drained by a number of streams, of which the Riachuelo was the largest. Seven blocks south of the Plaza de Mayo one crossed such a major "drain," a street named Chile, which had four-foot-high sidewalks. The accumulation of refuse, the lack of any sewer system, and the occasional overflowing of privies turned a number of streets into little more than open sewers. On hot summer days the smell of human wastes and garbage along Chile could become overpowering.

The Church made its presence much felt along Defensa. The initial southward expansion of the city doubtless accounted for the many churches in this zone. On Bolívar the parish church of San Ignacio, formerly a Jesuit establishment, served an area of forty blocks south of the Plaza de Mayo. Now on Defensa, two blocks south of the plaza, you came to the "Square of Churches," with its three religious establishments: the Church of San Roque; the Church of San Francisco, with its adjoining monastery of the Franciscan Fathers, founded in the seventeenth century; and the Convent of San Ignacio. Just across the street stood one of the city's oldest charitable institutions, the *Casa de Niños Expósitos,* or home for abandoned children, established in 1779. There five sisters of charity, four of them from Italy, supervised a household of eleven wet nurses, six servants, three seamstresses, a cook, and a lone male—an Italian doorman—as well as their thirty charges, who ranged in age from one year to ten.[7] One block farther south was the Church of Santo Domingo, with its convent and proud relics from the British invasions.

Along Defensa substantial family residences continued to appear. Just beyond the "Square of Churches" you passed the home of Tomás Gowland, an Englishman who, as a small child in 1811, had come to Buenos Aires with his father. In the 1820s he had established an auctioneering business which developed into one of the most important in the country. He married into an old and established Uruguayan family. In the 1850s he was awarded honorary Argentine citizenship and then took on increasingly important political and financial positions. His household, consisting of his wife, nine bachelor sons, two assistants, and five servants, occupied a two-story structure, twenty varas wide, at No. 112–14. Next door a more modest edifice, ten varas wide, housed the family of Juan Agustín García, a lawyer and national deputy who could trace his line back to the first founders of Buenos Aires. His dependents consisted of his wife and baby daughter, three servants, and two small sons, one of whom, also named Juan Agustín, would become a leading intellectual and jurist.[8]

But Defensa seemed to mark the eastern edge of substantial family residences, perhaps because the land here sloped steeply down to the river. At the foot of Potosí, only a block from the Plaza de Mayo, stood one of the city's largest conventillos. These structures, usually deteriorated patio-style residences which their owners had converted into high-density slum rentals, began to appear with increasing frequency after 1870 in the area south of the Plaza de Mayo. The edifice at Potosí No. 7 was an excellent example of the type of housing that developed as immigrant manual laborers

poured into the city in the late nineteenth century. Seeking close-
ness to work in the port and downtown area, and contact with
their fellow countrymen, they crowded into small rooms ranged
around the open patios of old private residences. The 207 inhabitants in this conventillo filled thirty rooms and took up the same
floor space which one well-to-do family of ten to fifteen members
and five to ten servants would have occupied. Some nuclear families lived in individual rooms: a Spanish washerwoman in her sixties
with her four children, the oldest of whom was widowed and lived
here with his six-year-old Argentine-born son; an Italian shoemaker
with his wife and three children, all born in Italy; a French mason
and his French wife, a washerwoman, and their four children, all
born in Buenos Aires; a widowed Spanish washerwoman and her
five children, the three oldest born in Uruguay and the youngest
two in Buenos Aires. More common was the group of men, some
single and others married to wives they had left in Europe, who
banded together to rent a single room. A number of these groups
lived at the Potosí address: six Spaniards, four working as peons
and two as night watchmen; four peons and four night watchmen,
all Spaniards; three peons, three night watchmen, two cigarette
vendors, and one cook, all Spaniards; nine Spaniards, seven employed as peons and two as night watchmen. Frequently the nuclear family and the male groups combined: eleven Spaniards, including a carpenter, a tailor, two male house servants, a peon with
his wife and four children, and a nineteen-year-old washerwoman;
one Argentine, from the province of Córdoba, and fifteen Spaniards, including three married couples; eight Spanish men and an
Italian couple.

Further traits of conventillo dwellers could be found among residents of Potosí 7. All of those who were employed worked at manual occupations, the majority of them unskilled. Males decidedly
outnumbered females (145 to sixty-two), confirming the fact that
many men came to Argentina either single or without their wives.
Although adults predominated, conventillos usually had a sizable
population of children; in this particular conventillo there were
forty-six children under fourteen years of age. Half the adults at
Potosí 7 could read and write, and of the twenty-seven school-
aged (six to fourteen years old) children, thirteen were in school.

The oldest child attending school, however, was eleven years old, and almost all those who were ten or over were employed. Despite the crowded conditions and mixture of sexes within a single room, the formalities of marriage were still important: of the twenty couples, only three lived in common-law arrangements, and only eight of the children were illegitimate.

Finally, the population of the conventillo was overwhelmingly of one nationality. In Buenos Aires in 1869 the Spanish-born constituted only 8 per cent of the population. But in this conventillo 116 of the 161 persons fourteen years of age and over had been born in Spain. And in this particular conventillo, the predominant immigrant group in the 1869 census—Italians, who made up 24 per cent of the city's population—was represented by a mere eight individuals. Four Frenchmen, five Uruguayans, and one Paraguayan completed the list of foreign-born. Of the twenty-nine Argentines, thirteen came from the city or province of Buenos Aires. At the manual labor level, some migration evidently took place from provinces near the city: seven of the Argentines came from Córdoba, four from Corrientes, two from Santiago del Estero, and one from Santa Fe.[9]

This area between Defensa and the river also provided sites for a few industrial establishments. As you passed the "Square of Churches," a five-story building and a tall square chimney on the left caught your eye—the San Francisco flour mill. At a time when most industry was housed in small artisan workshops scattered in homes throughout the city's built-up area, or was relegated to the outskirts, as sawmills, brick factories, leather-tanning establishments, and meat-salting plants were, the flour mill was an important innovation. As early as 1846 it had replaced wind power with steam, and its thirty-five-horsepower potential, along with its location two blocks from the Plaza de Mayo, doubtless contributed to its success. Along Defensa there were also other large establishments, such as the liqueur and candy factories of the Inchauspe and Noel families.

As you moved toward the street of México—the limit between the poorer parish of San Telmo and its relatively wealthy neighbor Catedral al Sud, on the Plaza de Mayo—the households and homes became more modest. The two sides of México in the block between Bolívar and Perú pointed to the changing composition of neighborhoods. A total of 214 persons lived in two dozen family-type residences and a few rooming houses along this *cuadra*—two facing sides of a block-long section of street. None of the powerful families seen in the vicinity of the "Square of Enlightenment" lived here. Instead, there was a mixture of small nuclear family groups, largely made up of skilled workers, some shopkeepers, and a few white-collar government employees—only a half dozen were day laborers or peons. The neighborhood had an adequate, if not affluent, living standard; it was inhabited for the most part by blue-collar and white-collar workers. Although the people of the area were varied in occupation and nationality, those of roughly the same occupational skills and standing and of similar nationalities tended to group together within residential units.

Several families were sufficiently well-off to have one or two servants. The two most affluent families, all of whose members were Argentine-born, lived opposite each other in the middle of the block. At No. 93 was a grandmother, two of her daughters, one married, seven grandchildren, two servant girls, one with two small children, and a coachman. At No. 102 lived a forty-five-year-old merchant and his wife, two older sons who helped in the family business, four other children, a maiden aunt, a maid, and a cook.

Small business establishments combined with residences occupied the corners at each end of the cuadra. At Perú an Italian grocer, aged twenty-nine, lived with his Italian wife and seven children—all under seven years of age and all born in Buenos Aires. Across the street two Italians ran a small eating house which employed three cooks and a cashier. At the other end of México, at Bolívar, a French candy maker with his French wife, child, and sister-in-law shared an address with a French shoemaker, his French wife, their baby, and a French saddler. Across the street stood a small café run by a Spaniard; he, his young Uruguayan wife, their three children, a Spanish clerk, and a Spanish cook also lived there.

Rooming houses also contained family units, although usually in fewer numbers and in less crowded conditions than in the conventillos. Next to the eating house on Perú, for example, several small apartments accommodated an Italian cartman and his Italian wife and two children; a group of four single men—two Italians and two Spaniards—with two employed as cartmen, one as a peon, and the fourth as a cooper; an Italian shoemaker with his Italian washerwoman wife and three children; and, finally, in a room by herself, an eighty-year-old German widow.

While the major immigrant groups—Italian, Spanish, French, English, German, and Uruguayan—were represented in proportion to their city-wide percentages, there was little mixture of different nationalities at the same address. Furthermore, marriages between people of different nationalities hardly ever occurred. In this particular cuadra, the only exceptions were the Spanish café owner, who was married to an Uruguayan, and the Spanish merchant, whose wife was an Argentine—it is likely that in both cases the wives were daughters of immigrant Spaniards.

Educational and marriage patterns reflected the higher socioeconomic status of such a neighborhood over that of a conventillo. School attendance showed a better record than at the conventillo on Potosí: at least one child was still in school at the age of fourteen. The people of the area adhered to social convention; there were no illegitimate children and no common-law marriages.[10]

Food, although of poorer quality and in less quantity, was remarkably similar to that served in wealthy homes. Breakfast often consisted of a mate or two. Corn and cornmeal, prepared in a variety of stews and mushes, constituted an important item in the diet. Meat, however, remained the principal staple. Puchero, principally of beef, squash, and potatoes, frequently comprised the noonday meal, and it was eaten again in the evening. Water was the universal beverage. Wines still were largely imported and expensive, and *caña*, native sugarcane brandy, was only brought out on festive occasions.

As you continued south along Defensa into the parish of San Telmo, the houses became even more modest. There were fewer shops and stores, and semiskilled or unskilled and manual laborers began to predominate. On the left stood an army barracks, one of several located strategically around the city. Further on, in the center of the parish, you came to the Church of San Telmo. Across from this church was the Medical School of the University of Buenos Aires and the adjoining Hospital General de Hombres, or General Men's Hospital, the city's oldest, whose badly run-down patios

12. The southern outskirts of the city in the 1870s. (Archivo General de la Nación.)

and wings sprawled over nearly an entire block on the riverbank.

The presence of hospitals, like that of garrisons and cemeteries, suggested that you were reaching the outskirts and the least desirable residential zones of the city. In an age which still knew little about contagion and the spread of diseases, the community sought safety by removing the sick to the fringes of the city. Few complained, since only the poor who were desperately ill went to such institutions anyway. All others received treatment and recuperated or died in their beds at home.

This impression of hospitals and outskirts grew stronger as you turned right up Brasil toward the Plaza Constitución. Immediately to the south lay newly constructed hospitals which had recently been established by the British and Italian communities. Farther on, past Plaza Constitución, in open fields belonging to the Hospital General de Hombres, stood scattered buildings for convalescents, a home for victims of the Paraguayan War, and two insane asylums, one for men, the other for women.

Along Brasil, you gained a rare sense of height and perspective in this almost flat city. The land sloped away sharply to the south

13. Calle Larga, looking south toward Barracas, in the 1870s. Compare with Illus. 5. (Archivo General de la Nación.)

14. Plaza Constitución in the 1870s. Compare with Illus. 2. (Archivo General de la Nación.)

and east. Toward La Boca, the closest houses were at least three-quarters of a mile distant, across low, swampy ground. Scattered one-story houses and cultivated fields and orchards paralleled the two main roads to Barracas: one was the southern continuation of Defensa, and the other a street called Larga (later to be named Avenida Montes de Oca) which ran from Barracas to Plaza Constitución. Brasil marked the southern limit of built-up Buenos Aires in 1870.

On arriving at Plaza Constitución, you found yourself standing in a huge open market, the traditional unloading place for carts and wagons from the south of the province of Buenos Aires. It now also served as terminus for the Southern Railroad. Bales of wool and hides, bags of grain, as well as garden produce and chickens testified to its commercial importance. Just beyond Plaza Constitución, to the west, the city's largest slaughterhouse took in a constant stream of cattle, and each day it dispatched the fresh carcasses to innumerable small butcher shops all over the city. Adjacent to the slaughterhouse stood the medical facilities, as well as the Southern Cemetery, which had opened in 1867 under pressure of a particularly bad cholera epidemic. It would soon be filled to overflowing, and then closed, by the disastrous yellow fever epidemic that would claim nearly one-tenth of the city's population in 1871. Still farther to the west lay the city's main garbage dump—now only a modest pile of smoldering refuse, but a sore that would grow and fester on the city's south side until its removal to the southwestern limits of the Federal District in 1911.

From Plaza Constitución you could take a horse-drawn carriage that followed a spur line of the Southern Railroad. After a ride of ten blocks you would arrive at Plaza Monserrat. The route led through two more parishes: on the right and left, respectively, stood the churches of Concepción and Monserrat. Here the houses and streets seemed newer than south of the Plaza de Mayo. The most typical structure was the modest one-story home built around one or two interior patios and occupied by a single family. Frequently, however, several families shared a larger one- or two-story building divided into apartments of two or three rooms that opened off corridors or patios. In these neighborhoods, artisans, skilled manual laborers, shopkeepers, and white-collar workers predominated. Unlike some of the blocks nearer the Plaza de Mayo, here the Argentine-born outnumbered the European-born, although it is probable that many of the Argentine-born were children of Italian, Spanish, and French parents who had arrived in Buenos Aires in the 1840s and 1850s.

From Plaza Monserrat, a brief walk along Lima brought you to the street Victoria, where the tone of wealth, elegance, and prestige returned. The shops and stores that lined the six blocks toward the Plaza de Mayo attracted the matrons of Buenos Aires' high society. Corseted and stuffed into somber-hued dresses that swept the dirty sidewalk, and accompanied by their slim and beautiful daughters, they came in the late afternoons to buy clothes imported directly from the Boulevard des Italiens in Paris. Along this street also strolled statesmen and merchants in search of the latest cut of waistcoat or the most recently arrived cravats. Tailors and seamstresses constituted large occupational groups in this city, since virtually all clothing was made up from imported yard goods. Rough cotton clothes were made for workers, and elegant fabrics were fitted and stitched to suit the tastes of the affluent.

Walking along Victoria, you passed the Victoria Theater, the Colón's only major rival, where French actors performed Molière and Spanish companies presented the latest zarzuelas from Madrid or the classics of Lope de Vega. Also to the right, on Chacabuco and Perú, respectively, stood those two prestigious social and political clubs, the Club del Plata and the Club del Progreso.

At Perú you could look south or north and see numerous elite residences. South from Victoria were the homes of Miguel Azcuénaga, heir of a powerful landowning family in the province of Buenos Aires, at No. 66, Ángel F. Costa, the famous Uruguayan jurist, at No. 82, and Juan N. Fernández, a leading cattleman, at No. 83. Looking northward you could see the residence of the Elizaldes at No. 27, in the block directly behind the Cabildo. Rufino, head of this household, had served as Minister of Foreign Affairs during the 1860s and only recently had been defeated by Domingo F. Sarmiento for the presidency of Argentina. Along with him, his widowed sixty-nine-year-old mother, his twenty-one-year-old Brazilian wife, and two small boys lived his four single brothers, one, like him, a lawyer and the other three ranchers in the province of Buenos Aires. Eight servants took care of the household. Further down the block, at No. 9, lived the Molinas, a powerful merchant family. In addition to the elder Molinas, this household consisted of Eduardo, the oldest son, who ran the family business, his wife, and four small children; three unmarried daughters and two younger sons; three clerks and four maids.[11]

As you crossed Rivadavia, the street that ran along the north side of the Plaza de Mayo, Perú changed its name and became Florida, a street that would assume increasing importance as the chosen location for elite residences in the 1870s and 1880s. Some leading families had already located their homes along Florida, usually at the center of each cuadra, where the deepest and largest lots were. There were newer names here, including some from the interior provinces, but names that would become increasingly familiar during the late-nineteenth-century expansion of the country: Estanislao Frías, a wealthy rancher and landowner in the province of Buenos Aires, at No. 79; Bonifacio Lastra, lawyer, journalist, and future Senator, at No. 135; Felipe and Pastor Senillosa, powerful landowners, at No. 192; a leading naval officer, Antonio Somellera, at No. 250; Carlos E. Pellegrini, the future Vice President and President, at No. 258; Manuel Zavaletta, lawyer, Congressman, and Judge, at No. 260; and the city's famous *Intendente*, or Mayor, of the 1880s, Torcuato de Alvear, at an unnumbered door between No. 286 and 288.

Commerce went hand in hand with elite residency along Florida and the adjacent streets. The lots toward the corner of each block were usually given over to small shops. Here stores selling French fashions, furniture, and perfumes had invaded the south end of Florida close to the Plaza de Mayo, indicating a trend in which Florida would soon replace Victoria as the center of shopping elegance. Parallel to Florida and one block to the left, Maipú had emerged as the location for several English commercial houses as well as for three of the city's six main hotels. As along Defensa, some of the city's industrial establishments also occupied locations close to the Plaza de Mayo. On the north side were Sackmann's steam sawmill just off Rivadavia, Bagley's liquor and cracker factory on Maipú, and the Peuser and La Unión printing plants on San Martín.

As you continued north along Florida, or along one of the parallel streets—Maipú on the left, or San Martín and Reconquista on the right—a slightly different tone and environment became evident. You were now in the parish of Catedral al Norte, with its Church of La Merced, located on Reconquista. Since families who dated their importance back to the colonial period had largely taken over the area immediately south of the Plaza de Mayo, those who had acquired wealth more recently moved north of the Plaza —close to the focus of power and prestige, yet with room to expand. With political consolidation and national unity after 1862, these newly wealthy—including a number of British, French, Italian, and Spanish merchants and entrepreneurs—became increasingly linked to European commerce, capital, and culture. Although often connected by blood or marriage with the Hispanic aristocracy south of the plaza, they began to establish different attitudes and ways of life for the city's elite.

The foreign merchants tended to congregate in this area north of the Plaza de Mayo. Their principal club, Club de Residentes Extranjeros, was located on San Martín, just across from the Cathedral. The Anglican Church of Buenos Aires, founded by British residents in 1831, stood around the corner from the parish church of La Merced, not far from a small chapel maintained by United

States citizens. Four blocks farther west, just off Cangallo, the German community had established a Lutheran chapel.

Along with this concentration of the foreign commercial elite came a clustering of the city's and the nation's financial institutions along Piedad (renamed Bartolomé Mitre in 1906) and Cangallo and extending into the adjacent blocks of San Martín and Reconquista. Both the Bolsa de Comercio, the stock and cereal exchange, which opened in 1862, and the country's leading bank, Banco de la Provincia de Buenos Aires, faced on San Martín. Around the corner on Piedad stood the Casa de la Moneda, the Government Mint, as well as the major foreign banking house, Banco de Londres y Río de la Plata. This area north of the Plaza de Mayo also included the offices of what were to become the city's two leading newspapers, *La Prensa* and *La Nación*, established in 1869 and 1870 and located, respectively, on Rivadavia and San Martín.[12]

The traffic of carriages along Florida, the stylishness of dresses worn to Mass, the elegance of furnishings in the home, all suggested an activity and display of wealth rarely seen south of the plaza. The processes which would lead to still further differentiation between the north and south sides had barely started in 1870, but changes in housing styles forecast the direction of the change. Many of the affluent homes north of the plaza replicated the one- and two-story structures centered on interior patios which sheltered the wealthy on the south side.

Occasionally, however, one came upon an Italianesque villa, with stucco walls and marble columns, and adorned with fountains and palms. Later, in the economic booms of the 1880s and the first decade of the twentieth century, these *petits hotels* would become the townhouses for Argentina's nouveau riche, who were centered in Barrio Norte—still in 1870 an unpopulated area at the northern edge of the built-up zone. In the gran aldea, however, only a few families, such as the Lumbs and the Anchorenas, had built such residences. These structures afforded an outward elegance, a facility for grand entertaining and conspicuous consumption, totally foreign to the patio-style construction. They bespoke a new era of wealth and extravagance unknown in the colony or the early formation of the nation. Also, since they could not be imitated on anything less than a grand scale, the less well-to-do could not—as was possible with the patio-style—merely make smaller and cheaper copies.

This new type of house was high and narrow. Its three stories made better use of the ever more costly land and provided better ventilation and light than did the low, one- and two-story structures. A large entrance hall with drawing and reception rooms took up most of the first floor; the second contained a dining room, a study, and a few small salons; while the third floor was reserved for bedrooms. Servant rooms and kitchen occupied the basement. When these *petits hotels* began to be constructed at the less crowded northern edge of the city, they frequently were set back somewhat from the street, thus allowing space in front for carriages and in back for a small formal garden.

In 1870 the similarities of these northern streets to those south of the Plaza de Mayo were, nevertheless, more pronounced than the dissimilarities. The sidewalks and streets were as narrow and irregularly surfaced as those on the south side. Near the northern end of Florida, where you crossed the street of Paraguay, the high sidewalks recalled that other natural drainage street, Chile. Until recently a swinging metal footbridge had enabled one to cross Paraguay even while a torrent from a recent downpour went raging toward the estuary.

Church institutions, although more spread out than they were immediately south of the Plaza de Mayo, still played important roles. In the parish of Catedral al Norte, in addition to the Church of La Merced and the adjacent Orphanage of La Merced for girls, was the Convent of the Cataline Sisters that enclosed within its high gray wall an entire block of Córdoba between Reconquista and San Martín. Four other churches, San Miguel, San Nicolás, Socorro, and the still incompleted Piedad, headed parishes of the same names located to the west of Catedral al Norte and thus served the remaining built-up area of the city.

Affluent residents of the area lived primarily on the streets of Maipú, Florida, San Martín, and Reconquista—all northward extensions of those streets along which the wealthy lived south of the Plaza. As on the south side, wealth and prestige seemed to decrease notably as you moved away from the Plaza. Reconquista, like Defensa, marked the eastern edge of prestige residences, and the blocks along the riverbank were largely given over to manual and semi-skilled workers and to cheap rooming houses and conventillos.

Unlike Defensa, Reconquista served as a dividing line of respectability, with a sprinkling of licensed houses of prostitution along or just off it and the street of 25 de Mayo. But even the houses of prostitution reflected the influence of the central plaza. Those nearest the Plaza de Mayo were pleasantly furnished, with salons for cards and conversation, and featured young, attractive French, Italian, or German girls. As you moved north along 25 de Mayo the women you met were older, often with heavy mixtures of Indian and Negro blood, and the houses clearly catered to sailors, peons, and laboring men in general.

At the northern end of Florida, ten blocks from the Plaza de Mayo, you reached the large, barren Plaza de Marte, renamed the Plaza San Martín in 1878.* Here the garrisons, wholesale markets, slaughterhouses, cemeteries, and the falling away of the terrain to the east and north brought to mind the southern outskirts. The edge of the city had again been reached. A block to the northwest of the Plaza de Marte stood the Church of Socorro, headquarters for this northern parish which you had entered upon crossing the street Paraguay. Adjacent lay several long buildings, the home of the Bieckert Brewery. Beyond, to the northwest, stretched an area of *quintas*—small farms and country houses—and orchards, with at most one or two homes to a block.

Still farther to the northwest, nearly a mile from the Plaza de Marte, the Church of Pilar administered a thinly settled rural parish that reached out toward Belgrano. Alongside this church was the Northern Cemetery, the Recoleta, which was soon to become the city's most prestigious graveyard and the final resting place for many of Argentina's best families. Behind the church was another small garrison. A few hundred yards to the west of the garrison, the area of the northern slaughterhouse, with its ring of shacks and small bars, had acquired a reputation for lawlessness, especially

---

* At the end of the eighteenth century this area, also given the name Retiro, had boasted a bull ring with spectator stands for the city's whole adult population. The color and movement associated with that popular Spanish spectacle had disappeared at the time of independence, when the ring was replaced by an army garrison and barracks.

15. View of the city of Buenos Aires from the passenger pier in the 1870s. Compare with Illus. 1. (Archivo General de la Nación.)

after nightfall. From here two main roads, both of which carried a considerable traffic in horses, carriages, and carts, continued through open fields toward Belgrano. Just this side of the stream bed of Maldonado, the city's official boundary, two miles distant, these roads joined to cross the Maldonado Bridge and then forked once again into the upper and lower roads to Belgrano.

Standing on the high ground at the Plaza de Marte, you could turn east or north and look down on a strip of low ground and beyond it see the yellow-brown estuary. Jutting out into the water were the sheds, piles of coal, and chimneys of the city's British-owned and managed gasworks, which since the 1850s had lit some of the downtown streets and homes. Immediately below the knoll stood the sheds and the brick station house of the Northern Railroad terminus, which had already acquired the area's name, Retiro.

From this railroad station, a horse-drawn car running on the Northern's spur line brought you back to the city's center. The Paseo de Julio along which you traveled was a broad dirt street that ran along the water's edge. On the river side, you had an excellent view of a scene still typical of the city—the wash of the

16. The Buenos Aires waterfront in the 1870s. Compare with Illus. 3. (Archivo General de la Nación.)

wealthy and not-so-wealthy spread out to dry on grass and dirt along the riverbank. Scattered along the shore, groups of washer-women, many of them black or mulatto, gossiped as they pounded and beat the shirts, sheets, and underclothes in the many shallow pools of stagnant water. On the right, rooming houses and bars pre-dominated in the narrow blocks between Paseo de Julio and 25 de Mayo. Here the population was almost entirely foreign-born, save for an occasional infant born to recent arrivals. There you found the usual mixture of Italians, Spaniards, Frenchmen, Germans, and Englishmen, but the large number of sailors and peddlers also con-tributed some nationalities rarely encountered elsewhere in the city —Danes, Greeks, Russians, Swedes, Poles. Along the narrow streets which climbed the slight rise to Reconquista were located other heavy concentrations of foreigners, divided by nationality into housing or family groups. A foreign tone, in accent, language, food, and dress, permeated this whole waterfront area.

On the left, near the foot of Cangallo, a wooden passenger pier extended 400 yards into the estuary. Three blocks farther on, the

17. View of the waterfront, looking toward the Riachuelo and La Boca area from the vicinity of Venezuela Station, in the 1870s. Compare with Illus. 3. (Archivo General de la Nación.)

Customhouse boasted a slightly longer pier for handling freight. These two rickety wooden structures constituted the major avenues by which transatlantic trade and passengers entered and left Argentina's major port. In 1870 the city had no facilities where ships could dock. Small ships, especially those in the coasting trade, could enter the Riachuelo and tie up alongside the bank at La Boca and Barracas. But the shallow mudbank, sometimes no deeper than five feet a mile from shore, forced large transatlantic steamers and sailing ships, which now weighed 400 tons and drew as much as sixteen feet of water, to anchor several miles offshore, in the open estuary. From there cargo and passengers were unloaded or loaded in a series of stages—first to lighters, then to launches or high-wheeled carts which were driven out into the river, and finally to the passenger or freight piers. Expense and inconvenience hobbled every step of this process. In addition, there were the peculiar dangers of the Río de la Plata, for the broad expanse of water and adjoining flat land allowed strong winds to turn the estuary into a sailor's nightmare. Not until the 1880s, however, did the porteños succeed in putting through plans to begin construction of modern port facilities along this waterfront.

Across the Paseo de Julio from the passenger pier, at a convenient distance for ship captains, was the Port Authority's Office. A few steps off Paseo de Julio, on Corrientes, stood a former horse barn, remodeled into the Immigrant Asylum, which furnished five days of free lodging and food to newly arrived third-class passengers. Most immigrants, however, immediately joined relatives or compatriots in one of the near-by rooming houses or conventillos. Only the more affluent turned toward the recently opened Gran Hotel Argentino. Here in the elegance of its comfortable rooms you could truly feel that you were at the center of the city, for you were directly across from the Central Station where the horse-drawn car had ended its run, with the Casa Rosada at your right hand and the Colón Theater only a few doors away.

This five-mile tour of the Buenos Aires of 1870 suggests some of the flavor of the gran aldea, an environment which was destined to undergo a rapid transformation during the next forty years. True, you had not reached out via the Western Railroad from Plaza del Parque to Plaza Once in the west, or beyond the city's limits to the town of Flores. You had seen neither the southern villages of La Boca and Barracas nor the outlying northern community of Belgrano. The federalization of the city in 1880 would bring all these settlements within the boundaries of Buenos Aires. A population explosion accentuated by massive European immigration, and a commercial expansion stimulated by European demand for meats, hides, wool, and cereals, caused astounding urban growth. Rapid development of the railroad and streetcar systems, which had been introduced at the critical moment of increasing population, caused the city to sprawl outward, far beyond the downtown streets of 1870. Buenos Aires not only enveloped separate villages such as La

Boca, Barracas, Flores, and Belgrano; it also added countless new suburbs. By the turn of the century, the pressure to push outward had increased still further, fueled as it was by renewed migrations of European peoples, especially in the boom years from 1905 to 1912, by electrification of the streetcar system and the consequent lowering of fares, and by the hunger of hundreds of thousands of acclimated immigrants, or of their Argentine-born sons and daughters, for a parcel of land to call home, even if it were located on the outskirts of urban settlement.

Locational Forces:
Port, Railroads,
Federal Capital

Around 1870, engineers, merchants, politicians, and other interested parties involved in working out three major problems—the location of port works, the development of a railroad system, and the establishment of a Federal District or national capital—pulled and tugged at the shape of Buenos Aires. By the first decade of the twentieth century, however, the solutions to these problems had moulded the city's form and growth.

Each of these problems had a long history. The mudbanks off Buenos Aires had served as an anchorage for ships since the first founding of the city. Oxcarts and mule trains in the seventeenth century had formed trails or roads to the west, south, and north, linking the city with its hinterland. Political authorities, whose control at times reached out beyond Argentina to adjoining countries, had used the city as a capital since its founding. There could be little doubt that the location of international and regional transportation systems and the seat of political authority would assume even greater importance during the period of rapid demographic expansion and intense technological change in the late nineteenth century. Nevertheless the final pattern that would emerge was far from clear in 1870.

Construction of a port at Buenos Aires did not prove easy. There were no sheltered bays or protecting hills like those found at Montevideo, at the mouth of the estuary, or at Bahía Blanca, which in

1870 was still a frontier outpost, far to the south. The vast river system that emptied into the estuary of the Río de la Plata brought huge amounts of silt from the interior of Brazil, Paraguay, Bolivia, and Argentina. At upstream ports along the Uruguay and Paraná rivers, such as Concordia, Concepción, and Rosario, the current kept open a channel close to the riverbank. At Rosario, this fast-flowing current and the high bank afforded easy loading of grain exports by means of chutes directed into the holds of ships. Below Rosario, however, the currents became sluggish, contributing to the vast delta of the Paraná River, which ended only twelve miles north of Buenos Aires. The silt of centuries had built a shelf of mud and sand in front of the city, and it kept the estuary's main channel several miles offshore.

Despite this handicap, Buenos Aires had acquired commercial momentum because it was the first location to be settled on the estuary. Of course, the size of vessels and cargoes also played an important role, since not until the mid-nineteenth century did draft and tonnage increase to a point where the mud flats presented more than annoyances. The city thus had grown slowly but steadily for 270 years and held tremendous advantages over possible competitors in population, commercial acceptability, and merchandising outlets, if not in physical location. No other city in the coastal zone approached it in size, to say nothing of wealth, prestige, and power.[*1]

Such primacy could not endure without port improvements. As the draft and tonnage of sailing vessels between Europe and South America increased, from the thirteen-foot, 200-ton average of 1850 toward the sixteen-foot, 400-ton figure of 1870, and as even larger steamships entered the Río de la Plata trade, the traditional methods of handling cargo and passengers began to wreak havoc with shipping schedules and freight costs. When it could be reported, as occurred in 1881, that a 500-ton vessel required 100 days to unload its cargo at Buenos Aires, as contrasted to ten to twelve days in

* The population of Argentina's ten largest cities, as recorded in the first national census (taken in 1869), speaks convincingly to the disproportionate weight given to the city of Buenos Aires (coastal river ports are italicized): *Buenos Aires*, 178,000; Córdoba, 28,500; *Rosario*, 23,000; Tucumán, 17,500; Salta, 11,500; *Corrientes*, 11,000; *Santa Fe*, 10,500; *Paraná*, 10,000; *Gualeguaychú*, 10,000; and San Juan, 8500. The second largest "city" in the province of Buenos Aires in 1869 was Chivilcoy, with 6500 inhabitants.

most ports, the disadvantages of the porteño waterfront clearly had telling financial impact on shippers, retailers, and consumers.[2]

All Buenos Aires, as well as the national government, recognized the need to endow the city with a port capable of handling efficiently the increasing flow of trade. The parties to the ensuing struggle, which, unfortunately, postponed an effective solution of the problem until nearly the end of the century, never questioned the need to modernize or to adopt new technology. They did, however, raise major questions as to location and construction methods—factors which decisively oriented the city's future development. The bitter conflict of those years has now largely been forgotten. Indeed, few porteños know that their city might have developed in any other way than with its waterfront and port located directly in front—that is, to the east—of the Plaza de Mayo.

Two quite different plans for port development emerged during the 1870s. The alternatives were, first, to deepen the channel and improve existing facilities along the Riachuelo, on the city's south side, or, second, to build new facilities on the shelving mud flats just east of the Plaza de Mayo (see Map 6). Each approach had logical appeal and each promised to contribute to the transformation of the city. To the successful side in this controversy would go a major share in determining the direction and style of the city's future growth—and accompanying spoils in building contracts and land sales.

Those interests who identified with the city's south side gradually allied themselves with Luis A. Huergo, an Argentine engineer with considerable local experience in dealing with hydraulic construction problems.* His supporters included most of the authorities

---

* Huergo was born in 1837 into an established merchant family of Buenos Aires. During the early 1850s he studied at a Jesuit college in Maryland in the United States. He then returned to Argentina to receive training as a surveyor and in 1870 became the first civil engineer to graduate from the Department of Exact Sciences of the University of Buenos Aires. During the early 1870s he served as Deputy and then Senator in the provincial legislature of Buenos Aires and was active in road and bridge construction as well as in several canal, irrigation, and railroad projects. For a decade, from 1875 to 1885, he devoted his principal efforts to locating Buenos Aires' port along the Riachuelo. His subsequent engineering activities included waterworks projects for the cities of Córdoba and Asunción, Paraguay; docks and railroad sidings in the port of Bahía Blanca; irrigation works in the province of Mendoza; and petroleum explorations at Comodoro Rivadavia in southern Argentina. He died in Buenos Aires in 1913 at the age of seventy-six.

of the province of Buenos Aires, who, in the 1870s, still resided in the city; the merchants and citizens located south of the Plaza de Mayo, especially those of La Boca and Barracas; the followers of *La Prensa*, a reform-minded and influential daily newspaper; and many others who felt that the nation as well as the city should evolve and develop gradually and steadily on the basis of local resources and capabilities. The Riachuelo had served as a second port for the city almost since its founding, and most of the coastal trade still operated out of La Boca and Barracas. Widen and deepen the channel, they said, straighten out the Riachuelo's worst bends, improve and expand dock, warehouse, and railroad facilities at La Boca and Barracas, and this port would be able to accommodate the increased tonnage and draft of overseas shipping. Thus the city's river and fishing port could become its overseas port as well. As commerce expanded, these facilities could be pushed northward from La Boca toward the Plaza de Mayo, with a single channel providing access to the main deep-water channel of the Río de la Plata. Furthermore, such a project could be accomplished with local technical expertise, with local capital, and without major expenditures.

Supporters of a port adjacent to the Plaza de Mayo early identified their spokesman as Eduardo Madero, an influential porteño merchant and politician.* Despite the tangled web of personal interests, political power, and financial considerations, the groups which most consistently backed the eventually victorious Madero included most of the top-level administrators of the national government, a majority of the foreign merchants and entrepreneurs resident in the city, most importers, exporters, and wholesale merchants, and leading daily newspapers such as *El Diario*, *La Nación*, and *La Tribuna*. Particularly influential were British financial and commercial interests, both in England and in Buenos Aires. Ma-

---

* Madero was born in 1832 into a powerful landowning family of Buenos Aires. He spent his early years in Montevideo, where his family lived in exile during the regime of Juan Manuel de Rosas. Shortly after his return to Buenos Aires in 1852 he established an import-export house with a branch office in Montevideo. As early as 1861 he initiated proposals to provide better port facilities for the city, and soon he became active in seeking British engineering and financial support for such projects. By the late 1860s he had become the leader of efforts to construct the port which would eventually bear his name. He died in 1894, four years before Puerto Madero was finally completed.

dero's approach satisfied many already entrenched political and commercial interests because it capitalized on the existing focus of the railroad network, retail and wholesale outlets, and financial credit institutions. The bulk of import-export trade already flowed to and from ships anchored in the open estuary in front of the city through the Customhouse, which was located immediately to the east of the Casa Rosada. Modern port facilities would, therefore, merely add efficiency and economy to existing operations. Furthermore, such proposals clearly appealed to those interested in grandiose projects: the dream of Argentina's commercial greatness seemed to find fulfillment in reclaiming the mud flats in front of the city and creating basins, docks, warehouses, and sidings that could handle the constantly rising flow of goods through the city. The enormous expenditures involved, the need for foreign credit, and the reliance on outside experts all seemed more than justified by the endless prospects for expansion and prosperity. In such a time of euphoria, the opportunity for individual profit-taking appeared to be part of the expected and acceptable pattern of development.

At the distance of nearly a century, it may be tempting to read into the subsequent clash of the Huergo-Madero projects still other motives. For some, Huergo represented the criollo heritage and the nationalistic development of the Argentine economy. At the same time, one could see in Madero the preoccupation of statesmen and writers of the "Generation of Eighty," who sought Argentina's modernization and progress on the basis of foreign capital and skills. This "Europeanization" of Argentina soon proved to be both the country's great strength and its greatest weakness. Those leaders of the 1880s not only contributed to the astoundingly rapid growth of the city and nation in the late nineteenth century; they also made the economy increasingly dependent on markets, factories, and resources outside Argentina.

Regardless of the implications of the Huergo and Madero positions, the victories gained by Madero and his followers during the 1880s and 1890s ensured that the city would continue to develop around a core centered on the Plaza de Mayo. Partly as a result of those successes, porteño expansion and development occurred increasingly on the northern side of the city, while the southern districts fell steadily behind in services, facilities, and opportunities. The foreign merchant and financier, the economy's commercial emphasis, and the prestige and power of a national government made up largely of provincials who had moved to Buenos Aires, all received reinforcement from Puerto Madero.

The outcome of the struggle between the two contending approaches remained in doubt for more than a decade, however, and Puerto Madero was not finally completed until 1898. The story of that conflict gives a sense of the forces involved, as well as providing some bench marks in the rapidly changing political and economic environment of Buenos Aires in the late nineteenth century.[3]

Eduardo Madero, whose import-export business was directly affected by the costly and dangerous loading and unloading procedures at Buenos Aires, in 1861 made a proposal that would have required financial assistance from Baring Brothers of London, the leading financial house and a long-time underwriter of Argentine credit operations. As it was presented to the provincial authorities, the project called for construction of a basin on the mud flats at the east side of the Casa Rosada, with an access canal cut south to the mouth of the Riachuelo and then east into the deep water of the estuary. Civil conflict within Argentina, along with serious doubts as to the feasibility of dredging such a channel and maintaining the dock facilities free of silt and sand, kept the provincial government from seriously considering this project.

Undaunted, Madero, with the backing of several supporters, traveled to England in the mid-1860s to secure technical assistance from British engineers. Out of these negotiations emerged a formal proposal, prepared by two British engineers and submitted to the national government by the especially constituted firm of Madero, Proudfoot and Company, to bring British capital and expertise to bear on the problem. In mid-1869, with the Paraguayan War drawing to a close, the Minister of Interior signed a contract with Madero for the construction of a port to be located in front of the Plaza de Mayo and to consist of two basins, one dredged eleven feet deep, the other seventeen feet; a dry dock; and a ship channel to deep water dredged to a depth of thirteen feet. Strong objections to this contract immediately arose from the provincial authorities, from several local commercial and engineering groups,

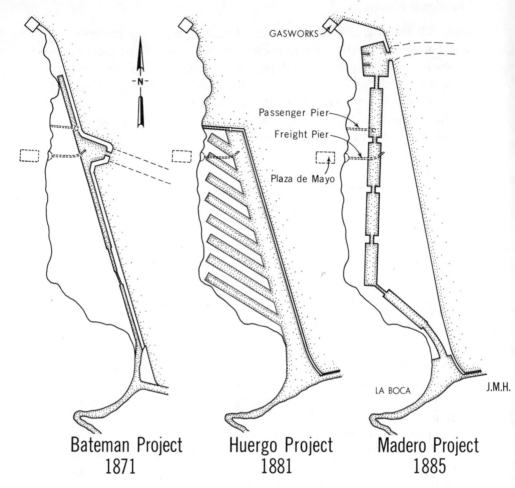

GASWORKS

Passenger Pier

Freight Pier

Plaza de Mayo

LA BOCA

J.M.H.

Bateman Project
1871

Huergo Project
1881

Madero Project
1885

6. Project Sketches of the Port of Buenos Aires: Bateman, 1871; Huergo, 1881; Madero, 1882.

and from the recently constituted but influential newspaper *La Nación Argentina* (soon to become *La Nación*), which was edited by former President Bartolomé Mitre. Mitre, recently elected to the Senate, made a particularly effective challenge to the contract in September 1869. His contention, never satisfactorily answered, was that Congress needed to study the port question more thoroughly before turning over such a vital matter to exploitation by a private concern. He succeeded in raising serious doubts in many

minds.[4] Although a substitute measure authorized the national executive to construct or contract for the construction of a port, the
1869 contract was withdrawn from consideration.

In the following year the national and provincial governments
collaborated in making a contract with John F. Bateman, engineer
for the London sewer works as well as for the docks on the River
Clyde, to give his technical appraisal of the port situation. After a
one-month visit to Buenos Aires, Bateman returned home in early
1871, leaving his sketches in the hands of the Argentine authorities. His plan called for a large ship basin located, as in the 1869
Madero project, in front of the Plaza de Mayo and reached from
deep water by a twenty-one-foot northern channel and by a shal-
lower southern channel to the Riachuelo (see Map 6). A deluge of
criticism from local engineers, mainly focused on Bateman's failure
to consider dredging and related financial and technical problems
during his hasty trip, soon discredited the project.[5]

Meanwhile, other designs continued to flow in, from both local
and foreign experts. Among these were Luis A. Huergo's plan to
straighten the mouth of the Riachuelo and build three harbor
basins on its right bank, where the town of Barracas al Sud (renamed Avellaneda in 1904) had begun to develop, as well as a fascinating project, suggested by Guillermo Rigoni, for a circular
ship basin located three miles offshore in the estuary, due east of
the Northern Railroad terminal at Retiro. The provincial government of Buenos Aires, with the blessings of the national authorities,
decided in 1875–76 to move ahead on one part of a revised project
presented by Huergo. It located the principal port at La Boca.[6]
These plans called for the alteration of the mouth of the Riachuelo
and the dredging of a nine-foot channel to this entrance. Huergo
was assigned the position of director of the "Riachuelo Works,"
and, despite the economic recession of the mid-1870s, dredging
operations moved slowly ahead. By the end of 1878, overseas shipping could enter the Riachuelo and tie up at warehouses in La
Boca. The opening of this channel stimulated commercial activity
on the city's south side and led the provincial legislature to author-
ize additional funds to increase the dredged depth of the channel
to twenty-one feet.[7] But rising tensions between provincial and national authorities—tensions that finally exploded in the brief civil

18. Port facilities in La Boca, around 1880. (Archivo General de la Nación.)

war of June 1880—cut off provincial funds for the project and resulted in the cancellation of a promised subsidy from the federal
government.

The solution of Argentina's "capital" question through federalization of the city of Buenos Aires restored stability to the political
scene and encouraged the Huergo and Madero camps to press for
a final decision on the "port" issue. Initially, at least, the advantage
seemed to lie with Huergo. At the end of 1880 the national government turned over most of its promised subsidy to the special commission charged with administering the Riachuelo port works, and
Huergo made a quick trip to England to arrange for the construction of two more dredges. Early in 1881 the provincial legislature,
in a repetition of its 1879 law, appropriated funds to dredge the
southern channel and the Riachuelo to a depth of twenty-one feet.[8]
Huergo thereupon brought forward a modification of his 1876

proposal. In addition to a twenty-one-foot channel and a dock at La Boca's northern edge, this project called for a series of parallel docks, protected by a breakwater, which could be built northward along the shore toward the Plaza de Mayo (see Map 6).

In the interim, the national government became increasingly convinced that it, rather than provincial authorities, should build and administer the port facilities. The municipal council had already excused itself, admitting that it lacked the funds and the power to carry out the construction operations.[9] In October 1881 the national authorities received congressional authorization to expropriate the Riachuelo port works and to float a loan in order to continue expansion of those facilities.[10] Adolfo E. Dávila, one of Huergo's staunchest defenders in Congress and the editor of *La Prensa*, subsequently crowed:

> At that moment [October 1881] the Argentine Congress gave its authorized opinion. It stated that this [Huergo's proposal for La Boca port] was to be the port of the Capital of the Republic or, what is the same thing, that this was to be the port of Buenos Aires and that the Nation should build it.[11]

Nevertheless, several other projects were still being studied by special committees during 1881–82, and the optimism expressed by Huergo's followers soon proved to be premature. One proposal that never received serious consideration involved building a seawall to protect the entire waterfront, from Retiro on the north to La Boca at the south. A local entrepreneur, Christopher F. Woodgate, advanced another; he advocated constructing a series of docks on his private property in La Boca. This project reached the floor of the Chamber of Deputies in 1881 at the end of the regular sessions. It immediately aroused such a storm of criticism that it was returned to committee, and it was subsequently withdrawn from the agenda of the extraordinary session.[12] In the following year Congress tabled the project after Dávila's minority report underlined the dangers of turning over port concessions to private control.[13] A more dubious proposal came from a certain J. W. Williams, who offered a port project "of tremendous importance to the country," but demanded a down payment of 50,000 pesos to unveil his blueprints; Congress quickly rejected the offer.[14] In 1882, during months of committee study and debate, the Ministry of War requested additional plans and estimates from Huergo on his project. These papers evidently never reached a congressional subcommittee and were not mentioned in any congressional debates; Huergo later implied that they had been deliberately withheld at this crucial moment in the struggle.[15]

Meanwhile, Madero and his followers had been working actively in Congress and in England to regain the ground initially lost to Huergo. In 1881 Madero had again traveled to London, where he secured the services of Sir John Hawkshaw, one of Britain's leading port experts, as technical adviser, along with the promise of funds from Baring Brothers. He returned home with a plan which drew heavily on his 1869 proposal as well as on the 1871 Bateman plan. North and south canals, dredged to a depth of twenty-one feet, would enable ships to reach two harbors located at opposite ends of a string of four connecting basins. This port would be constructed on land reclaimed from the estuary, with the docks themselves built immediately to the east of the Plaza de Mayo. The northern harbor would be situated adjacent to Retiro, while the southern harbor would lie at the northern edge of La Boca. At the end of June 1882, Madero formally presented these plans to the legislature (see Map 6).

Against the backdrop of discussions and delays, the sudden decision by Congress in late September and October 1882 to accept the Madero project came as a surprise to most. In a single day the Senate enthusiastically seconded Carlos E. Pellegrini's glowing speech of endorsement and unanimously approved the project. In the Chamber of Deputies, Dávila expressed amazement that the national executive had sponsored this proposal, which in effect canceled the "real port" under construction in La Boca and replaced it with an ill-considered and poorly prepared plan that Congress had had no time to study. His motion to postpone consideration of the measure, however, was defeated. The next day the Senate bill passed the Chamber of Deputies by a vote of 33 to 10, with only Dávila taking the floor to argue against the wisdom of such hasty action.[16]

Apparently the Huergo forces had been caught unprepared, or possibly they felt confident because of their past accomplishments. Only one editorial appeared in the usually vocal *La Prensa*, and it was a forecast of comments which that newspaper's editor would make on the floor of the Chamber of Deputies in October, urging that consideration of the Madero project be postponed until the next year.[17] Since the law had merely authorized the national executive to negotiate a contract with Madero for construction of the port, Huergo's followers perhaps judged that the already existing facilities in La Boca had sufficient impetus to win out over the Madero project. That view certainly gained strength when the large transatlantic steamer *L'Italia*, which drew fifteen feet of water, entered the Riachuelo in January 1883.[18] Not only had overseas shipping to La Boca increased since the opening of that port to transatlantic trade—from 197 vessels in 1879 to 1150 in 1884—but also the Riachuelo's trade, as a percentage of total shipping and tonnage entering Buenos Aires, had risen steadily. In 1879, 9 per cent of the ships and 7 per cent of the tonnage from overseas that entered Buenos Aires did so through the Riachuelo; by 1884 the flow through La Boca had risen to 23 per cent of the ships and 35 per cent of the tonnage.[19] Even the leading British newspaper in Buenos Aires, *The Standard*, showed unusual sympathy to the development of the Riachuelo and suggested that English shipping agencies should not be located north of the Plaza de Mayo along Reconquista, but rather in La Boca.[20]

During the course of 1883, *La Prensa* finally warmed to the task of demolishing the Madero project. After printing scattered editorials and articles early in the year, the newspaper published the report of a special government committee appointed to study and report on the Madero project. The report of the five-man committee, admittedly composed of several men who were hostile to Madero's plans, had a definitely negative ring to it:

> The payment of the port works in the form prescribed by the law and with the intervention of Mr. Madero is onerous and prejudicial to the national credit. . . . There is absolutely no reason to dredge a new canal. The Government should inform the Congress of the above-noted inconveniences and difficulties and of the advantages which will accrue to the country if the contract authorized by the law of October 27, 1882 is not carried out. . . .[21]

La Prensa then began a series of lead editorials and articles analyzing the financial and technical aspects of the contract, reviewing

the history of port proposals, and attributing all kinds of motives
to the Madero camp.[22]

The main thrusts of the arguments were directed against the expense, estimated at twenty million gold pesos (at this time, the gold
peso was approximately equal to the United States dollar, or to
four British shillings); the hasty improvisation of the plans; the
high return allowed Madero in his role as middleman between the
Argentine government and the English companies; and the sheer
waste of building a second channel.

> If the object is to give that gentleman [Madero] the total of *20
> million gold* pesos so that he can order others to build the port, and
> at the same time make his own fortune, let it be said with all frank-
> ness and not by twisting the background or the facts of the situa-
> tion.[23]

Clearly, Huergo's supporters still hoped that their project could
triumph:

> Even though all haste be made in the construction effort, it [the
> Madero proposal] will not be completed in the next two or three
> years given the slow pace of work here and in that time the port of
> Buenos Aires, proposed by Huergo and so severely attacked and
> disfigured by the Madero proponents, can be almost finished.[24]

Simultaneously, a propaganda offensive launched by Madero
backers supported the contract negotiations now under way in
England. *La Nación*, in a sharp reversal of the 1869 posture assumed by Mitre, ridiculed the Huergo project, calling it a mere ap-
pendage to the dredging of a channel, and questioning its location—
two miles from the commercial center of the city.[25] *El Nacional*,
a paper that spoke for the national government, also took the field
to establish the primacy of Madero's plans for a port and to criti-
cize the conception and location of a port in La Boca.[26]

Madero returned to England in 1883 to take advantage of the
promises of technical and financial assistance made two years
earlier. After much persuasion Sir John Hawkshaw, now an elderly man, agreed to accept the technical directorship of the port
works, but with the proviso that his son or his business partner
could represent him in Buenos Aires. With the guarantee of British
technical supervision thus secured, Baring Brothers agreed to pro-

vide financial backing, while several British firms contracted to supply machinery and actually construct the port. At the end of 1884, President Roca signed the final contract with Madero in a ceremony in which the three former Presidents acted as witnesses.

Nevertheless, the national government seemed inclined for the moment to support both projects—a deep-water port on the Riachuelo as well as the harbors and basins east of the Plaza de Mayo. In October 1883 Congress appropriated funds for further dredging and construction of the Riachuelo port works.[27] The arrival in that same month of the British ship *Macduff*, which drew nineteen and a half feet of water, strengthened arguments in favor of the Riachuelo project.[28] In the following year Congress approved widening and deepening the Riachuelo channel as far as Barracas.[29] The funds allocated for the task proved to be insufficient, however.

By 1885, government support for the Riachuelo port works had begun to erode. Despite the substantial flow of commerce through La Boca (see note 19), the streets that connected this area to the center of Buenos Aires remained nearly impassable except in dry weather; some credited this neglect to efforts to sabotage the development of the Riachuelo.[30] Faced with lack of funds and bureaucratic obstructionism, Huergo's position as director of the "Riachuelo Works" became increasingly difficult. The final straw came when the Hawkshaw consulting firm attacked technical aspects of the southern access channel to the Riachuelo. Huergo asked to see the statements and plans, but the government authorities refused, on the pretext that these constituted part of Madero's private property. Huergo took the only road left open to him—he withdrew. His resignation in January 1886 prepared the way for the Madero camp to appropriate the southern channel as its own and to relegate the Riachuelo once more to the position of a secondary port facility to be used primarily for the coastal trade. The combination of the newer commercial elite, foreign financial groups, and national authorities, all with interests oriented toward the Plaza de Mayo or to the area immediately west and north, had finally won out over those forces concerned with developing La Boca and Barracas.

The parting shots echoed for several more months. Huergo continued to defend his position in the press and in private publications.[31] The National Engineering Department condemned the

19. The Puerto Madero works (right) and the Central Railroad Station, 1889. (Archivo General de la Nación.)

Madero project; when the government refused to consider its report, the department head, Guillermo White, resigned in protest.[32] The local engineering society also published a report highly critical of the Madero plans.[33] The national government, however, continued imperturbably along its course. Hawkshaw himself never came to Buenos Aires, but in late 1885 his son made a three-month visit to the Río de la Plata. In March 1886 a council of ministers headed by Vice President Francisco B. Madero (an uncle of Eduardo Madero) approved the final plans for the port's construction.[34]

As the economic boom of the 1880s reached its climax—just before the crash and accompanying "revolution" of 1890—the accusations became more sordid. Cost estimates for the port works rose steadily, and Huergo leveled charges of fraud at Madero for his handling of the project.[35] Some saw curious relationships between Madero's decision to proceed with construction of the southern harbor and first basin and the acquisition of adjacent low-lying lands by a syndicate made up of highly placed politicians.[36] Subsequently, Madero's bid in 1888 to buy up all lands reclaimed by the port construction was undercut by competing bids and substantial public protest; a public auction then disposed of those lands.[37]

Scandals and rumors notwithstanding, the first section of the new port, the southern harbor, was inaugurated on January 28, 1889, in a colorful ceremony presided over by Vice President Pellegrini. The same man who as Senator had launched the Madero project in Congress in September 1882 now could eloquently forecast a new era in the city's commercial life and formally bestow the name "Puerto Madero" on the partly constructed port works.

The 1890s saw the completion of the Madero project, although at impressive costs in money and delays. The first and second basins (numbered from south to north) opened in 1890. In 1891, rising costs and the financial crisis combined to exhaust the twenty-million gold peso credit allowed in 1883, and work on the port was temporarily suspended. New and bitter accusations flowed, especially from the pens of *La Prensa*'s editors.[38] The national executive, however, successfully secured further credit to complete a third basin in 1892. In 1895, Congress, after extensive debate, approved an additional credit of more than six million gold pesos to finish the northern section of the port.[39] Successful completion of the port works had now become vital to the city's prosperity and commercial leadership, particularly since the recently completed facilities at Ensenada, port for the newly built provincial capital of La Plata, had begun to cut sharply into porteño domination of the import-export trade. By 1897 the fourth basin and the northern harbor reached completion, and the following year saw the opening of the northern channel, which had been so strongly combated by Huergo.[40]

For those concerned with the vitality of the Riachuelo, however, defeat was not total. In 1889 a corporation called Dock Sud, which numbered Huergo among its founders, began to buy up land on the right bank of the Riachuelo and build piers, warehouses, and other shipping facilities.[41] Funds for dredging operations in the Riachuelo continued to dribble out of Congress; it approved bills in 1891, 1897, and 1898.[42] In 1902 a revitalized corporation, with strong financial support from the Southern Railroad, took over Dock Sud. Two years later these facilities in Barracas al Sud (now renamed Avellaneda) could accommodate as many as twenty transatlantic steamers at one time.[43]

Although the completion of the Madero port works was to contribute forcibly to the direction of the city's expansion, the port faced problems during the first decade of the twentieth century that reflected on its design and foretold handicaps that would haunt future generations. Some of the difficulties sprang from the port's very success and some from the rapidly increasing exchange of agricultural exports for manufactured imports. The boom years from 1905 to 1912 were accompanied by a 50 per cent increase in the number of vessels and a doubling of tonnage entering and leaving the port of Buenos Aires. By 1910 the arrivals and departures had reached annual totals of 30,000 ships and eighteen million tons, a volume the Madero port proved inadequate to handle.[44] Moreover, technical miscalculations and the continued use of freight-handling methods that had been in vogue thirty years before compounded this lack of capacity. The northern harbor, for example, proved to be virtually useless because the wash from the river prevented ships from tying up safely alongside its wharves.[45] Launches, carts, and peons still slowly and painfully transferred freight from ships' holds to warehouses and back. The difficulty which the railroads experienced in building access routes to dockside resulted in exorbitant rail charges to the port. As a consequence, goods were often unloaded from freight cars into horse-drawn carts at the railroad terminals for the final trip to shipside. The resultant pileup of carts in the port area was such that from Plaza Once to the Madero port, a distance of thirty blocks, a carter could make only one trip a day.[46] The caricature of a tortoise unloading the ships, which appeared in 1906 in the popular magazine *Caras y Caretas*, had become a painful reality.

Belatedly, the government recognized that all was not well with the Madero facilities. In 1902 the government invited Elmer L. Corthell, the United States port expert, to look over the port and suggest remedies. He proved unwilling to tamper with the existing structure and limited himself to the suggestion of a breakwater and a parallel line of docks added to the east side of the Madero port.[47] Huergo returned to the offensive with a project to close the north channel, open the four existing basins into one continuous harbor,

¿Se halla el puerto abarrotado?
¡Claro está!
Mas siguiendo el iniciado
movimiento aquí indicado
• se desabarrotará.

20. Freight congestion in Puerto Madero inspired this cartoon. (*Caras y Caretas*, Feb. 10, 1906.)

and build a similar large basin just to the east.[48] The increasing size of ships and the challenge of Montevideo, across the estuary, which could accommodate vessels drawing thirty-two feet of water, provoked even more radical proposals. In 1899–1900, Congress discussed a project for a new port 100 miles south of the city of Buenos Aires, on the bay of Samborombón, and four years later, it actually voted funds for preliminary studies.[49] An initial project, prepared by Arturo Castaño, would have created facilities to accommodate ships drawing thirty feet of water; it allowed for depths which could be increased to forty feet. The Southern Railroad, among others, strongly opposed the project, not only because it would have detracted from porteño commercial dominance, but also because it would have required considerable restructuring of the railroad network. Although construction actually began on the Samborombón port in 1911, a year later a presidential decree stopped the operations, and the project collapsed.[50]

Meanwhile, the government wrestled to improve conditions at Puerto Madero. In 1903 it sent two Argentine engineers, Gustavo Jolly and Luis Curutchet, to Europe to study port problems and administration. Their report stirred no action, however, and it came to rest in a filing cabinet in the Ministry of Public Works.[51] An engineer in that Ministry, Abel J. Pagnarde, and a German-Argentine syndicate also developed plans for a costly canal connection to Ensenada, the port for the provincial capital of La Plata.[52] In 1906, Fernand Kinart, engineer for the port of Antwerp, came to Buenos Aires at the invitation of several commercial groups. He diagnosed the problem as lack of centralized administration aggravated by slow and antiquated loading methods.[53] Requests for funds by the national executive followed on the heels of each new proposal. In 1907 Congress voted nearly nine million gold pesos to "modernize" the port; within two weeks the executive branch was back with a new request for twenty-five million.[54] Experiments with administrative reforms in 1907–8 saved some money, but the demand for funds continued. The 1907 request was raised to twenty-seven million gold pesos in 1908, and it received congressional approval virtually without debate.[55] Congressional action also formalized administrative reorganization of the Port Authority in 1911.[56] But the problems remained, and they led finally to the construction of Puerto Nuevo, or New Port, completed in 1925–26, which extended facilities northward beyond Retiro in the form of a series of parallel docks projecting from the shore. The Huergo-Madero conflict thus had not only given form to the city's development; it had also left shipping problems that as late as the 1970s still plagued the port with one of the world's highest per-ton loading costs.

Although the history of the port of Buenos Aires remains to be written, it is evident that both Huergo and Madero brought significant talents and abilities to bear on the development of essential port facilities. Both men doubtless were honest and sincere in their bitter struggle. Huergo apparently commanded superior technical knowledge; he had had long experience as an engineer and as director of the Riachuelo port works. In the opinion of many trained and impartial observers, his projects possessed greater practical merits and involved far less expense. He actually engineered the southern channel, which first brought oceangoing vessels into the Riachuelo and which, for more than a decade, served as the only access to the Madero docks. Madero, on the other hand, had outstanding political and entrepreneurial talents. He represented the spirit of progress so sought after by Argentina's national elite, especially during the Roca and Miguel Juárez Celman administrations. He also boasted excellent connections in London financial and engineering circles as well as in the Argentine government. To him, therefore, belongs the credit for bringing the interested parties together.

Behind the proposals enunciated by Huergo and Madero, of course, stood the personal and financial interests of many politicians, landowners, merchants, and bankers. Far more research will be necessary to delve behind the "arrangements" that resulted in a particular executive decree, the signing of a contract, or the passage—without debate—of an appropriation. At this stage one can only speculate about the composition and loyalties of such interest groups.

Clearly, those associated with La Boca and Barracas and with the city's south side stood to gain by Huergo's project. The sizable investment in railroads, docks, and warehouses, the labor opportunities and the increased value of land, and the substantial increase in commercial activity all would have tended to orient urban growth southward. Therefore, the traditional Hispanic elite, who, in large measure, still clung to the south side of the Plaza de Mayo, supported efforts to locate the city's principal port in La Boca. The provincial authorities, closely linked by family ties and landownership to the south side, similarly struggled to make La Boca more than a center for the fishing fleet and the coastal trade. The creation of the Federal District in 1880 removed this influential force from the city, although the provincial government continued to pressure for the southern interests beyond the city—in the development of both Ensenada and Avellaneda.

Those who supported the Puerto Madero represented more complex and, ultimately, more powerful interests. The newer commercial group that had emerged since independence, and especially since the mid-nineteenth century, had tended to settle north of the Plaza de Mayo. For that reason, wholesale and retail outlets, real estate interests, and the transportation system largely focused on the areas west and north of the Plaza. Installation of the country's major overseas port facilities immediately to the east of the Plaza de Mayo would continue this focus and guarantee this group's prosperity and expansion. The national authorities, largely recruited—at least after the formation of a truly national authority under Mitre in 1862—from this newer commercial group and from politicians from the provinces who had come to Buenos Aires, also strongly supported the emphasis on the Plaza de Mayo and its western and northern accesses. After 1880, with the decision to locate the federal capital at Buenos Aires, the concern of the national government with the Plaza de Mayo became even more pronounced. In addition, the influential foreign banking and export-import interests, joined by financial commitments to the national authorities and newer commercial interests, strongly favored the Madero port. Above all, the British, because of their long-standing commercial involvement in Argentina as well as their recent investment in railroads, gasworks, streetcar companies, and loans to the national government, took the major role in providing technical assistance and capital for the Madero project. For all of these diverse groups, Madero's grandiose scheme also offered far more possibilities for speculation and enrichment than Huergo's more modest approach. The large amount of land to be reclaimed on the waterfront, the sizable number of men and machines needed for construction, the opportunities for speculation in real estate, and the promise for further expansion in commercial activity—all these served to generate intense enthusiasm.

All this suggests that the brave attempt on the part of southern interests, which inaugurated the southern channel and brought commercial prosperity to La Boca and Barracas in the years from 1879 to 1885, proved unable to sustain itself in the face of the powerful combination of a new commercial group, foreign banking and financial circles, and national authorities. These latter interests united around the Madero project and forced withdrawal of even limited support from La Boca–Barracas development. The building of the Madero port consequently reinforced the city's focus on the Plaza de Mayo. The plaza remained the core of prestige, power, and wealth in the city. Rather than expanding southward, as might have occurred with Huergo's design, the city continued to spread out from that core toward the west and north.

Location of the city's railroads provided the second major problem in Buenos Aires' growth.[57] The decisions made by engineers, politicians, and financiers, especially during the 1880s, determined the evolution of both the city's and the nation's railroad systems. These decisions, in contrast to the port issue, cannot be presented dramatically as confrontations between opposing groups of men or between strikingly different approaches. Nevertheless, the men who built the railroads responded to the same concern as that held by the port developers—the introduction of technology that would capitalize on the pampas agricultural potential. At first, terrain and inadequate local resources imposed some limitations on the location and extent of track construction. During the booming 1880s, however, the reliance on foreign expertise and capital gave British managers virtual control, and the railroad systems they built took the emerging Madero port as the hub and further stimulated the city's outward expansion to the west and north. The railroad thus reinforced dependence on foreign capital, increased the nation's wealth through agricultural exports, and emphasized still more the importance of the Plaza de Mayo area—results that had already been evidenced in the port's development.

The first three rail lines into the city followed paths laid down by oxcarts and mule trains in the seventeenth century. In the pre-railroad era the bulk of merchandise had flowed in and out of the city through two wholesale markets, one at Plaza Constitución and the other at Plaza Once. Since the building of railroads responded largely to the potential for carrying hides, wool, and grains, the Southern and Western railroads had established terminals for their lines adjacent to these marketplaces and thus had reinforced the existing commercial and transportation structure. The Western also reached into the center of the city with a spur to Plaza del Parque, subsequently named Plaza Lavalle. Meanwhile, the Northern Railroad had established its terminal at Retiro, on the northern edge of the built-up city. This access, which by a spur reached the Plaza de Mayo, constituted a logical route along the estuary's edge to towns north of Buenos Aires.

As with the port works, the capital and technical expertise demanded by railroad building soon became dependent upon British investments and interests. In 1862, for example, a group of British residents in Buenos Aires formed the Southern Railroad to serve the sheep- and cattle-growing zones. The contract that these men developed with the provincial government attracted additional capital from shareholders in England. A guarantee of 7 per cent on invested capital stimulated building, and three years later the first fifty-mile stretch of track was opened. Efforts to establish the Northern Railroad with local capital in the 1850s failed; thereupon, in 1863, British capital and management built the first twelve miles of the line, from Retiro to San Isidro. The Western—the first railroad built in Argentina—had initially been underwritten by local capital, but because of the railroad's increasing financial difficulties, the provincial government of Buenos Aires in 1863 took over the line. A first attempt to sell this railroad to foreign interests failed the following year, and the Western remained a state enterprise until its sale to a British company in 1889.

By 1870, therefore, the foundations for the city's railroad system had been laid, although a nationwide railroad network had not yet taken form. The Southern had reached Chascomús, 70 miles south of the city; the Western had pushed 100 miles west, to Chivilcoy; and the Northern had completed its link to Tigre, 20 miles north on the estuary (see Map 7). In addition, a four-mile stretch of track—the Buenos Aires and Ensenada Railroad—extended south along the waterfront to La Boca and Barracas.

During the 1870s railroad companies added a few more impor-

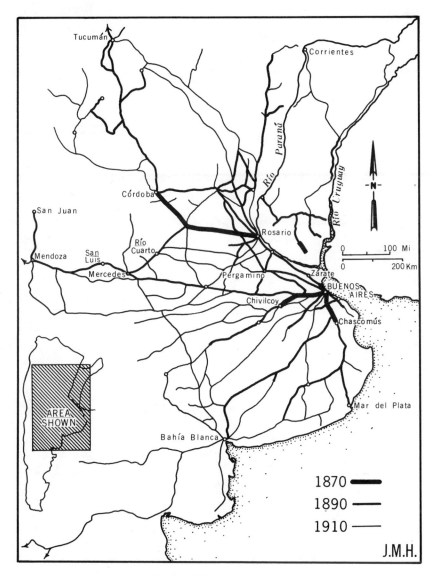

7. Expansion of the National Railroad System, 1870–1910.

tant links within the city, suggesting the marked northward shift of the next decade (see Map 8). The Buenos Aires and Ensenada line and the Northern Railroad connected their tracks along the estuary, and both companies began to use the Central Station, adjacent to the Plaza de Mayo. Access to the waterfront had become

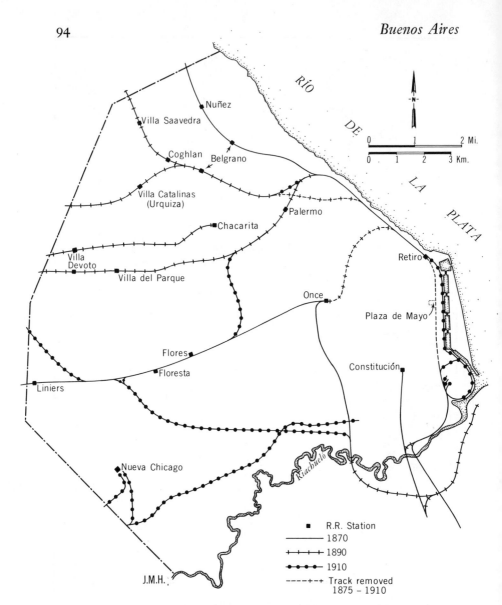

8. Expansion of the Railroad System in the City of Buenos Aires, 1870–1910.

significantly more important with the building of another freight
pier at the foot of the street Paraguay, as an addition to the original
freight pier and Customhouse next to the Plaza de Mayo. A spur
from the Northern Railroad reached out onto this new pier, thus

speeding up the handling of transatlantic freight. During this same decade, the Western connected its terminal at Plaza Once with the Northern's track near the cemetery of La Recoleta. The Western, along with the Buenos Aires and Ensenada, thus gained access to the Northern's track and to the freight and passenger piers that constituted the rudimentary port facilities of the early 1880s. On the city's north side, the Buenos Aires to Campana Railroad, begun in the mid-1870s and soon renamed the Buenos Aires and Rosario, added further impetus to this northward thrust within the city by using Retiro as its terminal.

Those few developments within the national framework that occurred during the decades of the 1860s and 1870s remained largely isolated from the railroad system emerging in and around the city of Buenos Aires, and only faintly forecast the remarkable boom of the 1880s. The British-owned Central Argentine Railroad from Rosario to Córdoba, completed in 1870, provided the principal thrust toward the interior. During the 1870s government-financed lines reached further inland, first north from Córdoba to Tucumán and subsequently south and west from Córdoba to Río Cuarto and Mercedes, the latter in the province of San Luis (see Map 7). The port of Rosario on the Paraná River continued to serve as terminus for this system.

During the next three decades, British railroad engineers and managers—and the increasing volume of freight that flowed in and out of the city—caused gradual readjustment of both the urban and the national railroad structures. What had initially been a local system oriented to the potentially rich agricultural zones of the south and west of the province of Buenos Aires gradually became the hub of a nationwide system that tied all the provinces to the port of Buenos Aires (see Map 7). This changed orientation tended to complement the development of the port works. The railroads' principal function—the transportation of wheat, wool, hides, and cattle destined for export to the coast, and of imported equipment and consumer goods to interior commercial centers—required access to the country's main port. The location of the Madero portworks, along with the amount of produce coming in from the pampas and the interior of Argentina, accentuated the role of Retiro and, to a lesser degree, of Once as terminals for the nationwide railroad system. The focus on the Plaza de Mayo and on its northern and western environs thus received still more reinforcement.

The 1880s brought the most important alterations in the nation's rail system. By means of concessions, mergers, and extensive new construction the port of Buenos Aires replaced Rosario as terminal for lines to the interior. Furthermore, the national government, particularly under President Juárez Celman, not only actively stimulated this climate of boom and speculation, but also sought to turn over to private—British—ownership and management as much of the railroad system as possible.

The Buenos Aires and Rosario Railroad reached Zárate and Baradero on the Paraná River in 1885, and Rosario in 1886. Shortly thereafter, in 1889, the Central Argentine bought out the Northern Railroad and thus acquired the key to Retiro and a northern access into Buenos Aires. The following year, in a further effort to secure connections with Buenos Aires, the Central Argentine built a new line from Cañada de Gómez in the province of Santa Fe to Pergamino in Buenos Aires and from there reached the Once station via a track leased from the Western Railroad. The interior system, which during the 1880s had been extended west to Mendoza and San Juan and north beyond Tucumán to Catamarca and Salta, thus became tied to Buenos Aires instead of to Rosario.

This trend of subordinating the provinces to the port and national capital received reinforcement with the formation of another British-owned and British-managed company, the Buenos Aires Pacific Railroad. Established in London in 1882 to carry forward the earlier dream of the Western to build a passage across the Andes to Chile, the company opened an initial section in 1885. By 1888 it had completed the connection between the Retiro and Palermo stations in Buenos Aires and Mercedes in the province of San Luis, thus providing a shorter route to the western provinces than was afforded via Rosario and Córdoba.

The Southern Railroad continued to expand the empire it had carved out in the southern part of the province of Buenos Aires. In 1884 it extended its track to Bahía Blanca, soon to become a major export center for wool and grain, and in 1886 it reached Mar del Plata. During the decade, the Southern added a total of 725 miles of track, to fill in this zone, which had only recently been liberated from the threat of marauding bands of warlike Indians by the so-called "Conquest of the Desert" in 1879–80.

The national government aggressively encouraged this fever of railroad building. In rails and locomotives it saw guarantees for Argentina's prosperity and unity. A veritable avalanche of concessions, permits, and privileges passed through Congress—from 1887 to 1889 alone, sixty-seven national concessions for railroad building were approved, three times the number extended in the preceding twenty-five years.[58] The keen interest of foreign investors, who saw enormous profits in this booming economy, combined with the government's increasing need for funds to underwrite public works and its growing bureaucracy, also led to the sale, in the late 1880s, of several government-built and -operated lines. The Juárez Celman administration apparently believed that the state should own and operate railroads only in remote frontier zones, where private investors were loath to venture and where defense interests obliged the national authorities to take action. Elsewhere railroads should be built and operated by private enterprise. As a result, in 1887, the Argentine Great Western snapped up the government-built line from Mercedes to Mendoza and San Juan. That same year, the Central Córdoba took over the Córdoba-Tucumán line. After a hotly contested debate over the merits of economic nationalism versus domination by foreign capital—a debate that raged in the city's best social clubs and in every local café—Congress finally, in 1889–90, authorized the sale of Argentina's first railroad, the state-owned Western, to a British-based company.

The 1890s and 1900s provided first consolidation, then controlled expansion. During the early years of railroad development the government had limited its intervention to building some lines in the less profitable zones and to guaranteeing the return on investments made in private ventures. In 1872 a federal law created the National Railroad Administration to supervise conservation of roadbeds and the policing and speed of trains. Four years later, further legislation established a federal body to review the technical details of construction plans. Neither entity had any authority over company finances or management or over general railroad development. The situation was further confused by the bewildering variety of terms, guarantees, and subsidies provided through concessions voted by provincial legislatures and the national Congress. Under the impact of the 1890 crisis, Congress, in 1891, established a Railroad Authority, the Dirección General de Ferrocarriles. For the first time, an effort was made to impose at least limited federal controls over the companies' responsibilities and rights and to regulate subsequent development of the railroad system.

The private companies themselves, under the impact of the depression, further restructured their systems in search of more effective control over their spheres of influence. The Central Argentine, having achieved access to Buenos Aires in 1889–90, led in this movement; it purchased several connecting links from the Western in 1892. For the moment, the Buenos Aires and Rosario Railroad continued aggressive competition with the Central Argentine. In addition to struggling for control of traffic between Rosario and the Federal District, the Buenos Aires and Rosario, in 1896, completed the Poblador Railroad from Belgrano to Tigre in a move to cut into the Central Argentine's monopoly of this delta area. The Southern, meanwhile, finally bought out the Buenos Aires and Ensenada and thus gained full control of the transport of passengers and goods in the southern part of the province.

In the years preceding World War I, Argentina enjoyed its longest and most prosperous period of economic development, with particularly expansive boom years from 1905 to 1912. In large measure this prosperity resulted from the efforts by the leading private railroad companies to extend their networks over most of the country's arable land and to consolidate spheres of influence that avoided undue competition. The two trends suggested during the 1880s now came to full fruition: the spokes of Argentina's railroad system all connected to the hub at Buenos Aires, and British investors rather than Argentine authorities determined priorities, rates, and construction of the railroad system.

Four British companies, each operating out of Buenos Aires, cooperated in dividing up and dominating the railroad system during these boom years. By purchases, transfers, and leases the Buenos Aires Pacific secured control of traffic between the Federal District and the western provinces of San Luis, Mendoza, and San Juan. The completion of the trans-Cordillera link to Chile in 1910, even though it brought little new traffic into the Buenos Aires Pacific's orbit, fulfilled the dream that had inspired railroad builders since the 1850s. The Central Argentine emerged as the dominant force in the northern and central provinces of Argentina. To achieve this, the Central Argentine swallowed up the Buenos Aires and Rosario in 1902. The Western continued to dominate much of the province of Buenos Aires and the territory of La Pampa, the heartland of the country's wheat-growing zone. The Southern, the largest of the four, controlled the cattle and sheep zones of the south that now extended toward Patagonia.* The degree to which the "Big Four" dominated the nationwide system cannot be read solely from the statistical record, even though that record is impressive: they held 51 per cent of the track; 61 per cent of the locomotives; 84 per cent of the passengers; 62 per cent of the freight by tonnage; 61 per cent of capital invested; 69 per cent of gross revenues; and 76 per cent of net revenues (see Table 3). Even more significant was the fact that all freight and passengers, in order to move anywhere in the most productive agricultural zones, or to reach or leave the port of Buenos Aires as well as the next two largest ports at Rosario and Bahía Blanca, had to be carried by one of these four companies.

The Argentine government, faced with the effective consolidation provided by the "Big Four," took little action to enforce the limited regulations suggested by the 1891 legislation that had created the Railroad Authority. Indeed, between that 1891 law and the 1947 Declaration of Economic Independence, in which President Juan D. Perón dramatically announced the expropriation of foreign-owned railroad companies, the only important measure was the Mitre Law, approved by Congress in 1907. Drawn up by Emilio Mitre, an engineer, and the son of former President Mitre, the law placed minimal restraints on the railroads.[59] Although it marked a

---

* The rest of the railroad system was filled in by nine smaller private companies, including the Central Córdoba, the Northeast Argentine (Nordeste Argentino), the Entre Ríos, the Santa Fe, and the Great Argentine Western (Gran Oeste Argentino), and five government-built and -operated lines located in frontier zones: the North Central Argentine (Central Norte Argentino), the North Argentine (Argentino del Norte), the Chaco (Chaqueños), the Eastern (Del Este), and the Patagonian (Patagónicos). One small railroad remained linked to the city of Buenos Aires: the Rural Tramway from Chacarita gained full stature with its reorganization in 1906 as the Central Buenos Aires, and it signed ferryboat agreements with the Entre Ríos Railroad which permitted it to tap the mesopotamian area of northeastern Argentina between the Paraná and Uruguay rivers.

departure from the extreme economic liberalism of the Juárez Celman administration, the railroads retained effective control over
their own internal organization and received generous financial and
tax advantages as well as a decisive voice in the development of Argentina's railroad facilities.

This national railroad system, built and controlled by British
companies and radiating from the city of Buenos Aires, in turn accentuated the focus on the Plaza de Mayo and the near-by Madero
port works. By 1890, all major companies ran their trains along the
waterfront and used the Central Station at the foot of Piedad (Bartolomé Mitre): the Southern and the Buenos Aires and Ensenada
came from the south, while the Western, the Central Argentine,
which had just assumed control over the Northern, the Buenos Aires
and Rosario, and the Buenos Aires Pacific arrived from the north
side. But as construction of the Madero port drew to a close, it became evident that this Central Station could no longer handle the
increasing freight and passenger traffic. A fortuitous fire leveled this
porteño landmark in February 1897. After a brief clash of wills
during which the railroad companies rebuilt ticket booths on the
ruins only to have them torn down by the municipality, the Buenos
Aires and Rosario, the Buenos Aires Pacific, and the Central Argentine agreed to establish new terminals at Retiro and tear up the tracks
along Paseo de Julio.[60]

After the turn of the century, expansion within the city consisted
primarily of access lines, spurs, and sidings for the recently completed port works along with additions to existing freight yards
and terminals (see Map 8).* The Central Argentine constructed
several large grain elevators alongside Basin No. 2. The Southern
built new freight yards on low-lying ground at the north edge of
La Boca and connected these to the southern harbor. The Western
took advantage of these new facilities by adding several lines on the

---

* During the 1890s, several new connections on the south and west linked the
tracks of the Western, Buenos Aires Pacific, and Southern. The major addition in
the 1900s consisted of the narrow-gauge track of the General Company of Buenos
Aires Railroads (Compañía General de Ferrocarriles de la Provincia de Buenos
Aires), constructed by Belgian and French capital (1906–11) as yet another link
with Rosario. This railroad sliced across the underpopulated southwest corner of
the Federal District and, along with a spur line of the Western, served the new
municipal slaughterhouse at Nueva Chicago.

south side of the city. A massive volume of export-import traffic thus moved through Retiro or via Constitución to and from the harbors and basins of the Madero port. Along with continued commercial expansion at the core, the flow encouraged concentration of settlement along the northern and western access routes to that core.

Railroads had little effect in the personal and daily life of porteños, at least in the 1870s. A number of merchants and bankers and some government officials and affluent landowners had begun to imitate wealthy members of the German and English communities, settling near Belgrano and other stations northward along the estuary. Flores, because of its higher elevation and reputedly healthier environment, had also emerged, first as a summer retreat but soon thereafter as a proper residence for the well-to-do. Passenger coaches serviced these near-by communities in the morning and evening hours, but the high cost of tickets limited any regular use of trains to those in the upper classes or in the top level of white-collar occupations. Freight provided the bulk of earnings for the railroads. Short hauls by the Northern brought a substantial volume of oranges, lemons, pears, peaches, plums, and garden produce to the city from the delta region. The Western thrived from the outset on grain and wool production, while the Southern brought hides and cattle as well as wool to the Constitución station.

By the 1880s, the volume of traffic moving along the waterfront and close to the Plaza de Mayo forced upon porteños a realization that trains had become part of their everyday life. Although the railroads' principal function remained that of carrying agricultural produce to the city and imported goods to the interior, passenger traffic increased, especially on the city's northern and western sides. This fast and dependable service to and beyond the edges of the Federal District encouraged the outward movement to chalets and bungalows. Since fares usually ranged from two to three times those charged by the streetcar, only the well-to-do and rising white-collar employees in government and commerce used the trains. Suburbs such as Villa Devoto, Saavedra, and Villa del Parque initially depended entirely upon such train service. Beyond Belgrano, settlements such as Nuñez, Coghlan, and Urquiza expanded at first because of the railroads, although subsequent extension of streetcar lines to these areas speeded up their growth. In addition, the Rural

Tramway, although at first little more than a streetcar running west from the area of the Chacarita cemetery, soon filled the growing need for passenger service in the northwest section of the Federal District.

These new communities developed around suburban stations as miniature replicas of traditional Hispanic settlement patterns—an adjacent plaza with a church, often a school, occasionally a district police headquarters, a scattering of commercial establishments along a near-by side street, and wealthy residences on or near the plaza. As one moved away from the station and the plaza toward unpaved dirt streets the houses became increasingly modest and the plots smaller—homes for minor bureaucrats and clerks. The common day laborer might still have to live within walking distance of his employment; the blue-collar worker by the 1880s had just begun to turn to the streetcars; but more and more white-collar workers took the train to and from their houses in distant suburbs.

At the same time that the railroad assisted the outward urban push, it also imposed handicaps on the city's transportation network. Since the railroad system's primary function was to carry cargo, not passengers, the rails were laid as spokes radiating from a central hub —namely, the port. As a result, if a porteño wanted to go from one outlying suburb of the Federal District to another it was far easier for him to board a train for Retiro and then take another train along one of the system's spokes to his destination than it was for him to struggle a mile or so across muddy rutted streets within the city itself. Streetcars compounded this problem by following the outline of the railroads and replicating the spoke system. Not until the 1930s did the *colectivo*, a small bus carrying approximately twenty seated passengers, provide much-needed cross-linkages within the Federal District.

The railroads' crucial need for access to the port also created serious downtown congestion. Porteños had long suffered from the annoyances and dangers of locomotives and trains operating through the downtown streets. Public outcry against injuries and damages finally led the Western to shut down its station at Plaza del Parque (Lavalle) in the early 1880s.[61] But not until 1888 did the municipal council order railroads that passed through parks or plazas to fence their tracks and place bars and a guard at every street crossing.[62]

Since the railroads received their concessions from the national government, the municipality found itself at a serious disadvantage in imposing its regulations on powerful British companies that wielded considerable influence with the national authorities. As *La Prensa* noted,

> If it [the municipality] orders the railroad to pave the area between the tracks, nothing happens; equally ignored are instructions to fence the track with iron pickets; the municipality does not even dare to control the movement of locomotives which goes on at all hours of the night.[63]

As traffic on the streets increased with the city's rapid expansion, the problem of railroad crossings became acute. The Congress adopted several token measures in 1893–94: it instructed the Western to take up its track along the street of Centro-América (Pueyrredón); it authorized the Buenos Aires and Rosario to build overpasses in Palermo Park; and it set up provisions that the Western's new connection to the Riachuelo pass through the least populated districts in the southwestern part of the city.[64] Nevertheless, the toll from trains continued to rise; an estimated eighty persons were either killed or badly maimed during 1897.[65] A particularly notorious accident at the end of that year, in which a carriage was hit and its two occupants were killed on a crossing at the street Avenida Alvear (since 1950, Libertador General San Martín), underlined the inadequate precautions taken by the railroads. The guards at the crossings invariably were old men or cripples who remained at their posts for twenty hours a day; in this particular accident, the guard, who had fallen asleep, had failed to lower the barrier in time.[66]

The tide of protest, along with the need for greater convenience, stimulated the construction of more underpasses and overpasses during the first decade of the twentieth century. In 1897 the Buenos Aires and Rosario completed several overpasses over major streets along its route from Palermo to Retiro and secured authorization to install overpasses to reach the port area from Retiro. The Buenos Aires Pacific built an elevated track from Palermo to Retiro in 1912. The Southern Railroad projected an underpass from its newly constructed freight yards in the northern part of La Boca to reach the Madero port. In the most dramatic move of all, the Western lowered its rails underground from Plaza Once all the way to the Caballito station, just short of the suburb of Flores. In 1907 the municipal council voted to require all railroads to install underpasses or overpasses at all crossings within the Federal District.[67] Like so many other municipal ordinances, however, this order was almost totally ignored. As a result, railroads had to cut across many main arteries in order to reach the port area—a problem that remained to haunt the city. In fact, even today railroads still intercept such main avenues as Santa Fe, Corrientes, and Córdoba, along with a large number of north-south streets. At frequent intervals, impatient drivers in cars, colectivos, and taxis are backed up for several blocks along these streets while barriers, often lowered manually, announce the passage of one of the numerous trains to and from Retiro station.

Despite such frustrations and handicaps, the introduction and expansion of railroads in Argentina exercised enormous influence on the city's development. The control by major British companies over all rail transport to and from Argentina's principal ports, and the encouragement given to commerce to flow through the emporium of Buenos Aires, dramatically strengthened the city's domination over its hinterland. These railroads consequently seconded the Madero port in reinforcing the centripetal attraction exerted by the area around the Plaza de Mayo. At the same time passenger service, offered as a supplement to the principal freight-carrying function of the lines, helped to transport the moderately well-to-do—business managers, merchants, government officials—between their downtown places of work and their homes, which were located near a suburban station. The rail lines also provided the transportation structure—a pattern of spokes oriented toward the city's western and northern sections—subsequently imitated by the streetcar companies.

The third major problem that shaped the city's development toward the end of the nineteenth century was the location of the national capital.[68] The administrative preeminence which Buenos Aires had possessed ever since its establishment finally received ratification in 1880. The city's influence then reached out over the fourteen provinces and nine territories—at a moment when technological and political developments within Argentina permitted a high degree of centralization of power in the hands of the national authorities.[69] During the next three decades, influence and power accrued to the city as seat of the national government, indicating that Buenos Aires had acquired wealth as well as prestige from its role as residence for presidents, ministers, congressmen, judges. The development of the port and the railroads had made the city the economic head of Argentina; federalization confirmed it as the effective political master of the country.

The "capital" question had simmered throughout Argentina's early years as an independent nation. Tariffs collected at the port of Buenos Aires constituted the only substantial and readily available source of income for the national government during most of the nineteenth century. As a result, control of the city became virtually synonymous with control of the nation, and any truly national authority took the city as its seat. At times, provincial caudillos from both the coastal areas and the interior of Argentina rebelled against the control—economic and political—exercised by the port. In simplest terms, provincials resented and distrusted porteños.

In 1852 the overthrow of Rosas, Argentina's de facto ruler, by his rival Urquiza reopened the issue of where to locate the national capital. For nine uneasy years the province of Buenos Aires—including the port and city of Buenos Aires—maintained itself as an autonomous state, independent of the Argentine Confederation formed by the remaining thirteen provinces. When Mitre, Governor of the province of Buenos Aires, won election in 1862 as President of a reunited Argentina, the "capital" question assumed yet another dimension. The localist sentiment of those who wished to retain the wealth and power of the city for the province of Buenos Aires now replaced the resistance of provincials to domination by the port as the principal obstacle to establishment of the national capital in the city. A clash of wills between the national Congress and the Buenos Aires provincial legislature just before Mitre's inauguration prevented the permanent solution—location of the capital in Buenos Aires. Instead, in a temporary five-year compromise, they declared the city of Buenos Aires to be the seat of the national government. Former provincial offices—the Treasury, Customhouse, Ministry of War, and Postal Service—were nationalized.

Federal authorities agreed to underwrite expenses for the municipality without changing its administrative structure. At the same time, the provincial government also continued to be based in the city, from which it maintained control over banks, courts, and other public institutions that belonged to the province. The exact delineation of jurisdictions within the city was not so easy to resolve, however, and this led to extensive correspondence, debates, and recriminations between national government, provincial authorities, and municipality.

For the next several years the national Congress and the provincial legislature periodically discussed proposals aimed at a permanent solution to the "capital" question, but they could agree only to continue the unsatisfactory dual location of national and provincial authorities within the city. None of the many other cities mentioned seemed able to overcome the traditional role of Buenos Aires as seat for the Argentine government. Presidents—whether porteños by birth, as with Mitre, or by adoption, as with Sarmiento from San Juan and Nicolás Avellaneda from Tucumán—consistently opposed moving the capital elsewhere.

During 1867 both the Senate and the Chamber of Deputies wrangled over projects to locate the capital in Rosario or along the projected line of the Central Argentine Railroad between Rosario and Córdoba. The provincial legislatures of Córdoba and Santa Fe promptly offered the cities of Córdoba and Rosario as sites for a federal capital. In 1868, the Rosario proposal almost made it through Congress, only to falter in the Chamber of Deputies because of strong opposition from the executive branch; although it was passed the following year, its supporters could not muster enough votes to override the presidential veto. Two years later, in 1871, Congress approved a project to build a new capital in southern Córdoba, but it also failed to override a veto. Yet another effort to make Rosario the capital fell to a veto in 1873. Meanwhile, in an effort to conciliate the Buenos Aires provincial authorities, Congress in 1866 had agreed to turn back municipal government to the province; in the following year the national government returned to the province legal jurisdiction over the city.

By the end of the 1870s a permanent solution seemed no closer than it had been in 1862. The "capital" question became a central issue in the presidential election of 1880, when Tejedor, a staunch porteño and the Governor of the province of Buenos Aires, ran against Roca, a native of Tucumán, the Minister of War, and a hero of the "Conquest of the Desert." Behind these two men and around the so-called Autonomist and Nationalist tendencies were mobilized the fears and hopes of those who were concerned over Buenos Aires' fate as seat of government. Porteños, as well as those from the province of Buenos Aires, found themselves divided. Some favored establishment of the Federal District composed of the city, or even of a large portion of the province, as the logical confirmation of Buenos Aires' historic role in the area of Río de la Plata. Others feared that if the city were federalized, the province would somehow lose its traditional influence in the national government. They foresaw a city captured by politicians from the interior and thereby lost to porteños. Meanwhile, the distrust of porteños held by those from other provinces had not vanished. But federalization seemed to guarantee that the city would belong to all of Argentina, and provincials had generally come to support the solution of the national capital in Buenos Aires.

As 1880 opened, the lines between the two groups hardened. Followers of Tejedor formed a volunteer militia and began to drill in Palermo Park. In response, incumbent President Avellaneda ordered several cavalry regiments into the city as reinforcements for the national government. Conflict nearly broke out on February 15, when the Tejedor volunteers planned a gala review. Despite active mediation efforts by a number of leading politicians, both sides mobilized their men, and by evening small armies, with loaded rifles, faced each other across the Plaza de Mayo—the national troops positioned around the Casa Rosada, the provincial forces located under the arches of the Cabildo. An eleventh-hour armistice led to an interview between Governor Tejedor and President Avellaneda and the restoration of a tense peace between the two camps.

The April elections gave the presidency to Roca. Tejedor carried only the provinces of Buenos Aires and Corrientes. His followers now promised revolution. New conciliation efforts, including public manifestations in favor of peace and a meeting between Te-

jedor and President-elect Roca, resolved nothing. The return of
San Martín's remains from France at the end of May and the accompanying celebrations that installed Argentina's independence
hero as the symbol of national pride and unity postponed civil war,
but only temporarily.

June opened with rebellion by the Buenos Aires government.
President Avellaneda had ordered an army battalion to La Boca
to intercept a substantial shipment of arms destined for the provincial government. Tejedor countered with a battalion of provincial
guardsmen, city firemen, and local citizenry who unloaded the rifles and ammunition and carried them off to the governor's executive offices, only three blocks from the Plaza de Mayo. Faced with
insurrection, Avellaneda immediately abandoned the Casa Rosada
and took shelter with a cavalry regiment stationed at the nearby
Chacarita cemetery. Shortly thereafter he established the national
capital in the village of Belgrano. On June 20 and 21 sharp fighting
broke out along the Riachuelo and at Plaza Constitución between
provincial and national forces. Nearly 20,000 men were involved.
These battles made it clear that Buenos Aires could not hold out
for long against the superior national forces. Although the city's
defenders continued to throw up fortifications in preparation for a
last-ditch stand, the appointment of former President Mitre as com-
mander in chief of the porteño troops reopened the door for negotiations. By the end of June, Tejedor agreed to resign as Governor,
and the national government extended amnesty to the rebels.

Although Roca did not assume the presidency until October, he
soon became involved in the complicated task of reuniting the nation, an effort which occupied the intervening months. Federal intervention in the province of Buenos Aires laid the groundwork
for the election of a new legislature and governor more amenable
to the changed situation. In late August Avellaneda sent his proposal for the federalization of Buenos Aires to the national Congress, which was still meeting in Belgrano. In the final session held
in that town, the Congress approved the project, and on the following day, September 21, 1880, Avellaneda signed into law a measure
establishing the municipality of Buenos Aires as the national capital. The law also provided that the province would retain control
over its own institutions, such as the provincial bank, and that the

provincial capital would be based in Buenos Aires until a new site could be selected. At the end of November a newly constituted provincial legislature ceded the city to the nation.[70] Thus the "capital" question drew to a close, leaving to ensuing years the determination of exactly what these decisions meant to Buenos Aires and to the nation.*

Contrary to the fears of some porteños, federalization resulted in the "flowering" rather than the "pillaging" of Buenos Aires. The 1880s witnessed the city's period of most rapid growth, with efforts made by all sectors to beautify and modernize the capital as the showplace of Latin America. The momentum generated by the port works and railroads, as well as the final selection of the city as federal capital, resulted not only in increased trade, investment, and immigration, but also in a rising tide of politicians, lawyers, educators, merchants, and landowners from all over Argentina. These men, known to literature and politics as the "Generation of Eighty," worshipped at the altar of progress and science. They worked closely with foreign investors and entrepreneurs and sought by means of technology, immigration, and finance to tear themselves away from the stereotype of Latin American backwardness. They adopted the city as their own. In physical attributes, at least, they found it an easy city to "modernize."

Roca, in his first term as President, appointed the Intendente who did the most to alter the city's façade—Torcuato de Alvear, who served from 1880 to 1887. Alvear's program spoke to the concerns of a generation intent on remodeling the city into a modern, progressive metropolis—for the purposes of this study, the most important legacy of the 1880 solution to the "capital" question.

* The political decision to locate the capital in Buenos Aires was the key factor in bringing the full resources of the national government behind the development of the city and in accentuating the attraction of this center for all Argentines. The complex changes in the administrative and political structure of the city did not directly affect the urban ecology, and consequently they fall outside the main focus of the present study. Another fascinating legacy—the building of the planned city of La Plata as residence for the provincial authorities—also lies beyond the scope of this work. The newly elected Governor of Buenos Aires, Dardo Rocha, made this program the main objective of his administration. In 1882 the provincial legislature declared the municipality of Ensenada the capital of the province and ordered the construction of the new city of La Plata six miles inland from the port of Ensenada.

In light of continued congressional wrangling over the basic law for municipal government in Buenos Aires, the designation and installation in September 1880 of a municipal council headed by Alvear proved particularly fortuitous. The measure of the man who was to become Buenos Aires' most famous Intendente might well have been taken from scornful comments which he, as municipal councilman, had leveled at the council two years earlier, when it had hesitated to vote funds to pave intersections in the center of the city:

> Postponing this project will be the equivalent of saying that the people of Buenos Aires are satisfied with the mud and yawning holes of their streets. . . . It is very regrettable that the municipal employees are due several months' back salaries, but I beg you to remember that the municipality has not been created merely to benefit its employees, but rather to serve the citizenry. . . . It is to be deplored that this body seems to think it natural and honorable to pass out leaflets pleading for money from the citizens in order to spend twenty thousand pesos on revelries for July 9, a vulgar display more in keeping with villages and hamlets, while at the same time it raises such opposition to as useful and economical a proposal as this.[71]

As president of the municipal council, and, subsequently, as Intendente, Alvear demonstrated much the same drive and determination as he had expressed in that speech.[72] Early in his administration he put into motion projects to develop the city's sewer system and expand the public water supply, to complete two new city hospitals, and to widen and pave avenues such as Alvear, Callao-Entre Ríos, Santa Fe, Corrientes, Rivadavia, and Independencia. Paving stones gradually replaced the mud and dirt of many of the downtown streets. He ordered shrubs and trees to be planted in barren plazas such as Marte (San Martín), del Parque (Lavalle), 6 de Junio (Vicente López), Lorea (Congreso), and Constitución. Many citizens, of course, disagreed with Alvear's tactics, and many deplored his tastes—in particular his predilection for sprawling masses of concrete, stone, shrubbery, and ironwork. He built several of these so-called "grottoes," including a famous one located in the magnificent park built on the banks of the estuary near the Recoleta cemetery.

His most dramatic act—the reuniting of two plazas into a single

Plaza de Mayo—best represents the concerns of the "Generation of Eighty" to remodel the city. The Recova Vieja, an arcade dividing the Plaza de Mayo in two, had been built by the cabildo at the beginning of the nineteenth century to shelter shops and facilitate commercial activity on the plaza. During the Rosas period it passed into private hands. From time to time newspapers and public figures discussed elimination of the unsightly and deteriorating structure, but nothing happened. In mid-1882, Alvear requested estimates and plans for the removal of the arcade from the municipal architect, Juan A. Buschiazzo. The enthusiastic support of Roca helped push the necessary legislation through Congress in 1883, and the following year the Supreme Court handed down its decision on the valuation of the property. When the paper work was finally completed, Alvear aggressively set to work to implement his dream. He personally directed the operations, and in two weeks—barely in time for the patriotic celebrations of May 25—workmen had cleared away the Recova Vieja and filled over the area with paving stones. A historical commission, headed by three past Presidents, Mitre, Sarmiento, and Avellaneda, had managed to keep Alvear from tossing away as unusable the modest pile of brick and mortar erected in 1810 to commemorate the city's first move toward independence.[73] But little else stopped him, certainly not the comments of bitter opponents in the municipal council who suggested that his palm trees encircling the Plaza de Mayo threatened to turn Buenos Aires into "a Jamaican village or a Paraguayan or Brazilian sugar plantation or horse farm."[74] It is said that at one stage in the clearing operations, when the telephone company procrastinated in relocating its lines, he cut the telephone wires attached to the walls of the Recova Vieja and left a number of offices without communications.[75] Regardless of the methods he used, Alvear significantly revitalized the real as well as the symbolic importance of the Plaza de Mayo as center of the city.

Linked with the removal of the Recova Vieja was Alvear's project to cut an avenue west from the Plaza de Mayo through the centers of the blocks between Victoria (Hipólito Yrigoyen) and Rivadavia. This effort to endow downtown Buenos Aires with a vista and a boulevard and thus bring to mind comparisons with Paris rather than Lima had had antecedents in the 1870s, but none

21. Plaza Victoria and Plaza 25 de Mayo were unified to form the Plaza de Mayo.
This was taken in 1885, after the shops were removed. (Archivo General de la
Nación.)

had prospered.[76] Although Congress gave approval to the plan in
1884, even Alvear's impetuous direction could not carry this ambitious project to immediate fruition. The city's attempt to pay for
the construction of the avenue by expropriating not only the land
needed, but also the whole area between Rivadavia and Victoria,
resulted in lengthy legal snarls. Construction on the avenue did not
begin until 1889, when an arrangement was made which freed
owners who donated the land actually needed for the avenue from
municipal taxes and left them with the remainder of their lots, pre-
sumably of far greater value because of their frontage on the avenue.[77] The dusty, dirty process of tearing down walls and leveling
back patios continued intermittently over the next several years.
Nevertheless, the inauguration of the Avenida de Mayo in mid-

1894 largely resulted from Alvear's vision and drive in starting the dramatic restructuring of the gran aldea's center in the 1880s.

The mould within which Buenos Aires would expand from 1870 to 1910 had thus been formed by three critical elements—the port, the railroads, and the federal capital. The 1880s proved to be crucial to each. By 1885 the supporters of the Madero port had won the battle to locate the city's harbor east of the Plaza de Mayo, confirming the plaza area as the center of commerce and wealth. The addition of the Buenos Aires and Rosario line in 1876, the building of the Buenos Aires Pacific and the Rural Tramway in 1888, and the purchase by the Central Argentine of the Northern Railroad and Retiro Station in 1889 turned the city's growth toward the north and west. These developments brought the flow of commerce and passengers from all over Argentina to Retiro, the port, and the Plaza de Mayo. The selection of Buenos Aires as permanent seat of the federal authorities in 1880, and the subsequent efforts by the "Generation of Eighty" to remake the gran aldea on the Parisian model, accentuated the plaza orientation. The three branches of national government remained on the plaza until 1906, when Congress moved to its new edifice, at the opposite end of the Avenida de Mayo from the Casa Rosada.

The Plaza de Mayo remained of paramount importance during the city's transformation from gran aldea to metropolis. Those with wealth and power continued to live close to this traditional center of prestige. But, since the plaza's environs also provided substantial employment opportunities for manual and semiskilled workers, recently arrived European immigrants congregated in this same area. How the city's core evolved as a residence for both wealthy, traditional families and newly arrived, penniless Europeans forms the principal inquiry of the next chapter.

4

Plaza and Conventillos

In the gran aldea, the Plaza de Mayo and adjoining blocks formed the center of commercial, financial, social, and intellectual activity. Persons with wealth and power sought to live in this center, and a pattern developed in which one's prestige roughly equated with one's proximity to the plaza. Thousands of laborers who had come from Europe also sought to live near the Plaza de Mayo, in order to be close to work and to save on transportation. By 1910, despite vast expansion—there had been a sevenfold growth in population—the center around the Plaza de Mayo still remained the heart of the city, the residence of the powerful as well as the home of the newly arrived laborer.

Although this center is shown only imperfectly in published census data, a limited perspective of certain characteristics can be seen in an arbitrarily defined zone which may be called the *Central City*.[1] This rectangular area of 250 blocks, consisting of six districts (1 through 6) in the 1869, 1887, and 1895 censuses and of two districts (13 and 14) in the 1904, 1909, and 1914 censuses, increased in population from 83,000 to 138,000 between 1869 and 1914. There occurred, therefore, no overwhelming influx of population into this area, nor any sharp increase in density. The outward spread of the city was reflected in the proportion of the city's total population who lived in the Central City: nearly half did in

114

1869, one-quarter did in 1887, and one-tenth did in 1909 (see Table 4). The foreign-born predominated. The percentage of foreign-born in the Central City exceeded that for the city as a whole, and the spread between the two figures increased steadily. In 1869, foreigners in the entire city comprised 50 per cent of the total population, while in the Central City they amounted to 52 per cent. By 1914, with the city-wide figure virtually the same (49 per cent), the Central City claimed 64 per cent. In like fashion, the percentage of foreign-born in the Central City was always slightly higher—between 2 and 4 per cent—than it was in Buenos Aires as a whole (see Table 4).

The census of buildings tells a parallel story. The number of buildings in the Central City actually declined, from 8000 to 7000, between 1869 and 1914. However, those over two stories in height increased enormously in the same period—from 162 to 1678 (see Table 4). Details on conventillo population emerge only in the censuses of 1887 and 1904. These figures show nearly one-third of the area's population living in conventillos in 1887: the absolute number of conventillo dwellers remained virtually the same in 1904, amounting then to a little over one-quarter of the area's total population (see Table 5).

Such data suggest a stable, built-up area and underline the predominance of immigrants, conventillos, and tall buildings in the Central City. For a fuller explanation of the considerations and conditions that bound both newly arrived workers and elite to the Plaza de Mayo, one must turn to maps, city directories, newspapers, and other contemporary reports.[2]

Throughout the period of rapid population growth, all services important to the activities and comfort of the city's merchants, politicians, and professional men remained concentrated in the blocks immediately adjacent to the Plaza de Mayo. By 1910 the two blocks of Bartolomé Mitre (known before 1906 as Piedad) between 25 de Mayo and San Martín served as the focal point for banking, exchange, and credit operations. A number of banks also appeared on Reconquista and San Martín, in a block on each side of Bartolomé Mitre. This location for the city's financial institutions had been set in 1862, when the Bolsa de Comercio, the stock exchange, opened its doors on the west side of San Martín, between

22. At the heart of the financial district—a view along Piedad (subsequently Bartolomé Mitre), around 1900. (Archivo General de la Nación.)

Cangallo and Cuyo. Two decades later, in 1885, this prestigious
focal point for the financial and commercial community moved
back toward the Plaza de Mayo, establishing its offices in a handsome two-story edifice that fronted both on the Plaza de Mayo

9. Real Estate Values in Census Districts 1 and 2, City of Buenos Aires, 1887.

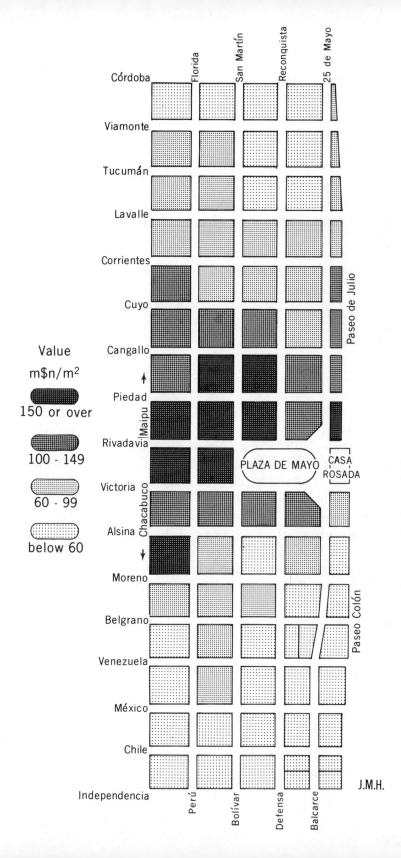

and on Piedad (Bartolomé Mitre). The collapse of the Banco
Nacional during the crisis of 1890, and its replacement by the
Banco de la Nación, reinforced this shift toward the plaza. The
new national bank occupied the edifice of the Teatro Colón on the
plaza. Other major banking institutions preferred Piedad: the
Banco de Italia y Río de La Plata, established in 1872; the Banco de
Londres y Río de la Plata, which moved to that street in 1867;
the Banco Carabassa which opened offices here in 1880, only to be
absorbed by the Banco de Londres in 1891; the Banco Inglés y Río
de la Plata, until it moved to Reconquista in 1884; and the Banco
de Comercio, which opened in 1884.

Concentration of the city's commercial activity took place in
similar fashion around the Plaza de Mayo. By the 1880s the value of
land and buildings on the north side of the plaza had increased
slightly over those on the south side, but the sharpest decline of real
estate values could be seen as one moved away from the plaza in
any direction (see Map 9). This same pattern appeared in the number and liquid assets of commercial establishments recorded by
block.[3]

The hotels, restaurants, and shops frequented by the elite remained close to the Plaza de Mayo, particularly on the Perú-Florida
axis. Gathering places for porteño notables were the Rotisserie
Francesa and the Confitería del Águila on Florida, the Café de
París on Cangallo, and hotels such as the Hotel de Londres and the
Casa del Señor Leloir on Piedad, the Hotel de la Paz, Hotel de
Provence, and Hotel de Roma on Cangallo, and the Hotel Argentino on Rivadavia. More and more of the clothing and retail establishments that catered to the city's upper class—among them Sas-
trería Parenthou (1870), Sombrería de A. Manigot (1853), and
the Peluquería Ruiz y Roca (1876)—moved to choice locations
along Florida. There was also a cluster of expensive stores along
Perú and Victoria, just west of the Plaza de Mayo, including Zapa-
tería de J. Bernasconi (1855), Imprenta y Librería de Mayo
(1853), A la Ciudad de Londres (1873), El Progreso (1875), and
Mueblería de Paris (1851).

Social clubs selected the Perú-Florida axis for their facilities. The
first two gathering spots for the elite, the Club del Progreso (1852)
and the Club del Plata (1860), opened just off Victoria, on Chaca-

23. Florida, the center of porteño elegance and prestige, around 1900. (Archivo General de la Nación.)

buco and Perú, respectively. The Sociedad Rural Argentina (1866), exclusive club of the country's livestock growers, established its headquarters at Perú 35. By the 1880s the elite clubs were choosing Florida for their centers: the Jockey Club (1881), the Club Naval y Militar (1881), and the Club de [Gimnasio y] Esgrima (1885). The elite of the foreign communities showed a similar preference for this same area. The Club Español (1866) was located in the section just west of the Plaza de Mayo, while the Club de Residentes Estranjeros (1841), the Club Francés (1867), the Circolo Italiano (1880), and the English Literary Society (1876) had their headquarters north of the plaza. The theater district, originally centered on the Plaza de Mayo—the old Teatro Colón, completed in 1855, and the Teatro Victoria, just west of the plaza—had begun to move northwest with the opening of new establishments such as the Odeón, Opera, San Martín, and Comedia. This outward move along Cuyo and Corrientes received dramatic confirmation in 1908 with the opening of the city's new opera house, named the Teatro Colón after its predecessor on the Plaza de Mayo. It occupied a whole block at the corner of Cerrito and Tucumán. Several new establishments—Apolo, Politeama Argentino, and Nuevo—also appeared farther out on Corrientes, while the famous Teatro Victoria moved five blocks farther west.

After 1900 the rising cost of land began to push some governmental and educational institutions out of the downtown center. In 1906 Congress moved from its cramped quarters alongside the Casa Rosada to an imposing edifice at the opposite end of the Avenida de Mayo. The Supreme Court in 1880 had transferred its offices from the Cabildo to the center of the financial district on San Martín. In 1904 the cornerstone for Tribunales, the national court building, was laid near the new Teatro Colón, but delays postponed the final opening of the Supreme Court chambers until 1942. Only the national executive—admittedly, the most important and powerful branch of government in Argentina—failed to move from its long established base on the Plaza de Mayo. The President and his staff, as well as the ministries—which were increased from five to eight in 1898—remained in the rambling Casa Rosada. The city government also remained at the plaza, although in the 1890s these authorities moved from the Cabildo to a Parisian-styled, five-story building fifty yards away, on the newly opened Avenida de Mayo.

Despite increasing rents, considerations of tradition and prestige served for many years to keep upper-class educational facilities close to the Plaza de Mayo.[4] The country's most important secondary school, the Colegio Nacional de Buenos Aires, was situated on Bolívar, a block from the plaza. University activities clustered near by. Exact Sciences and Engineering remained in the original buildings of the University of Buenos Aires at the "Square of Enlightenment." In the 1880s the Law Faculty moved two blocks southeast, to Moreno, but it did not transfer its operations to new buildings at Azcuénaga and Las Heras, four blocks northwest of Entre Ríos-Callao, until after 1910. With the formation of the Faculty of Philosophy and Letters in 1896, a new center of university activity opened at Reconquista and Viamonte, seven blocks

24. Teatro Colón, around 1910. (Archivo General de la Nación.)

north of the Plaza de Mayo. Only the Medical Faculty remained outside this orbit, largely because of the tendency to locate hospitals on the urban outskirts. In 1890 this faculty moved from the vicinity of the General Men's Hospital at the city's southern edge, to occupy an entire block at the intersection of Córdoba and Junín, four blocks beyond Entre Ríos-Callao. Legislation in 1909 set aside four blocks just north of this site for a polyclinic, but not until 1941 were the new teaching facilities completed. When Agronomy and Veterinary Science opened in 1909, it also took its place on the outskirts, in a large park area west of the Chacarita cemetery.

While most facilities for the upper class remained—as in the gran aldea—within an easy walk of the plaza, several developments in the late nineteenth century started the movement of the elite toward the north side of the plaza and eventually toward Barrio Norte. A yellow fever epidemic in 1871; the increasing commercialization of prime residential streets, including the Perú-Florida axis; the changed housing and architectural styles; and the steady accretion of the immigrant laboring mass in the downtown conventillos all served to encourage new members of the upper class to settle on the plaza's north side. The plaza area still served as the center for work and play, but members of the upper class sought near-by, somewhat segregated zones for their homes.

The powerful families of Buenos Aires had traditionally congregated immediately south of the Plaza de Mayo, in an area of fifteen blocks enclosed by Belgrano, Chacabuco, Rivadavia, and Defensa, but in the late 1860s prestige locations began to develop north of the plaza, along several blocks of Florida and San Martín. A few wealthy families also had summer homes in Flores or Belgrano, where they could enjoy the country breezes and escape the sultry heat of the downtown streets. During the summer and fall of 1871 this slight northward and outward trend received strong reinforcement from an epidemic which made those summer retreats highly desirable and also cast serious doubt on health conditions in the southern part of the city.

There had been several "scares" in the 1860s which, momentarily, had focused public attention on the city's lack of sanitation; however, most porteños still dumped waste and garbage in the public thoroughfare, and some streets that ran down toward the river served as little more than open sewers. Irregularity in street levels and inadequate paving allowed stagnant pools of water to form. Furthermore, privies in the back patios of each house were only infrequently cleaned and emptied and thus easily contaminated the shallow wells located on the same lot. Disease thrived on these conditions, particularly among the rapidly increasing numbers of poverty-stricken immigrants from Europe. In 1867, soldiers returning from the Paraguayan War brought cholera to the city. The epidemic afflicted 5000 persons during April and May, and left behind more than 1500 dead. Cholera visited the city again the next year, but strict quarantine measures limited its spread. In 1869, typhoid reached epidemic proportions, with some 500 deaths in Buenos Aires; but the population resignedly accepted typhoid, smallpox, and diphtheria as periodic and expected killers.

Yellow fever, which first struck in 1870, was a new visitor to the Río de la Plata. Travelers to Brazilian ports greatly feared the disease, and strict quarantine of vessels to the Río de la Plata always followed its appearance at Santos or Rio de Janeiro. The last outbreak of yellow fever in the Río de la Plata had been in 1857, across the estuary at Montevideo, where it had left a heavy death toll. But the unexpected appearance of the disease in Buenos Aires in March of 1870 claimed less than 200 victims and was soon dismissed as a capricious and unusual event.

Then, in early 1871, yellow fever returned.[5] Several cases occurred at the end of January in a house close to the San Telmo church. As the disease reached epidemic proportions in February, the newspapers lashed out at a number of presumed causes: the wastes discharged by the meat-salting plants along the Riachuelo; the crowded, often dirty conventillos, where the recently arrived immigrants congregated; the filthy conditions of barracks and hospitals close to the downtown area. Not until a decade later, in Cuba, would anyone seriously suggest the mosquito as the carrier of yellow fever, and only in 1900 did scientists prove how the virus spread. But journalistic diagnoses at times came unwittingly close to the culprit. Particularly suspect was the unsanitary system for disposing of human waste. Some journalists recalled that heavy rains in late 1870 had flooded all the low-lying areas of the city; latrines had overflowed and fecal material had been spread through houses, patios, and streets. As the hot summer months advanced, the swarms of mosquitoes became more of a plague than ever before. One newspaper noted that "the spread of yellow fever seems to follow the drainage courses" and observed that the worst ravages occurred along the streets which served as drains for the city.[6]

At first the disease was confined to the parish of San Telmo and the area of La Boca. As it became epidemic and began to spread outward, the authorities began to take belated public health measures. Decrees and orders, like the newspapers, struck out wildly at all possible causes, but, unfortunately, they came nowhere near the real carrier. Whenever a case appeared, the inhabitants of the house were immediately evicted; as the epidemic progressed, the entire population was removed from any seriously infected block. It was decreed that bodies must be buried within six hours after death. Funeral processions were limited in size. Latrines were to be disinfected and dug deeper. Dirt and rubbish could no longer be dumped in the river. Meat must be thrown out as garbage if not sold the same day as slaughtered, only live fowl could be sold in the markets, and the meat-salting plants on the Riachuelo were closed.

By early March more than 100 persons were dying from yellow fever each day, and in April the municipal authorities had to open an emergency burial ground in the northwestern section of the city, at Chacarita. Panic seized the population. Everyone who could do so abandoned the city, and free train tickets hastened the exodus. As it became clear that few deaths from the fever occurred in higher locations, such as Flores and Belgrano, rents in those towns rose astronomically. Provincial authorities attempted to ease the housing shortage by putting up large tents and erecting barns near towns such as San Martín, Morón, and Luján, in the province of Buenos Aires.

During the first two weeks in April, the death rate climbed to over 300 a day, and on April 10 yellow fever carried away a record 563 persons in a single day. By then the city appeared deserted, especially in the usually busy plaza area. Somewhere between 50,000 and 100,000 persons had left the city.[7] A few courageous doctors and priests remained at their posts, but church services were suspended. All government offices were closed. Garbage collection, police patrols—indeed, all normal services—ceased, and for a while thieves and burglars who were foolhardy enough to brave the epidemic had a free hand with hastily abandoned houses.

Then, with the return of colder weather in May, the epidemic slacked off; deaths slid below 100 a day and by the middle of the month declined to twenty per day. Gradually, both inhabitants and sanity returned to the city. The beginning of winter in June marked the end of the yellow fever, leaving behind a grim toll of nearly 14,000 dead—double the city's normal number of deaths in a year.

The epidemic had dramatic impact on the plaza area. It caused the wealthy to question the wisdom of remaining in the older, deteriorating, patio-style buildings south of the Plaza de Mayo. It also helped to develop among the well-to-do the habit of sending their families out of the city, at least for part of the summer. Many foreign-born merchants, especially the English, had long before moved to outlying homes along the riverbank north of the city; it was they who, in the 1860s, had all but built several of the towns

25. Typical suburban quinta of upper-class porteños. This was the summer home of the Rodríguez family in Almagro, built around 1895. (Archivo General de la Nación.)

along the line of the Northern Railroad. Now even the Argentine upper class began to see advantages of a summer or weekend retreat to a quinta, with its fruit trees and gardens.

The initial move was to Flores, on the Western Railroad's line, in large measure because of its proximity to the Plaza de Mayo. Land values increased sharply in Flores during late 1871, in anticipation of the exodus expected during the following summer, and by early 1872 the town boasted new attractions—a social club, a band, a theater, and public baths.[8] By the middle of the decade the town had established a solid reputation as a summer retreat for the better families. As one contemporary observer later recalled: "San José de Flores was one of the elegant places to go for the summer. There were a number of splendid quintas and the local activities and parties attracted a great deal of attention."⁹

At the same time, the porteño upper class, although willing to rent or buy a second home in an accessible suburb, showed great reluctance to abandon the plaza area. What took place during the 1870s, therefore, was a movement out of the area south of the Plaza de Mayo and a relocation along streets north of the plaza. New-comers to the upper class contributed even more significantly to elite settlement on the north side. Provincial politicians and profes-sional men who had settled in the city, foreign merchants and bank-ers, and porteños who had recently made money almost always bought or rented along Florida, San Martín, or near those two streets.

By 1880 Florida had replaced Bolívar and Perú as the home of the elite. Its southern end, near the Plaza de Mayo, had also over-taken Victoria as the elegant shopping district. At first the com-bination of high-class shops and prestige residences seemed to blend well. Gradually, however, a struggle broke out between the store-keepers, who desired to restrict Florida to pedestrian traffic, and the wealthy residents, who wished to drive their carriages up to the street entrances of their homes. One can gauge from this relatively obscure conflict that Florida remained the residence of the elite until roughly 1910. In 1887 the municipal council experimented with a measure to close off traffic along the five blocks of Florida closest to the Plaza de Mayo between 7:00 and 10:00 p.m., but the measure faltered and never was implemented because it "would prevent those living on the street from coming home in their car-riages."¹⁰ For the next two decades the upper-class residents of Florida defeated similar measures.*¹¹

But control of Florida, and of the municipal council, finally passed into commercial hands. In 1909 the council approved a measure prohibiting vehicular traffic on Florida during the evening hours. Although residents objected to it and gained a temporary repeal, the regulation gained final acceptance in 1913.¹² Meanwhile,

---

* Contributing to the problem faced by the upper class was the fact that almost no blocks in Buenos Aires had alleys or corridors which might have given access to a rear entrance. The elongated house lot, characteristic of the patio-style construc-tion, undoubtedly discouraged such alleys.

in 1911, the prestigious newspaper *La Nación* bemoaned the passing of an era in an article entitled, "The Death of Florida:" "Florida —elegant and aristocratic—suffers today from boorish vulgarization and is dying."[13] By then yet another displacement of the upperclass families was under way. Although they remained within a short distance of their offices and stores in the plaza area, the elite expanded their northward push into Barrio Norte and the streets northwest of the Plaza San Martín.

Changes in housing and architectural styles were also an integral part of the readjustment of upper-class residential patterns around the Plaza de Mayo. Architecture within the city had changed substantially only once prior to 1870. Toward the end of the eighteenth century local production of kiln-baked bricks and tiles had radically altered housing for the city's well-to-do. Sun-dried adobes and straw thatch soon began to give way to the new materials. With added strength of walls, the height of ceilings could be increased toward a twelve- or fourteen-foot standard—a noticeable advantage during hot humid porteño summers, even though it made the rooms drafty and chilly in the damp winter months. Builders occasionally added a second story. The tiled roof also provided a valuable side benefit: well-to-do families increasingly turned to rainwater collected in cisterns rather than using water from shallow, often contaminated, wells or purchasing daily supplies from water carts filled in the muddy estuary. The traditional patio-style house, the elongated structure described earlier in the tour of the gran aldea, thus emerged.*

During the 1840s and 1850s a few adjustments were made in this patio-style construction.[14] Stylistic innovations, generally lumped together under the rubric "Italian influence," dominated the ornamentation and façades of buildings, especially churches and public edifices. Several Italian architects, most notably Nicolás and José Canale, and a host of Italian masons and carpenters who arrived in Buenos Aires in these years dominated the construction industry. In applying their trades and techniques, they modified only slightly the appearance of the patio-style house. The simple, unadorned house front which had predominated since colonial times continued to be in vogue. Balustrades and square columns were occasionally

* See pp. 44–47.

26. Changing architectural styles. An example of the ornamentation and balconies that were added to housefronts along Maipú in the 1850s and 1860s. (Archivo General de la Nación.)

added to the façade, and some ornamentation appeared over windows or at the roof's edge. The few windows that faced on the street still featured iron grillwork, but they were now frequently filigreed and decorated, and second-story windows usually had balconies adorned with grillwork or balustrades.

Rising land values around the Plaza de Mayo caused more and more second and third stories to be added onto the elongated patio-style floor plan. The result was a two-family dwelling with adjacent entry ways from the sidewalk: one opened into the traditional, formal first patio, now covered with a ceiling and designated as a hall; the second gave access to a flight of stairs which ended in a similar hall or patio on the second floor. Servants' quarters, along with a kitchen for the downstairs family, were located in a basement area near the front of the house. Those serving second-floor residents had their cubicles and a kitchen and laundry area on the roof. With such adjustments, the architects had accomplished about as much as could be done within the confines of a lot measuring 57 by 199 feet, or, more frequently, within the even narrower limits of 28 by 85 feet.

After 1880 the burgeoning of the country's agricultural exports and the accompanying commercial-bureaucratic expansion of the city brought a marked change in upper-class housing styles and construction. Wealthy residents of Buenos Aires, many of them successful politicians and merchants from the provinces, saw modest income from lands, goods, and agricultural produce blossom into veritable fortunes. At the same time, increasing travel abroad, along with the admiration for progress and science engendered by the rising tide of positivist thought and philosophy that swept through Argentine educational and elite circles, filled the country's ruling classes with shame for their humble colonial origins and Hispanic background. Nouveau riche in spirit if not in origin, the porteño elite sought to remake their city in the style of the most modern of Europe's capitals. Alvear's dramatic reuniting of two plazas to form the Plaza de Mayo, and the plans for the Avenida de Mayo, merely highlighted the elite's admiration of Georges Haussman's design for the great Parisian boulevards.*

* See pp. 110–13 for a description of the formation of the Plaza de Mayo and the building of the Avenida de Mayo.

27. The Unzué residence, on Cerrito. Compare with Illus. 10. (Archivo General de la Nación.)

The porteño upper class turned quickly from a taste for the Italianesque to a wholesale acceptance of currents emanating from the world's leader in architectural design, the École des Beaux-Arts in Paris. Italians were replaced by French-trained architects led by such figures as Carlos Agote, Alejandro Christophersen, Julio Dormal, Jacques Dunant, Pablo Hary, and Eduardo María Lanus— all of whom had studied either in France or Belgium.[15] Supported by a few German and English architects, they remodeled the city into the Paris of South America. The crisis of 1890 and the ensuing depression years slowed but did not stop the trend toward more ornate and sumptuous styling, both in public and in private edifices. With the boom of 1905-12, the elite became eclectic, although the French influence, with its grand entrances, foyers, and vestibules, sweeping command of space, and harmonic balancing of lines, pre-

28. The palacios of the Anchorenas and the Peñas on Plaza San Martín, around 1914. Compare with Illus. 10. (Archivo General de la Nación.)

dominated. Italian-oriented architects, however, regained some popularity with their exuberant and exaggerated ornamentation of façades.

The impact of the École des Beaux Arts on housing for the upper class, along with increasing land values at the city's center, stimulated the move toward Barrio Norte at the same time that it encouraged construction of the three- and four-story *palacio*, or mansion, and the *petit hotel*. The elongated lot, so effectively used in patio-style construction, could not serve the French style, which demanded space. Although the narrow lot was still used for the new houses being built in the suburbs,* the wealthy who moved

---

* For a discussion of the outward expansion of non-elite groups, see pp. 178–80.

from Florida toward Plaza San Martín and Barrio Norte acquired square lots, often a quarter of a city block, or at least rectangular lots with a depth not more than three times the width.

In its most pretentious form, the new style gave birth to mansions and palacios that occupied an entire city block. One of the most striking, the palacio of José C. Paz on the Plaza San Martín, completed in 1912 and still used in the 1970s as the social center for the Círculo Militar, took up a wedge-shaped block. The design for the building was drawn up in France by a leading French architect, Louis Sortais. Similarly, René Sergent sent prepared plans from Paris for the Errázuriz family's fabulous mansion, built in 1911 on Avenida Alvear (renamed Libertador General San Martín in 1950); today that building serves the city as the Museo de Artes Decorativas. Two years earlier the mansion of Mercedes Castellanos de Anchorena had risen on the Plaza San Martín—an entire block highlighted by a striking oval reception hall at its center.[16] The tone of such stately, baroque mansions had already been set by the Ortiz Basualdo/Peña families, whose palacio was also located on the Plaza San Martín. This three-story house, winner of the municipality's architectural prize in 1904 and at that time valued at 500,000 pesos, or roughly a quarter of a million dollars, came from the drawing board of Julio Dormal.

Not only the exterior of these dwellings, but also the rich and ornate interiors expressed the spirit, ambitions, and values of an upper class eager to parade its wealth and accomplishments and emulate the world's most current fashions. The mosaic billiard rooms, the mirrored and ornate salons, the special rooms set aside to exhibit art collections suggest how much the elite's environment and attitudes had changed from the era of the gran aldea.

The new styles and tastes also affected those members of the porteño upper class who could not afford the sybaritic level of the palacio or the petit hotel. The chalet type of construction that appeared increasingly after the turn of the century appealed to families of comfortable means. Typical was the chalet described in an advertisement in 1906:

> Attractive chalet in Belgrano. . . . First floor: salon, study, large dining room and antechamber, powder room, magnificent entry hall, kitchen and toilet, washroom, and a garden for vegetables.

29. The billiard room of the Ortiz Basualdo mansion. Compare with Illus. 11. (Archivo General de la Nación.)

30. Salon of a typical palacio. Compare with Illus. 11. (Archivo General de la Nación.)

> Mezzanine: one bedroom and two rooms for servants. Second floor:
> three bedrooms, charming drawing room, bathroom. Recently built,
> gas and running water installed.[17]

Further down the scale, yet within grasp of modest professional
men, were houses such as this one, advertised in 1907: "New . . .
10 by 27 yards. First floor with hall, study, living room, two bedrooms, dining room, bath, kitchen; upstairs a servant's room. Gas,
running water, and sewers."[18] In this case not too much had
changed from the patio-styled design, except that this was a more
compact type of housing.

While the Ortiz Basualdo palacio had a value of half a million
pesos, the selling prices of those two houses stood at 43,500 and
18,500 pesos, respectively. Yet even those prices were well above
the 1000 pesos which a skilled artisan might invest in a narrow lot
and one-room house.*[19]

* See the discussion of costs of worker houses on pp. 178–79.

The wealthy of Buenos Aires for a few decades at least sought to have the best of two worlds—proximity to the compact downtown area centered on the Plaza de Mayo, yet the enjoyment of spaciousness, elegance, and luxury which they could attain by moving out toward the Plaza San Martín and Barrio Norte. The outward push by the well-to-do thus came in more muted form and at a much later stage in Buenos Aires than in many commercial, industrializing urban areas. After 1920 the upper classes, assisted by the automobile, tended to follow the earlier lead of many of the foreign-born upper class—notably the English and Germans. Increasingly, they spread out into Belgrano, Villa Devoto, and Flores and beyond the Federal District to the north into Vicente López, Olivos, La Lucila, Martínez, Acassuso, and San Isidro. But Barrio Norte retained its attraction for the upper class; even today it is the most concentrated and prestigious place of residence for the porteño elite.

Despite the elite's preference for the Plaza de Mayo area, most of those who lived in the city's center were manual laborers, artisans, skilled laborers, small shopkeepers, and clerks. Many had only recently arrived in Argentina. Since the demand for manual labor in the urban center was great and the streetcar fare was expensive until after 1900, these newcomers congregated in downtown conventillos, cheap boardinghouses, and apartments. Consequently, their working and living conditions formed the other part of changing patterns around the Plaza de Mayo.

Argentina, particularly Buenos Aires, attracted immigrant labor throughout most of the years from 1870 to 1910. In Europe economic depression, overcrowding, and lack of advancement encouraged workers to leave their homelands, and Argentina possessed the powerful drawing card of economic opportunity. In Buenos Aires, wages for manual labor, especially in skilled and semiskilled fields, were at times double and triple those in Italian, Spanish, and French cities and occasionally were substantially higher than those in London or Liverpool. The demand for construction workers attracted masons, carpenters, painters, and day laborers in proportion to increases in total population; the percentages of workers employed in each activity also remained fairly constant (see Table 6).

Although workers in construction headed the list, those employed in other occupations also increased proportionately to total demographic growth. The city's total population increased nine times between 1869 and 1914; during that period the number of shopkeepers multiplied by eight, servants by seven, butchers, bakers, shoemakers, and seamstresses by five. Furthermore, the development of certain processing industries, such as meat-packing, wool-washing, distilling, brewing, cigarette-making, biscuit and pasta production, and flour-milling, opened up a whole range of occupations that were virtually unknown in 1870.

The foreign-born predominated in these occupations in striking fashion. Even by 1914, when numerous sons of immigrants were included in the Argentine-born figures, the foreign-born outnumbered the Argentines by impressive ratios: 5.6:1 for masons; 4.2:1 for carpenters; 9.8:1 for day laborers. The need for strong backs in railroad and port construction and in loading ships—lines of work little favored by the native-born—rose sharply during the economic booms of 1884-89 and 1905-12. As crop farming expanded on the pampas—initially through owner-colonists and subsequently through tenant farmers—the demand for harvest laborers grew enormously. These opportunities attracted an annual influx from the start of the wheat harvest in central Santa Fe and Córdoba in late November to the end of the corn harvest in the south of the province of Buenos Aires in late March. An estimated 50,000 *golondrinas*, or migrant workers—literally, swallows—entered Argentina each year during the 1890s; twice that number came during the first decade of the twentieth century.[20] The pay was several times that offered on European farms; it provided the thrifty worker with enough to cover a round-trip third-class passage—plus a substantial nest egg, which he acquired during Europe's slack winter season. Although no certain answer can be made as to how many of these migrant laborers also fed the city's labor force, memoirs and contemporary accounts suggest that, for many laborers, a few years of rural summer work served as the introduction to permanent residence in Buenos Aires.

The economic attractiveness of Argentina and of Buenos Aires did not remain constant during these forty years, even when measured in wages.[21] An estimate of fluctuations in remuneration can be secured by reducing the wages paid in paper pesos to day laborers and skilled constuction workers to the common unit of the gold peso (see Table 7). In 1870 wages stood at particularly high levels, several times those in Italy and Spain and somewhat above those in most parts of England and the United States. The common laborer earned approximately 1.20 gold pesos per day, while skilled laborers received upwards of 4.00 gold pesos. With the depression of the mid-1870s this figure fell, until by 1880 the day laborer commanded no more than 75 gold centavos per day, and the mason or carpenter 1.50 gold pesos a day. Economic recovery in the early 1880s pushed wages to two or three times those in Spain and Italy; the differential remained considerably less for workers from France and Germany. By 1885 a day laborer could expect a gold peso per day, while skilled labor received between 1.90 and 2.10 gold pesos daily. The depression of the early 1890s cut these wages by more than half: by 1892 the daily wage of a common laborer stood at 30 to 50 gold centavos, and that of a skilled worker ranged from 75 to 100 gold centavos. Some recovery occurred late in the decade, and by 1905 Argentina could again draw from depressed areas of Europe, particularly Spain. Common labor commanded close to a gold peso a day by 1905, while skilled labor topped two gold pesos. By 1910, another peak, nearly as high as that of 1870, had been reached: common day laborers were receiving 1.20 to 1.50 gold pesos and skilled laborers could secure 2.50 to 3.50 gold pesos per day. The trend once again turned downward with the depression of 1913-14: common laborers' wages slid to 75 gold centavos daily and skilled laborers' dropped to 1.00 to 1.50 gold pesos. Wages in the city of Buenos Aires acted as a magnet for Spanish and Italian workers throughout the period, with the exception of the early 1890s. For other nationalities, the attraction proved more sporadic.

The city's attractiveness for foreign laborers also varied with the local prices and the cost of living.[22] Real wages fell drastically during the depression years of 1874–78 and 1890–93. The high cost of rents, food, and services in the city completely overrode the attraction of wages at least in 1891 and accounted for a net emigration during that year of 30,000 foreigners. During the long periods of recovery that followed each of these depressions, immigrants and laboring people in the city made do by reducing the quantity and quality of their food, by mending and re-mending worn-out clothing, and by seeking out miserable, low-cost hovels of tenements.

Even in boom years, living costs bit deeply into apparently handsome wages. The slope of a real wage curve between 1870 and 1910 does not replicate the high peaks of 1868–72, 1884–89, or 1905–12 apparent in gold-peso wages, but only shows moderate increases for those years. In 1871, for example, a commercial report to the British Foreign Office noted that in Buenos Aires bread cost three times as much as it did in England, fuel four times, and groceries twice as much. Although meat was cheap and constituted the staple item in the diet, it was so sinewy and tough that it took three pounds to go as far as one pound of beef would in England.[23] Two years later another British diplomat quoted a comment, made by one of the local bankers, to the effect that "the cost of living in this city has risen . . . at least 25% since the year 1871," and the diplomat added that the cost of lodging and clothes made the salary paid his secretary look ridiculous.[24] The rent of a tiny tenement room, shared with five or six other men, took at least one-fifth of a common laborer's monthly earnings. In 1873 a modest, furnished room cost the equivalent of 37 gold pesos a month, one and a half times the monthly wages of a day laboror or half those of an accountant. A lightweight summer suit cost an accountant more than a month's wages, and a hat absorbed nearly a week's salary.

As the effects of the mid-1870s depression began to be felt, and wages declined sharply, there was no accompanying fall in rents or in the price of food and clothing. Many Europeans returned home, discouraged and embittered. During late 1876 the streets of Buenos Aires were reported to be almost totally deserted, even during the middle of a normal working day.[25] Many of those who remained suffered real hunger, which was relieved only in part by the municipal council's efforts to distribute, at cost, mutton and fish—both highly unpopular foods in Argentine eyes. The number of beggars in the downtown streets increased noticeably, and in the evenings bands of fifty to 100 of them gathered outside the kitchens of the Colegio Nacional or of the two Jesuit secondary schools to fight over scraps of meat and bread.[26]

As wages slowly recovered from the lows of the depression, the city faced a rare phenomenon—an extraordinary rise in the price of the basic food staple, meat. The armed conflict of June 1880, which concluded with the federalization of the city of Buenos Aires, along with intranquillity and disorder in the countryside, had caused a momentary jump in meat prices. But after settlement of the conflict prices did not come down, and repeated attempts to lower prices actually cut the production of the meat needed to satisfy rising urban demand. An effort to establish a chain of cooperative butcher shops failed, as did the projects of the municipal council to regulate prices and to distribute meat free to the poor. The temporary lifting of taxes on butchers and the provision for free railroad transport of live animals into the city also accomplished little.[27] Those most affected by meat costs, of course, were the manual laborers, who looked to beef as those in other countries might look to beans, potatoes, rice, or bread.

The white-collar workers fared only a little better, for rents cut sharply into their salaries. The head of the British diplomatic mission in Buenos Aires had tripled the salary of his secretary over that paid in the early 1870s; yet he complained that the cheapest, unfurnished, small house his secretary could find required a half-hour ride by streetcar to his work and absorbed two-thirds of his annual salary.[28] The intense land speculation of the 1880s, and the tendency to build one- and two-story buildings, contributed to steadily climbing house rents. This caused, as *La Prensa* noted, "a critical problem which affects . . . numerous families of middle income who have certain social standards to maintain and who have to spend more than half their income on rent."[29]

The abortive political revolution of July 1890—a protest against the financial speculation as well as the political corruption of the national government—accompanied one of Argentina's worst economic depressions. The initial climb in meat prices—in response to the threat of civil war—quickly ended: in 1891 the municipality began to distribute meat free to the needy and established rigid price controls over meat stalls in the city markets.[30] Rents declined an estimated 20 per cent during the second half of 1890, although many landlords preferred to leave houses and apartments vacant rather than lower the rents. Dramatic declines in jobs and wages, however, far exceeded any fall in the cost of living and made the city an unrewarding place for immigrant labor. For example, on a single day in late 1891, 7000 men were discharged from port construction projects.[31]

Public works projects subsequently helped to stimulate a slow recovery from the 1890–93 crisis. The Avenida de Mayo, a swath cut westward from the Plaza de Mayo through the downtown area, reached completion in 1894, and the final basin of the new port works was opened in 1898. Nevertheless, an overabundance of labor slowed any appreciable rise in wages. On several occasions during 1899–1900 as many as 20,000 to 40,000 workers were reported unemployed in the city. In 1899 the secretary to the chief of police had the temerity to say in a public statement that the unemployed were not working because they did not want to; the next day several thousand fliers appeared on the streets; they offered employment and gave the secretary's home address as the place to which to report. The following morning unemployed workers packed that street and the adjoining blocks. Police reinforcements finally had to be called in to disperse the crowds.[32] In August 1901 thousands of unemployed paraded down the Avenida de Mayo to the Plaza de Mayo. President Roca himself appeared on a balcony of the Casa Rosada, but his promises to study the problems were drowned out by the whistles and jeers of the angry crowd. A year later, again in the plaza, another sizable crowd gathered to protest the President's failure even to look into the situation.[33] Others registered their dissatisfaction by leaving Argentina in droves; in 1902 there was a net immigration of only 17,000, one of the lowest of the preceding three decades.*

Living standards for manual laborers remained depressed for more than a decade following the crisis. In a series of articles on labor conditions published in late 1901, *La Prensa* concluded that workers with families could hardly survive in the city. The top monthly wage a day laborer could earn amounted to 70 pesos

---

* A net loss of 30,000 had been recorded in 1891 and a net immigration of only 16,000 in 1875, the only two years below 1902. In 1902, 96,000 immigrants entered Argentina, but 79,000 left the country.

moneda nacional (m$n), or the equivalent of 30 gold pesos.[34] The estimated minimum expenses for an average worker family totaled 100 pesos m$n, or 43 gold pesos. Conditions did not improve further up the scale: it took 265 pesos m$n a month to support a typical white-collar family of five at a time when clerks made less than 150 pesos m$n per month.[35] Survival, of course, lay in putting wife and children to work and in cutting living standards below the estimated minimums. Even for those who did not have to watch their expenses so closely, life in Buenos Aires proved costly. In 1905, the British envoy exclaimed in a dispatch to the Foreign Office that Buenos Aires is "far and away the most expensive place that I have ever been in my life."[36]

By 1905 wages for the urban workingman finally began to move upward. Unemployment virtually disappeared, and the city and the country embarked on an economic boom without precedent. For those whose skills and profits were linked with rising exports and trade, life in the city once again acquired a rosy hue. The unmarried manual laborer or the skilled worker with several teenaged, and consequently employable, children benefited considerably. These groups fueled the exodus to small plots of land, to outlying houses, and to the suburbs.

But those on the fixed salary of a white-collar job, or possessing skills and training not urgently required by the country's expanding commerce, bureaucracy, and agriculture, did not share in this prosperity. For them the rising prices that accompanied the general increase in wages meant continued hardship. Fruit, vegetables, butter, milk, and eggs—never common items in porteño diets—disappeared from the table of the laboring man. A vegetarian who had been attempting to attract followers in the city with well-publicized feats of strength commented that one could live comfortably on fruit for five centavos a day. One wit sardonically estimated the amount of fruit that five centavos could buy in Buenos Aires in 1908: two grapes, one cherry, two strawberries, half an orange, half a peach, one banana, the stem of a pear, one-fifth of an apple, and one-sixtieth of a melon.[37] Bread of the cheapest quality had risen in price from 13 centavos a kilo (2.2 pounds) in 1900 to 22 centavos by 1909. In Argentina, a country that had become the world's third and sometimes second largest exporter of wheat, bread cost more than it did in Paris, London, Amsterdam, or New York. In a further extension of irony, by 1910 meat often cost more in a Buenos Aires butcher shop than Argentine beef did in a London market.

Marketing procedures and the tax structure contributed much to the woes of those on fixed salaries or pensions. As truck-garden zones gradually moved away from the city's center, transportation costs and rising land values affected food prices. The many middle-men involved in food retailing and the high overhead in the thousands of small shops scattered across the city further padded food prices. Import duties and internal taxes weighed heavily on the lower echelons of the population. Import duties on most items were levied by weight or volume rather than by value. The wealthy might pay only a tiny percentage on their cases of French champagne, British marmalade, or Spanish olives, but the poor could pay over 100 per cent on protected items such as sugar or wine, or upwards of 75 per cent on items such as kerosene, paper, rice, coffee, starch, oil, and beans. Also, in the 1890s and 1900s a substantial part of the national revenue came from internal taxes levied on sugar, matches, cigarettes, beer, and wine. Since unit intake of such items obviously could not increase proportion-ately with income, the manual laborers and the blue-collar and white-collar workers carried an inordinate share of expenses in ex-panding national budgets.

Working conditions—in addition to fluctuations in wages and living costs—affected urban laborers and European immigrants. The most common type of employment, and one that absorbed large numbers of recently arrived Europeans, consisted of the lift-ing and carrying associated with the waterfront, the construction sites, the railroad stations, or the wholesale and retail outlets. Dock workers were hired each morning between 5:00 and 6:00 a.m. in gangs as employment opportunities presented themselves.*[38] This work might involve twelve trips an hour down a gangplank, un-loading 220-pound bags of sugar, or 150 trips a day from ship to

---

* In Buenos Aires, perhaps because of cultural and linguistic similarities between the host society and the Italian and Spanish immigrants, there was less of the labor boss, or padrone, system which exploited immigrant labor, especially Italian labor, in United States cities.

shore, balancing unwieldy, 130-pound stacks of lumber on one's shoulders.[39]

Skilled and semiskilled workers, especially carpenters, blacksmiths, mechanics, masons, and painters, as well as those who clothed and fed the urban populace—butchers, bakers, tailors, shoemakers—also found ready employment. These men worked in small groups. Rarely did construction jobs or artisan shops employ more than ten persons. The fact that laborers were accustomed to working alongside their *patrón*, or employer, and the relative absence of large industrial plants, helped to postpone development of working-class consciousness. Twelve- and fourteen-hour days were common, and jobs tended to be labor-intensive rather than machinery oriented. There were, however, fewer industrial hazards and more healthy surroundings in Buenos Aires than there were in most European and United States cities.

In order to supplement family incomes, women and children often worked as long hours as men, frequently in cramped, unhealthy surroundings. Most children in the city attended the first grades of elementary school, but those from poorer families went to work at the age of nine or ten. Producers of cigarettes, matches, hats, buttons, and burlap bags invariably turned to cheap labor—women and children. These shops, which employed anywhere from a dozen to several hundred workers, also saved on light, ventilation, and space. Rarely did women and children, as marginal wage earners, effectively protest such economies. In addition, piecework from garment stores, as well as the city's laundering and ironing, afforded thousands of women employment at home, in the crowded patios and rooms of conventillos and apartment houses.

During the first decade of the twentieth century, certain workers, especially those possessing special skills or involved in transportation of agricultural exports, gained some improvements in working conditions. In the 1890s in particular, socialist and anarchist agitation, fueled by experienced and dedicated organizers from Spain and Italy, promised to mobilize labor into an aggressive and effective force. The sharp reaction of Argentina's ruling merchant-landowner elite at the beginning of the twentieth century, combined with the turning of the economic cycle—an overabundance of labor from 1890 to 1903, followed by a period of rising wages and opportunities from 1905 to 1912—handicapped the labor movement. What emerged were trade union organizations that affected skilled workmen, such as carpenters, masons, bakers, or printers, and the specialized sectors of railroad and tannery workers.[40]

A look at agitation and regulations concerning Sunday rest, reduced working hours, and accident compensation affords further insights into working conditions for the average urban worker. The upper class slowly changed certain of their attitudes toward the working masses during the debate over Sunday holidays. In September 1881 the municipal council revived an earlier ordinance that closed all establishments except drugstores, cafés, hotels, and restaurants on Sundays; stores dealing in food items could open in the early morning and late evening. Store owners and the public in general protested vigorously, and a new ordinance was passed, substantially extending the list of exemptions and permitting all establishments to remain open until 10:00 a.m. on Sunday.[41] Although the British diplomatic representative observed that the regulation "seems generally to be little regarded,"[42] shopkeepers renewed the battle against any restrictions in 1883. Such regulations, it was argued, prejudiced the freedom of commerce, discriminated against religious groups that did not observe Sunday rest, and handicapped workingmen who needed to earn additional money by Sunday labor. One of the municipal councilmen, Francisco A. Tamini, summarized these viewpoints with the comment: "The laziness of a Sunday off will merely stimulate all sorts of vice, since this is what the working class generally indulges in anyway on Sundays."[43] Despite a veto by the Intendente and a lengthy debate involving anticlerical issues, the commercial interests won the day, and by the end of 1883 all establishments remained open on Sundays.[44]

After 1900, Sunday closing, strongly supported by Catholic labor groups, re-emerged as a safe issue around which all labor could rally. At the end of August 1902, 1500 employees of the downtown stores marched down the Avenida de Mayo to present a petition with 50,000 signatures to Congress.[45] Such pressures continued through 1903 and 1904. Even the merchant-bureaucrat-landowner elite acceded to the idea of Sunday rest on behalf of religion, family, and health. The same newspapers which in the 1880s had rejected Sunday closing as an attack on individual freedom now accepted it as a basic need of the working class.[46] Congress, prodded by reform-oriented Catholic deputies and by its first Socialist representative, got around to debating the problem in 1904, and in the following year it passed a law closing all stores in the Federal District on Sunday.[47]

Measures for shorter working hours did not fare as well. By and large, hours remained governed by the supply of and demand for laborers in various trades, or by special arrangements that workers could make with employers. Indeed, not until the 1890s did pressure for shorter hours even develop. In 1894 a municipal councilman and an early champion of labor causes, Eduardo Pittaluga, introduced a project to establish an eight-hour day for all municipal workers. Supporters of the project led marches along the recently completed Avenida de Mayo, and there was extensive newspaper debate, but eventually the argument that such regulation inhibited the freedom to work carried the day and the proposal was sent "to the archives."[48]

In 1904 the executive branch introduced in Congress an all-inclusive labor measure, including provisions for shorter working hours. It was claimed that two years of study had gone into drafting this complex proposal, and the accompanying eloquent message from President Roca stated that its passage would improve conditions for both the working class and capitalists.[49] The press, soon supported by congressional debate, cast serious doubts on the intentions of the executive branch. According to rumor, the project had been designed purely for propaganda purposes; after serving this function, it would be allowed to die in committee.[50] That is, in effect, what happened.

A few sections of the 1904 proposal subsequently were put forward as individual projects. In one such effort in 1906, the Socialist deputy Alfredo Palacios introduced a measure for a forty-eight-hour week and a maximum of ten hours' labor a day, with still shorter hours established for women and children.[51] The following year an emasculated law that provided for an eight-hour day for those under sixteen years of age and permitted women to work or not, as they chose, immediately before and after child-

birth, finally emerged from Congress.[52] Nevertheless, employers
flagrantly violated even these limited provisions. The flurry of So-
cialist-sponsored projects introduced in Congress in 1913 and 1914
—a forty-eight-hour week in factories, an eight-hour day for government and railroad employees, a half-day of work on Saturdays,
regulations for nighttime work, and an end to the long hours still
demanded of clerks in most commercial establishments—were
promptly referred to committee, where they died. Shorter hours
had to wait for a greater concern on the part of the general public
and a more popular representation in Congress.

Congress and the public at large found it even more difficult to
accept the idea that employers in some way bore legal responsibility for accidents involving their workmen. Accidents, according
to the popular view, occurred because of the carelessness or stupidity of the individual; they should not involve management.
Concerned legislators of both socialist and conservative tendencies
kept accident compensation proposals constantly before Congress
after 1902.[53] Not until 1913, however, was the first step taken, with
indemnification established for all federal employees: payment of
up to a maximum of 1000 days of wages in event of death, and
compensation, on a sliding scale, for injuries.

Housing—even more than working conditions, cost of living, or
wages—was a mark of the way of life of the non-elite groups that
resided in the center of the city. Although conventillos, according
to the municipal censuses of 1887 and 1904, sheltered only one-
quarter to one-third of the population in the Central City, the living conditions in this type of dwelling were in most respects the
same as those of all of the non-elite who lived in the downtown
area (see Table 5). The 60 to 70 per cent of the population who
did not live in conventillos or in individual family units—in the
city's center such units were usually reserved for the upper classes
—occupied boardinghouses, small apartment buildings, or narrow
two-story houses that accommodated two to four families.* But
life in these dwellings differed little from that in the conventillo in

---

* Some individual family units not belonging to upper-class families were owned
by shopkeepers. Especially in the buildings on the small, square lots at the corners
of blocks, which often housed food stores—*almacén, panadería, frutería, carnicería*
—the owner and his family lived in a back room or an upstairs loft.

31. Deteriorating elite residences became conventillo dwellings. This is Casa Balcarce, on Belgrano, south of the Plaza de Mayo. (Archivo General de la Nación.)

size of rooms, crowded conditions, or facilities. Indeed, the number of inhabitants sheltered in one building—usually over thirty—seems to have been the conventillo's principal distinction.*[54] The large number of inhabitants also gave the conventillo visibility in contemporary sources—a visibility not shared by other housing for non-elite groups. Such visibility substantially facilitates examination of the conventillo.

Conventillos had first emerged in the city in the 1850s, when the shells of deteriorating patio-style homes south of the Plaza de

* There is no definition of "conventillo" in the 1887 and 1904 censuses; in the manuscript census materials for 1869 and 1895 the notation "conventillo" occasionally appears on a booklet, but no standard criteria for such notations emerge. The 1904 municipal census suggests, however, that, in addition to the census takers' subjective evaluations, the factor of size played a major role. That census gives the total number of conventillo rooms in the city, dividing them into categories by the number of inhabitants in the conventillo. Only 14 per cent of the total room capacity of conventillos occurred in buildings with thirty or fewer inhabitants.

Mayo were turned into multiple dwellings. Crowded tenement housing returned high income on increasingly valuable commercial land near the center of Buenos Aires, and conventillos thus competed with office and wealthy residential utilization of that land. Such profits added to the pressures that were bringing changes within the plaza area. Plaster-covered adobe or brick walls of patio-style homes frequently showed considerable deterioration after forty or fifty years. These older buildings, often with only slight interior remodeling, brought substantially higher profits for owners as tenement rentals than as housing for the affluent classes.

Outright construction of tenements also added to the supply of conventillos in the plaza area. One of the earliest recorded instances concerned a group of Italian merchants who, in 1867, leased a number of vacant lots along Corrientes and Lavalle on twenty-year contracts and put up cheaply constructed tenements. By the end of that year two newly built conventillos on Corrientes between Talcahuano and Uruguay had been filled. Each had thirty large rooms measuring 16 by 16 feet. The initial monthly rental, four gold pesos per room, was a real bargain, since it approximated only 20 per cent of a common laborer's monthly wages.[55] The construction of new conventillos led *La Prensa* to comment, early in 1871:

> The practice has now become general to build in a small area a great number of rooms made with cheap materials and under conditions that they produce a monthly profit of 3 to 4 per cent; at the same time, because of the low rent these rooms are within the reach of day laborers and persons who do not care how they live, packed together like animals without any concern for morals or health.[56]

By 1880 nearly 300 of the 2000 conventillos in the city were new construction built expressly as rental property.[57]

Whether remodeled from older housing or built new for speculation, the conventillo conformed to the elongated rectangular house lot which characterized the patio-style home and the subdivision of blocks generally in Buenos Aires. The conventillo's depth, therefore, was three to six times as long as its width. The usual frontage was ten varas (28.4 feet), especially in the plaza area, where streets and blocks dated from the seventeenth century. Building materials and size of rooms varied somewhat, according

32. The patio of a typical conventillo, around 1910. (Archivo General de la Nación.)

to location and time of building; a conventillo also might consist of a single story or be a "double-decker." But the outline and structure of the conventillo was remarkably consistent during the entire period from 1870 to 1910. The framework of the patio-style building remained, with a single street entrance, a number of rooms opening off interior patios, latrines at the rear of the building, and no exterior windows except for the few barred ones on the street. Rooms usually measured twelve by twelve feet, with ceiling heights of fourteen feet common in the older buildings but a general decline toward nine feet by 1900. Since every square foot had value, patios often shrank until they were little more than corridors.

At the same time, tenement housing, by crowding as many as

350 persons into a building that formerly had accommodated twenty-five family members and servants, sharply reduced individual rents. By this means alone, the newcomer to the city frequently closed the gap between his living costs and his wages. Single men banded together in groups of six or seven to share a room. Families of five or six members rented a single room and often took in a few additional relatives or compatriots to share expenses.

In these surroundings, life certainly never lacked for activity, commotion, and proximity to one's fellows.[58] Each unit or room afforded some privacy as long as the door remained closed and a curtain covered the single window that opened on the patio. Community kitchens existed only rarely in conventillos, and most groups did their cooking on a charcoal brazier placed on a box or shelf at the entrance to, or occasionally inside, the room. Other boxes at the entrance might hold a basin for washing or serve as receptacles for collecting garbage. Furnishings were sparse. A double bed or some iron cots might accommodate a number of sleepers during the course of a twenty-four hour period, especially among a group of single men. A pine table, a few benches or chairs, some old trunks, perhaps a sewing machine, and more boxes completed the furnishings. In summertime, light came from the open door and window; in other seasons and at night one relied on an oil or gas lamp, or sometimes on a bare electric light bulb. Pictures of popular heroes, generals, or kings torn from magazines, an image of the Madonna and of a couple of saints, perhaps a faded photograph of family members still in Europe appeared on the once whitewashed walls.

The average day began early—at 4:30 in the summer and at 6:00 during the winter—as the men left quietly, often without breakfast in order not to wake the children in these cramped quarters. Shortly thereafter the women and older children began to stir: they put water or milk on the brazier, went to market, or haggled in their doorways with street vendors selling bread and meat. By 9:00 the children were off to scour the streets for odd jobs; those aged seven or eight might attend the first or second year of primary school. The women were long since at their piecework—sewing, rolling cigars, ironing, or doing laundry. At 11:30 the men

33. A conventillo room and some of those who lived there. (Archivo General de la Nación.)

returned for a hasty lunch of watery puchero or some cornmeal pudding. Afternoon brought the bedlam so often associated with conventillos. Despite all the landlords' precautions against taking in large families, half a conventillo's population usually was under fifteen years of age, and fifty to 100 shrieking, fighting, playing youngsters were the rule in any conventillo patio. Men returned from work by 6:00 or 6:30; a dinner of stew was eaten shortly thereafter; by 10:30 nearly everyone was in bed. Religious or patriotic holidays provided a break in this routine. Then accordions, violins, and guitars playing Old World dances enlivened the gray surroundings. A bottle of wine or, occasionally, caña injected warmth into tired bodies, and the conventillo acquired for a moment a vivacity and sparkle it usually lacked.

The conventillo and housing in general for non-elite groups in the downtown core served to condition great numbers of new-comers to the porteño environment. Over this bridge many European-born poor crossed into Argentina permanently. Only the 1887 census distinguished the native-born from the foreign-born among conventillo dwellers, registering 72 per cent as foreign-born in the Central City, while for the city as a whole the figure stood at 66 per cent.*[59] An examination of conventillos from Census District 1 (bounded by Paseo de Julio, Rivadavia, Maipú, and Córdoba) in the 1869 manuscript census suggests even greater foreign-born domination of conventillo population (see Table 8). Of the 707 individuals registered in eight conventillos, 468, or 66 per cent, were foreign-born. If one adds, however, the 180 children under fourteen years of age who were born to immigrant parents, the "foreign" component increases to 92 per cent.

Further characteristics emerge from study of the several conventillos in this district. Occasionally, an entire conventillo was composed almost completely of one ethnic group. The conventillos at San Martín 256/258 and Tucumán 17 drew 93 per cent and 87 per cent of their adult population from Italy (see Table 8). More frequently, although one nationality might predominate, the conventillo housed a number of nationalities. In these cases, however, each individual room inhabited either by a family or by a group of single men represented a single nationality, with all residents born in France, in Germany, or in Italy. One can surmise that such persons also came from the same region and perhaps even from the same town. Likewise, little intermarriage occurred between nationalities. French tended to marry French, Italians married Italians. Occasionally, when older children had been born in Europe and young siblings were Argentine-born, the date of arrival in Buenos Aires can be estimated. Otherwise, one can only guess at the length of residence and whether the marriage occurred in Europe or in Buenos Aires between two persons of the same nationality.

Paralleling the predominance of foreign-born and the clustering of those from the same ethnic background was the similarity of occupations among conventillo dwellers (see Table 8). Of the 111 employed women (roughly half the adult female population) in

---

* Both figures are considerably higher than the total foreign-born figure for the Central City, 60 per cent, or for the entire city, 53 per cent (see Table 4). The fact that in the 1904 municipal census 35 per cent of the registered conventillo population were under fourteen years of age (1904, p. 132) reinforces the likelihood that most of the Argentine-born were children born in Buenos Aires to immigrant parents.

this district all except one—a cigarette vendor—were occupied as washerwomen, seamstresses, or house servants. All the men worked with their hands. Day laborers, peons, and servants constituted a little over half the male work force; the remainder were carpenters, masons, shoemakers, tailors, and store clerks.

The conventillos, largely because of their size and occasionally because of their foreign composition, periodically attracted public attention. During the yellow fever epidemic of 1871 the glare of newspaper publicity quickly turned on the conventillos, not only because the epidemic first broke out in a conventillo in the parish of San Telmo, but also because the disease spread rapidly into other conventillos in the city. In the desperate search for a cause of this often fatal disease, the crowded conventillos came under scrutiny, as did meat-salting plants, latrines, and garbage-strewn streets. Public health committees established in each parish to attempt to control the spread of the epidemic used a heavy hand on the conventillos. In the San Nicolás parish by the end of May more than half of the conventillos had been forcibly evacuated.[60] Such forced expulsion only resulted in worse crowding elsewhere, as those evacuated from one zone moved in with friends or relatives in other conventillos. Quite unrealistic regulations followed. The municipal council decreed that conventillo rooms must be at least thirteen feet high and that each occupant should have thirty cubic yards of space—meaning a maximum occupancy of two per conventillo room. Further ordinances prohibited dirt floors or patios, required a yearly whitewashing inside and out, and ordered that boards be laid under any zinc or corrugated metal roofs.[61] When reports reached the council's ears that crowded conditions had resulted in persons sleeping in the patios and roofs of the conventillos, it passed an ordinance which shut off even the relief of a breeze on hot summer nights by ordering that no one could sleep in the open.[62]

The specter of the yellow fever epidemic continued to guide public concern over this type of housing for several years. The repeated regulations, ordinances, and inspections suggest, however, that the municipality waged a losing battle with the new arrivals' need for cheap rooms and the owners' desire for profits. It was observed that, despite the vigilance of public health committees:

In practice, the committee may approve a room with 2 or 3 beds, but at night 8 or 10 individuals cram into this room to sleep on the floor while the beds are occupied 24 hours a day by individuals who take turns sleeping in them.[63]

At the same time, conventillo and apartment ownership paid handsome dividends. *La Prensa* noted, in 1874, "The conventillos give a 30 to 36 per cent annual return to their owners, who figure among the richest and most respectable men of Buenos Aires."[64] In 1875, in an effort to extend the regulations to cover small apartment houses, where abuses proved most exaggerated, the municipal council put into effect a new licensing system that required inspection of any establishment renting four or more rooms.[65]

Unfortunately, the municipality lacked the power to enforce its reforms. Expulsion of inhabitants remained the council's only weapon in face of threatened epidemics. Fear of another yellow fever outbreak in late 1879 resulted in new expulsions: a particularly dramatic incident occurred in the parish of Monserrat, where the authorities descended in the dead of night and pushed men, women, children, and furniture out into the street.[66] Attempts to move conventillos out of the central part of the city by means of taxation yielded no better results. Such taxes merely fell on the shoulders of tenants in form of higher rents.[67] Even the approach suggested by Alvear in the 1880s—that the municipality construct and operate several model conventillos—came to grief because of the belief that the government should not compete with private business.[68]

Since conventillos effectively met the laboring man's need for cheap shelter while affording handsome profits to the owners, they increased steadily in number until the 1890s. Thereafter, although the number of tenement dwellers increased, the number of registered conventillos in the city remained in the vicinity of 2500 (see Table 9). Once the fears of yellow fever faded, the general public little heeded the health problems of these cramped islands of newcomers. Hardly any of the conventillos in La Boca met the city's minimum standards for construction, latrines, or maintenance.[69] Although diseases such as tuberculosis, scarlet fever, and diphtheria were common among conventillo dwellers, the relatively ineffectual inspection and expulsion activities of public health committees in each parish remained the only weapons used to combat them. Indeed, municipal inspectors frequently accepted the inevitability of the conventillo and performed their duty by reporting lower occupancy figures than actually existed.

Rising rents encouraged further crowding. The conventillo room which in 1870, at the height of a boom, cost four gold pesos had doubled in rent by 1890 (see Table 9). Illustrative of the crowded conditions is a newspaper report of 1887:

> The conventillo at Salta 807 has 8 rooms with 48 persons. In room No. 5, 5 yards by 6, slept a married couple, a 15-year old girl, and 6 men. In room No. 2, 5 yards by 5, slept a woman whose husband was in the quarantine hospital and 5 other men. The two kitchens sheltered 11 men, and in room No. 7, 6 other men lived.[70]

A few years later, in a surprise night visit to conventillos in La Boca, the head of the city's public health service found rooms in which as many as twelve persons were sleeping. Conventillo rents showed little inclination to fall during the depression of the early 1890s, and they resumed their upward climb during the boom that started in 1905. By 1910, the basic price of a conventillo room had reached twelve gold pesos, triple the price in 1870. Housing costs for the poor thus stood at figures eight times that charged for equivalent shelter in Paris or London.[71]

Despite the crowding encouraged by steadily rising rents, health conditions in the conventillos perceptibly improved during the first decade of the twentieth century. Central Buenos Aires now had running water, sewers, and garbage collection. Conventillo dwellers benefited enormously from access to these municipal services, which were made possible in large measure because of the concentration of these conventillos in the downtown area.

Owners still resisted regulations, as they had in 1893, when they were ordered to provide at least one shower for men and one for women.[72] Extensions, exceptions, and outright evasion followed; yet the council returned in 1899 with a further refinement, insisting on one shower per ten rooms.[73] In practice, such facilities never reached the standards set by the municipality; by 1904 there was still an average of only one shower for sixty persons.[74] But this type of ordinance suggested that new improvements could be sought and, occasionally, obtained.

Conditions, although far from ideal, showed improvement from the standards of the 1870s. By 1900 the average conventillo had a concrete patio, in some cases as much as fifteen feet wide, and toilets and some type of bathing facilities. One report noted, however, that often between twenty and seventy people might have to use a single latrine, and "the ammonia vapors are so strong that anyone who penetrates in these [latrines] feels ill and has tears come to his eyes."[75] The room size had decreased somewhat from 1870, but construction materials and methods had improved. Each room now had a window and a door, whereas in 1870 many had lacked windows, and doors had consisted of old boards. The building of sidewalks, the paving of streets, and the raising of houses above the level of the streets also served to eliminate some of the flooding and humidity common to the earlier era.

The improvement of conventillos at the city's center did not have any parallel on the outskirts. Along with expanding squatter settlements there was an increase—one that cannot be measured or located—in the number of households that rented out two or three rooms or took in several roomers. Those with less than five rooms for rent or less than five tenants escaped any muncipal supervision. Rents might be cheaper than in the conventillos, but often far worse conditions existed, in large measure because such housing was beyond the reach of water and sewer lines.[76]

At the city's center the improved conditions in conventillos had come at a high price—in steadily rising rents. These rents constituted such a substantial and inelastic portion of the workingman's budget that increases began to spark tenant protest. In 1890, for the first time, tenants organized a committee to propose action against the landlords.[77] The movement then faded, only to renew itself again in 1893. But it soon succumbed to the general lack of unity among conventillo dwellers.[78]

Very substantial rent increases in 1907 generated renewed protest from tenants and led to the famous "Tenant Strike." This strike, which gathered momentum in late 1907, seems to have started as a spontaneous refusal of tenants, in a number of conventillos south of the Plaza de Mayo, to pay the higher rents resulting from increased municipal taxes levied on the landlords. From the vicinity of Plaza Constitución the movement spread rapidly through La Boca and Barracas and then jumped to the north side of the city, around Palermo. Parades of children shouldering brooms "to sweep away the landlords" marched around La Boca and other areas, whipping up enthusiasm for the resistance.[79]

The landlords, through their association, adopted a hard line and showed clear determination to press for court action to evict striking tenants.[80] In this they were assisted by a practice which had developed during years in which landlords had enjoyed a seller's market. The landlord in Buenos Aires invariably required that a tenant provide a guarantee or bond, pay several months in advance, or pay the first two months' rent without receipts. In this last case, the landlord only gave a receipt when he received the third month's rent, and this receipt was marked and dated for payment of the first month's rent. Consequently, any tenant who was cited for nonpayment appeared in court already two months in arrears. Furthermore, the cases came before a local justice of the peace, an appointed political figure who wielded considerable authority in the parish or police district. Such officers more frequently responded to the interests of an influential landlord than they did to the individual tenant, who often was illiterate, foreign, dirty, and a day laborer.

As the struggle dragged on into October and tenants persisted in their demands for a 30 per cent reduction in rents, violence began to mark the forced eviction of tenants. After several brushes between strikers and police, blood was drawn in the San Telmo parish. A youth of eighteen, Miguel Pepe, died, and three others were wounded in an exchange of shots. The funeral for Pepe, and the accompanying protest march from Plaza Once past the Congress, down the Avenida de Mayo, and then to Plaza San Martín drew crowds estimated at 15,000 and led to more incidents and shootings.[81] The police responded to the demonstrations with massive shows of force. Subsequent evictions brought out a standing escort for a justice of the peace consisting of 100 firemen armed with Mauser rifles, an additional squad of firemen with hoses, fifty armed policemen, and fifty mounted police from the city's special security squadron. Often the Chief of Police also appeared to lend a hand with on-the-spot negotiations which sometimes brought landlords to terms with their tenants.[82]

34. Police security forces involved in an eviction at Defensa 830 during the Tenant Strike, October 1907. (Archivo General de la Nación.)

In late October and early November, during the height of the protest, it was estimated that as many as 2000 conventillos and 120,000 persons were involved in the strike.[83] Ultimately, the tenants proved no match for the better organized and supported landlords. In early December the landlords' association responded to strike mediations with its conditions: two months' deposit from any tenant, along with evidence of having paid the last four months' rent in the previous place of residence. In addition, the association agreed to blacklist any delinquent or undesirable tenants.[84] Gradually the tenants were evicted, moved out, or, in return for promises of repairs or improvements, settled for slightly higher rents. Several months later little but memories remained of the Tenant Strike. In mid-1908 a newspaper reporter observed that almost all the conventillos involved in the strike were in worse condition than before and that the owners paid little heed to municipal regulations.[85]

The Plaza de Mayo was a powerful magnet, pulling both the

poor immigrant and the wealthy porteño toward the center of the city. The conventillo dweller was drawn to the plaza by the proximity of employment, and he was kept there by his inability to pay the high cost of transportation to outlying suburbs. The wealthy, although shifting his residence from the plaza's south side to its northern approaches, also refused to abandon the plaza for the suburb. The high concentration of social, economic, and political institutions around the plaza, as well as the powerful tradition that equated residential proximity to the central plaza with prestige, bound the upper class to the city's center.

The conventillo and the palacio typified the evolution of the Plaza de Mayo's environs. The conventillo provided the most identifiable and striking sort of worker housing in the center of the city. It constituted a principal shelter for new arrivals, and many of its aspects reappeared in other types of housing available to non-elite groups in the downtown area. The palacio gave exuberant expression to the materialism and conspicuous consumption that overtook the city's upper class in the economic booms of 1884–89 and 1905–12. Those who could not afford a palacio sought to emulate its opulence on a smaller scale in chalets and individual family dwellings.

The thrust away from the plaza was made by other groups. The boom years brought not only demographic growth, but also expanding opportunities. For the worker acclimated to the porteño environment and possessed of skills or savings, the road upward led toward the suburbs. The sons and daughters of immigrants thus sought a plot of land and a home on the outskirts. After electrification and unification of the streetcar system, low fares powerfully supported these efforts and moved the common man outward.

5

Streetcar and Neighborhood

Buenos Aires sprawled outward because of the mobility offered by the streetcar system. The process began with horse-drawn vehicles, but it accelerated rapidly after 1900 with electrification of the lines and the accompanying lowering of fares. In this change from a plaza-oriented city to a downtown core surrounded by suburbs, the local neighborhood, or *barrio*, with its smallest unit consisting of the cuadra—two facing sides of a block-long section of street—proved extremely important. The barrio and the cuadra provided the common denominator of urban life for all those persons who escaped the downtown conventillos but could not aspire to a mansion or chalet. The streetcar and neighborhood thus constituted major elements in Buenos Aires' development.

Horse-drawn carriages running along railroad spurs had been used in Buenos Aires for several years before 1870. One such line carried passengers from Plaza Constitución to within several blocks of the Plaza de Mayo; another linked Retiro station to the central plaza. But the year 1870 marked the first systematic application of rail transport to city streets by means of independent companies whose function it was to carry passengers.

Despite locomotives that came within eight blocks of the Plaza de Mayo at the Western Railroad's station at Plaza del Parque (later Plaza Lavalle), and the subsequent joining of the Northern's and the Buenos Aires and Ensenada's track along the waterfront at the east side of the Plaza de Mayo, horse-drawn streetcars were not introduced into the city without misgivings. In 1868 the provincial assembly, which legislated for the city until 1880, discussed various applications for streetcar concessions, some of which dated from 1862. It finally passed a law that extended specific approval to projects after companies had submitted detailed plans, rate schedules, and an agreement to build and maintain paving between the rails. Few legislators disputed the fact that one could hardly move around the city except on horseback during the rainy winter months and that any carriage trip across the irregular cobblestones, deep ruts, and muddy potholes constituted an excruciating and dangerous experience. But all questioned whether appropriate jurisdiction lay with property owners whose lots fronted on streets along which the cars would pass or with municipal, provincial, or national authorities.[1]

The authorizations extended by the provincial government caused further furor. Three groups of entrepreneurs—Mariano Billinghurst, Julio and Federico Lacroze, and Teófilo and Julio Méndez—pressed for concessions. Meanwhile, property owners besieged provincial authorities with requests to deny access to streets along which they held land. Such distinguished statesmen as Nicolás Avellaneda, who was to be the next President, echoed common fears that streetcars would introduce new obstacles and dangers to the narrow downtown streets and that they would depress land values. Others voiced concern that vibrations along the rails would weaken foundations and cause buildings to collapse. One leading newspaper, *El Nacional*, promised to leave one column blank in order to record accidents and casualties that certainly would occur from the streetcars' outrageous speed—six miles per hour. A few of the many petitions that flooded into the Governor's office even suggested that the passage of the cars would prevent easy access to the churches.[2] But many citizens who favored progress and economic development continued to support the newly formed companies.

The first two streetcar lines, those of Lacroze and Méndez (the latter was also often referred to by the name of the other concessionaire, Agustín Rodríguez), opened for service on Carnival Sun-

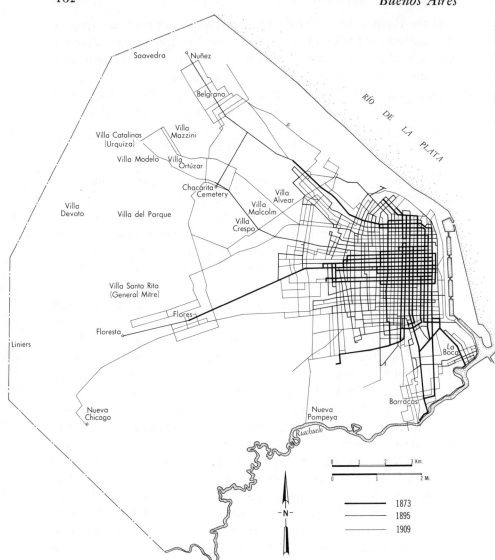

10. Expansion of the Streetcar System in the City of Buenos Aires, 1873–1910.

day, at the end of February 1870. The two lines ran parallel to each other from the center to Plaza Once, the first along Cangallo and the other along Cuyo (later renamed Sarmiento). Even during the test runs in mid-February, public sentiment began to acclaim this new element of progress. With the inauguration of service, fears turned to praise, and Carnival crowds pushed and struggled to get seats.[3]

New applications for concessions poured into the Governor's office. It was soon noted that the streetcars, rather than increasing the rate of collision, caused fewer accidents than did carts, wagons, and carriages.[4] Some who owned lands in the downtown area initially feared for their profits: "[The opposition] springs from the fact that with the establishment of this new means of locomotion the families who have lived in the center are seeking locations farther out in order not to pay the exorbitant rents."[5] But most landowners understood that the streetcars increased the commercial value of their properties, and they sought out entrepreneurs to lay track along their streets.

Another section of track opened in late April of 1870, when the Southern Railroad extended its spur line to Plaza del Parque. On the last day of June, Billinghurst inaugurated his first line, running from the Recoleta cemetery to Rivadavia. In August the Ciudad de Buenos Aires Company, which soon absorbed the Southern Railroad's spur, built a line along Buen Orden (Bernardo de Irigoyen) past Plaza Constitución to Barracas. Yet another concession to the Lacroze brothers (it was soon transferred to the company of Unzué and Zemborain) was opened along Defensa from the Plaza de Mayo to La Boca on September 1, and the first section of the Billinghurst line to Flores, along Rivadavia, reached completion just before Christmas. Within a year the outline of the new transport system had taken shape (see Map 10) and *La Prensa*'s prophetic words, "The furor of the streetcars has captivated all those with money to invest," had been realized.[6]

Although the municipality of Buenos Aires had failed to assert any authority in the matter of concessions, it now took measures to regulate the streetcars. Companies were to post or publish the departure times from their terminal stations. Each streetcar had to be drawn by two horses with bells on the harnesses, and thirty-yard intervals were to be maintained between cars. A horseman in a green blouse preceded each car or series of cars at a distance of at least thirty yards—in order to clear the track and warn all passersby and other vehicles by blasts on his horn. The maximum speed was

35. Streetcars in front of the Cathedral, 1874. (Archivo General de la Nación.)

set at six miles per hour; horses had to be slowed to a walk at intersections; no one could get off or on a car until it stopped; no more
passengers were allowed on board than there were seats; passengers were cautioned from "proferring indecorous words or actions"
—so went the detailed instructions.[7] The penurious municipal council also voted to tax the streetcars: each company, in addition to
maintaining the pavement between the tracks, had to purchase an
annual municipal permit.[8]

Enforcement of regulations was another matter. Porteños soon
had to become adept at boarding or descending from a car at
a brisk trot. Typical was the incident in which an elderly man ran
alongside the final late evening car of the Ciudad de Buenos Aires
line while the conductor yelled, "Get on if you can. I'm not stop-
ping."[9] The installation of rails in badly paved and unleveled streets
frequently upset what little drainage had existed and channeled

torrents of water into houses—or added new mudholes to an already plentiful supply.[10] The line to Barracas early displayed what would become an increasingly common failing of the system—a shortage of cars. Instead of a car every ten minutes, as promised in the schedule, one passed each hour. "Seats for all" soon proved impossible with the press of eager passengers: "Gentlemen cannot even move and the trip from Barracas to Cinco Esquinas [Juncal and Cerrito] lasts two and a half hours."[11]

The provincial government continued to extend concessions with a generous hand. Nearly thirty new authorizations, not including transfers or rerouting of lines, received approval between 1869 and 1873.[12] But problems of regulation remained in the hands of the municipality, which was handicapped, as always, by a small number of employees and a lack of authority for its inspectors.[13] These limitations, of course, did not prevent more rules from being issued. Revised ordinances in 1872 and 1873 imposed more safety requirements on the lines: the conductor now was supposed to descend at all intersections within seven blocks of the Plaza de Mayo and wave on the driver; every streetcar was to be equipped with a large bell to be rung by the conductor ten to fifteen yards before each intersection; and no other vehicles or horses were to carry bells. A more practical requirement forced the companies to deposit a substantial sum in the provincial bank to cover injuries to persons hurt by their streetcars.[14]

The streetcar system was initially developed as an extension of existing railroad lines. The first streetcar companies provided connections between the three major railroad terminals and the central plaza, or paralleled the railroad service to outlying villages such as La Boca, Barracas, Flores, and Belgrano. Soon, however, the companies moved to fill in the Central City with a gridwork of north-south lines crossed by a number of east-west lines (see Map 10).

In this expansion the streetcar had an immediate effect on land values. Auction notices now carried pointed references to the presence of lines: a sale of fifty lots in Barracas in 1870 promised a streetcar every five minutes; an offer of eighteen lots on Corrientes near Plaza Once assured prospective buyers that one could be at the Plaza de Mayo in twenty-five minutes; an auction in 1871 of eighteen lots on Rivadavia at Caballito, on the way to Flores, stressed the presence of the "Tramway Billinghurst"; and flyers for a forty-four-lot sale in 1873 near the Recoleta advertised that the property was "only two blocks from the Tramway Billinghurst and three from the Tramway Nacional."[15] In similar fashion, an article in *La Prensa* in mid-1871 emphasized that the original Billinghurst line had opened to substantial settlement an area that had previously been the haunt of vagabonds and squatters on the north side around the Recoleta cemetery:

> The area around the Recoleta is being built up in an amazing fashion with attractive homes, beautiful buildings, and even business enterprises of all kinds. The price of surrounding lots and the advantages that become more evident each day support the rising demand for land and the desire of not only small but also large landowners to settle there. The streetcars have connected these suburbs with the center of the city and promise shortly to turn this locality into a downtown area, continuing the preference, now more marked than ever, to build and live on the north side of the city.[16]

The horse-drawn streetcar thus established itself in Buenos Aires during the 1870s. As early as 1870 the rash of concessions had provoked a comment in the municipal council that there was hardly a downtown street that had not been taken up by some entrepreneur.[17] Toward the end of the decade city authorities boasted that Buenos Aires was the "streetcar capital" of the world, with an estimated 100 miles of track.[18] Six major companies emerged from the initial deluge of concessions. Based on all criteria—passengers carried, trips made, miles covered—the Ciudad de Buenos Aires outstripped its competitors. After that line, in order of passengers carried, stood the Central (Lacroze concession), the Argentino (Billinghurst concession), the Belgrano (Billinghurst concession), the Nacional (Méndez and Rodríguez concession), and the Boca y Barracas (Lacroze, then Unzué and Zemboraín, concessions) (see Table 10).

In a fashion reminiscent of Argentina's railroad experience, local capital financed most of the initial streetcar construction. British investors, possessing resources and experience not available to local entrepreneurs, soon moved into this profitable new venture. The Ciudad de Buenos Aires represented the first major British commitment. Then, in December 1876, the Anglo-Argentine Company was established in London. At the beginning, it acquired the Argentino line to Flores. Its purchase, a year and a half later, of the Nacional made British capital the principal underwriter for the city's transport system and set a pattern for control and management which lasted until the 1940s.

The expansion of the streetcar system, from an estimated fifteen miles in 1873 to 100 miles by the end of the decade, was accompanied by a modest increase in the number of trips made by streetcars—from 438,000 in 1873 to 621,000 in 1879. The number of passengers carried, however, hardly varied from the twelve million figure first set in 1873 (see Table 11). Undoubtedly, the depression years, which lasted from 1873 until nearly the end of the decade, put a damper on construction toward outlying areas or on any reduction of fares that might have brought the streetcar within reach of substantial new segments of the population.

The streetcar thus remained principally a vehicle for those who could not afford a carriage yet earned a salary and held a status well above those of the skilled laborers, artisans, or small shopkeepers— namely, many professional men and the higher paid white-collar employees in government and commerce. To board a car even for a short ride in the Central City cost two paper pesos—the equivalent of eight gold cents.[19] In a decade when the skilled laborer's daily wage gradually fell to 1.50 gold pesos, few from this group indulged in a luxury that, for regular transportation to and from work, would absorb 10 to 20 per cent of their earnings. Longer rides cost proportionately more: the fare from the center to Flores totaled twenty gold cents. Furthermore, the absence of consolidation or agreements between companies prevented transfers and increased the cost to a worker whose route necessitated using more than one streetcar line. Indeed, on the basis of the cost of fares and the number of trips made, one can speculate that probably not more than 8000 to 10,000 persons used the streetcars with any frequency during a decade when the urban population increased from 185,000 to 270,000 inhabitants.*

---

* Such an estimate is based on the fact that men at this time, especially members of white-collar and professional groups, ate lunch at home, necessitating four trips per day. Figuring an average of 250 working days per man, the twelve million recorded trips would suggest 12,000 regular users. Since allowance must be made for non-regular users, the correct figure must be somewhat lower.

Although the streetcar did not become the vehicle of the common man until after 1900, the 1880s brought some broadening in its use. Rising wages, consolidations in the system, and a major new orientation toward the northwest, between Belgrano and Flores, encouraged a steady climb in passenger traffic. Total mileage increased only moderately during the decade, from 100 to 150 miles, but the number of passengers carried each year quadrupled, from fourteen million to fifty-six million. The companies showed no inclination to lower rates—in fact, in the early 1880s the absence of small coins in circulation meant that one usually paid the equivalent of ten gold centavos instead of eight. In 1884 the companies fixed the rate for the shortest ride at ten gold centavos, and despite protests and sabotage the increase remained.[20] The companies even successfully resisted a proposal to create a "short ride"—twenty blocks or less—for which only five gold centavos would be charged.[21]

Skilled workers still could not afford streetcar service, since fares increased as rapidly as wages did.* But salaried white-collar workers increasingly turned to the streetcar. As noted in the porteño press: "The employees in all the government offices live in outlying barrios where the rents harmonize with their salaries, and they calculate their budget and regular attendance at their jobs on the basis of economical streetcar transportation."[22]

The 1880s also witnessed a start in consolidation of the system that encouraged more use of streetcars, since passengers now could often avoid frequent changes. The absorption of the Boca y Barracas line by the Anglo-Argentine in 1887 left three major lines— Ciudad de Buenos Aires, Anglo-Argentine, and Central-Lacroze, in that order—dominating the system. Nevertheless, the exuberance of the economic boom of the late 1880s spawned new companies in 1888. One served the southern reaches of Flores, while three others centered their operations on an intermediate belt ten to thirty blocks from the Plaza de Mayo.[23]

The most significant concession during the decade was acquired in 1887, by Federico Lacroze, to complement his Central lines and provide service to the northwestern suburbs lying between Flores

---

* Although wages for skilled construction workers, for example, had climbed slightly during the decade, to the equivalent of two gold pesos a day, any regular usage of the streetcar would have taken 20 per cent of their daily wage.

and Belgrano. The new line tied into the Central at Plaza del Parque and then ran northwest along Corrientes toward the Chacarita cemetery.* A concession from the provincial government also allowed Lacroze to build a Rural Tramway northwest from Chacarita to the village of San Martín outside the Federal District.[24] This new streetcar orientation underlay the development of Villa Crespo, located four miles from the Plaza de Mayo. By the early 1890s this community boasted more than 4000 inhabitants; several important factories, including the Fábrica Nacional de Calzados, or National Shoe Factory; twenty-eight shops; a theater; a *colegio*, or secondary school; and a plaza.[25]

With the increased passenger load carried by the streetcars the municipality made new attempts to regulate and tax the companies. In 1885 the national Congress, now legislating on matters within the Federal District, approved a 6 per cent tax on gross profits payable to the municipality to replace the previous and often ignored obligation of the companies to maintain paving between and alongside streetcar tracks.[26] The following year the municipality issued a new streetcar ordinance which authorized the Intendente to grant concessions, extensions, and route changes subject to council approval, ordered companies to submit schedules of rates and times of departure from terminal stations, reiterated the 6 per cent tax on gross profits, and placed a sixty-year limit on future concessions. In 1888 safety requirements were again issued. In addition to previous regulations—posting a bond for accidents, coming to a complete stop for passengers to descend or board, permitting only as many passengers as there were seats, and sounding a horn at all intersections—each company was required to pay the salary of one municipal inspector appointed by the city.

A wide gap remained, however, between the letter and the application of such regulations. Open cars called *jardineras*—flower

---

* An initial line of track had been laid down hastily in 1871 to serve the newly opened Chacarita cemetery and handle the bodies from the yellow fever epidemic. In 1887 the municipal council once again concerned itself with funeral services because of the severity of the cholera epidemic that year. The concession for a Rural Tramway extension beyond Chacarita to suburbs in the province was authorized by the provincial government on February 4, 1886. Initially, the use of horse-drawn cars made this Rural Tramway no more than a streetcar line, but in 1891 locomotives began to pull the cars and the line then effectively became a railroad.

pots—which were capable of carrying even more passengers repeatedly appeared on the lines, even on rainy days and winter nights, when regulations specifically banned them. Conductors permitted passengers to cram aboard far in excess of the number of seats; sometimes an extra horse had to be used to get overloaded cars moving. The animals were scrawny, underfed beasts. Horses that had to pull the huge two-deck "Imperials" accommodating seventy passengers reached their destination nearly dead. Cars always seemed to be in short supply, especially at rush hours in the morning and evening. Invariably, the upkeep and cleanliness of cars left much to be desired. And drivers, because they were late or ill-disposed toward the world, frequently ignored the gestures of potential passengers and kept the horses moving at a steady trot.

The streetcar's impact on land values, first noted in the early 1870s, began to be felt again during the boom years of 1884–89. Urban land values had fallen sharply after 1873; many of the speculative ventures based on expected rapid growth collapsed to one-fifth or one-tenth of their 1871 high.[27] But these prices more than recovered during the 1880s as streetcar lines once more led buyers and mortgage money toward the outer fringe of the city. "Suffice it that a distant street be paved or a streetcar line approach and the district becomes habitable."[28] The 1887 New Year's Day financial review of *La Prensa* noted that the sharpest rise in land prices during the previous year had occurred in the northwest section of the city—precisely the area along Corrientes where the new Lacroze line had begun operations: "Those districts that only yesterday were isolated from the center, today have new developments connected with the older parts by pavement, served by several streetcar lines, and covered with luxurious and well-built houses."[29] A few months later Antonio Galarce, head of the national tax bureau, published a study of urban land values that quoted the average price per sale. In 1868 it had stood at 4280 pesos; in 1882 it had risen to 5115 pesos and in 1886 it was 9442 pesos. He also observed that almost all sales in 1868 had involved centrally located properties, while in 1886 most sales were in suburban lots. Furthermore, land along streets served by streetcars brought markedly higher prices.[30]

Auction notices show that there was continued preoccupation with advertising the actual presence or projected plans of streetcar lines. Some of the less scrupulous auctioneers even laid a few well-placed rails near lots to be sold in order to give the impression that construction on a streetcar line had begun. Although high fares still placed streetcars beyond the reach of the average workingman, for the first time advertisements made appeals to lower-paid occupations: "A Major Auction Especially for the Poor," or "Attention: Employees, Masons, Carpenters, Workmen, Peons! A Chance for Anyone to Buy!"[31]

The 1890s, so inauspiciously begun in financial and political crisis, marked a period of steady expansion for the streetcar system. The 56 million passengers transported in 1890 more than doubled by 1900, to 123 million, while the length of track increased from 150 to 280 miles (see Table 11 and Map 10). In gold terms, streetcar fares actually decreased somewhat during the decade because of the sharp depreciation of the paper peso. Companies in 1891 were allowed to increase rates in paper currency 25 per cent, although the major companies—Ciudad de Buenos Aires, Anglo-Argentine, Buenos Aires y Belgrano, and Lacroze—strenuously objected to the accompanying municipal supervision of rates and did not accept that condition until 1893–94.[32] Even with this increase, the fare declined to approximately three centavos in terms of the gold standard. But the skilled worker's daily wage also slid downward—from two gold pesos to one gold peso (see Table 7).

Laborers, therefore, depended on streetcars only for the shorter, cheaper rides. If trips were limited to two daily, the 6 per cent of earnings paid in streetcar fares could be justified in terms of lower rents. In 1895, in an effort to enable workers to travel further, and to relieve congestion in downtown conventillos, the municipality ordered companies to run "worker cars," for one hour in the early morning and one in the evening, in which laborers could travel at half price.[33] The companies neutralized the measure by using open or broken-down vehicles and by having such irregular and infrequent runs that no worker could be assured of the promised savings or of getting to work on time. Nevertheless, a well-developed streetcar system facilitated the marked increase in population density that occurred during the 1890s in an intermediate area beyond the Central City—a zone that extended outward forty blocks from the Plaza de Mayo.

At the same time, high rates charged on lines servicing areas di-

rectly north of the Plaza de Mayo discouraged laborers from settling in this zone. *La Prensa*, in 1896, noted:

> Such abusively high fares have contributed heavily to the de-
> population of a large area between Centro América [later Pueyr-
> redón] and Palermo, since the poor prefer to rent in zones where
> they can save 30 per cent in the daily cost of streetcar fares. . . .
> Those who live along the aristocratic and developed streets in the
> direction of Palermo have to pay 15 centavos . . . instead of the 10
> charged by other companies for even longer rides.[34]

A growing area of wealthy residences in Barrio Norte between
Plaza San Martín and the Recoleta cemetery also fostered higher
fares. Intendente Emilio V. Bunge eloquently underlined the dangers of lower rates to such upper-class locations in his arguments
against a concession for an electric streetcar along Avenida Alvear
(subsequently Avenida Libertador General San Martín) before the
municipal council. Such a line, he argued, would bring an invasion
of conventillos and cheap worker residences and depreciate the ex-
clusiveness of Palermo Park.[35]

Despite the increasing use of streetcars in the 1890s, the system
still labored under the painfully slow pace of its horse-drawn vehicles. By 1880 the city had spread beyond the one-mile radius centered on the Plaza de Mayo, but for nearly two decades more one
could reach one's destination as quickly by walking as by riding in
a streetcar. A car usually covered thirty to thirty-five blocks per
hour. With biting accuracy, the *Revista Municipal* concluded:

> Within the city we are no better off in facilities and speed than we
> were forty years ago . . . and except for the time needed to reach
> a railroad station one can go faster to Ramos Mejía, Adrogué,
> Tigre, or San Fernando [all towns at a distance of ten to eighteen
> miles from the Federal District] than from the Plaza de Mayo to
> that of Once.[36]

Nevertheless, the municipal council, in 1895, voted down a simple
measure to speed up the horse-drawn vehicles—a provision for stops
only at intersections rather than wherever a passenger chose to flag
down a car.[37]

Also contributing to slowness were congestion in the downtown
streets and the lack of extra cars to handle the heavy late afternoon
traffic. All concessions granted before 1891 had permitted street-

36. An electric streetcar speeds travel to the outskirts. This is along Rivadavia, around 1910. (Archivo General de la Nación.)

cars to circle the Plaza de Mayo or to come within a block of it.[38] The need for access to the city's center caused companies to fight off all proposals to remove streetcar tracks from the vicinity of the plaza. Indeed, the Lacroze line overcame repeated vetoes by the Intendente and pushed through authorization for a loop that brought it within a block of the plaza in 1901.[39] Public uproar, provoked by the temporary suspension of traffic around the plaza while wooden paving blocks were being laid in 1900, finally forced the municipality to make an exception for streetcars.[40] With regard to rush-hour problems, one observer noted that the *completo*, or "full," sign seemed part of the standard equipment on all cars leaving the downtown area between 4:00 and 6:30 p.m., when banks, government offices, and most commercial houses closed their doors.[41]

Replacing horses with electricity solved many of these problems, and it also brought in its wake more changes than the introduction of the horse-drawn streetcar in 1870. The same process that had developed a few outlying suburbs and had pushed the built-up zone outward another twenty blocks from the outline of the gran aldea now encouraged suburban fingers and nuclei to stretch out over most of the Federal District, especially to the north and west (see Map 10). With lowered fares, the vehicles that had transported the city's professional and white-collar groups came within reach of artisans, skilled workers, and even day laborers.

As with many technological innovations, the changeover from horse to electric power came gradually. The major companies, which had both investments and long experience in the horse-drawn system, viewed with skepticism the capital outlay and restructuring required to transform their lines to electricity. Thus, a few new companies led in experimentation. The first proposal for electric cars came in the mid-1890s. Congress and the municipal council soon received applications for a wide variety of concessions: aerial cables, underground cables, alternating or direct current, or batteries. There were even proposals for elevated electric systems.[42] Three new companies—Capital, Gran Nacional, and Nueva—began to use electric streetcars along short sections of track in 1896, and at the same time test sections opened on the Buenos Aires y Belgrano and the Anglo-Argentine track and along a new trolley line to Belgrano. In 1897 the Ciudad de Buenos Aires followed suit with its first section between Retiro and the Plaza de Mayo. New requests for electric streetcar concessions continued to appear at the rate of one a month.[43] Two requests that year contained proposals for underground systems, thus anticipating developments that finally led to the completion of a subway under the Avenida de Mayo and Rivadavia in 1912-14.

The adaptation of electricity to the system promised to remove the handicaps of slowness and high rates, but other problems appeared that delayed complete acceptance of electricity until 1907. Technical problems gradually were solved, although only after considerable newspaper and public outcry. The overhead wires, added at a moment when electric power lines and telephone lines were also being rapidly extended throughout the central part of the city, contributed to an unattractive and sometimes dangerous tangle. Some property owners tried to slow the growth of this web by refusing to allow sustaining wires to be attached to the fronts of their buildings; the streetcar companies, backed by the municipality, soon overcame this resistance.[44] Streetcar and telephone companies, however, soon clashed over jurisdictions: such a conflict held up electrification of the first section of the Anglo-Argentine for several months before the telephone company finally agreed to raise its wires.[45] Accidents from fallen wires often added a bizarre and frightening touch to city streets. The 500 volts used by streetcars were not supposed to kill humans, although dampness or other complications occasionally refuted the scientific reassurances. But horses frequently fell victim to a sizzling line. Streetcar conductors all carried insulated gloves for just such an emergency, but these incidents nonetheless unsettled bystanders.

Speed constituted electricity's major advantage, but speed caused more accidents. In outlying districts where settlement was sparse, the streetcar's rate of twelve to thirteen miles per hour greatly improved service. Nearer the center, the regulated limit—eight miles an hour—was twice or three times the speed of horse-drawn vehicles.[46] The trip from the Plaza de Mayo to Flores, Belgrano, or even Puente Alsina on the southwest edge of the Federal District now took a mere forty minutes, instead of two or three hours. The pace was also quickened because electric cars stopped only once in each block. But the same reluctance displayed by drivers of the horse-drawn vehicles to stop for passengers was found in motormen who were haunted by tight schedules and by company rules to conserve electric current.*[47] Accidents increased in direct relation to the exhaustion and inexperience of drivers and to the unrelenting pressure by companies to keep cars on schedule.[48] Porteños continued to mount or descend agilely, for the streetcars made little more than a perfunctory "running stop" at intersections. The cost of a misstep at the higher speeds, however, was often a severed limb or even a life, and the newspapers periodically regaled their readers with graphic accounts of such tragedies.

The cheapness of electricity exerted the decisive pressure on both the public and major companies to push toward electrification of the whole system. A technical study completed in 1901

---

* One investigation revealed that several companies had installed meters to measure the consumption of electricity in each car and awarded prizes to the drivers with the lowest consumption. Obviously, one could save considerable current by not coming to a full stop.

showed that the operating costs of horse-drawn cars absorbed 80 per cent of gross revenues, while those of electric cars took only 65 per cent.[49] At first the giants—the Ciudad de Buenos Aires and the Anglo-Argentine—refused to move beyond the experimentation stage, but they began to lose passenger traffic to newer lines (see Table 12). Only when this trend became clear did the large companies shift to electricity. By 1904 the Anglo-Argentine had converted entirely to electricity. The Ciudad de Buenos Aires reacted more slowly. Partly because of resultant losses, it was absorbed by the Anglo-Argentine; the changeover on these lines reached completion in 1907. The last to convert was Lacroze, which remained entirely horse-powered until 1906, but then completed the shift to electricity in two years.

The principal benefit of electrification for the consumer—lower fares—remained linked not only to acceptance of electricity by the major companies, but also to consolidation and unification of the system. At first the fares of electric streetcars remained as high as those of the horse-drawn vehicles. Until 1903 the trip from Plaza de Mayo to Palermo cost fifteen centavos (seven cents gold), while the companies charged twenty or twenty-five centavos (nine or eleven cents gold) for the trip to Belgrano or Flores.[50] A renewed proposal to divide lines into sections with a five-centavo charge for each section encountered strong opposition from all leading companies.[51] They also did little to implement provisions for half-fare "worker cars." Repeated instructions and regulations by the municipal council suggested that, in reality, these savings did not exist for laborers.[52] Fares started downward in 1903–4; the Anglo-Argentine then lowered its rates to Flores from twenty-five to fifteen centavos. When the first drop in fares occurred, the increased traffic caught the company without sufficient cars to carry the added passengers.[53] Further lowering of rates was rumored and then became fact when the Anglo-Argentine absorbed the Ciudad de Buenos Aires and implemented (in 1905) a uniform ten-centavo rate on its far-flung system. Immediately the public responded, and the Anglo-Argentine once more faced difficulties—it had to move an estimated 7000 passengers a day on its Flores line.[54]

The 1904 developments—electrification of the Anglo-Argentine and its absorption of the Ciudad de Buenos Aires—marked a trend toward further mergers. Efficiency, centralization, standardization, and economies became more important as the number of passengers increased. The 123 million passengers carried in 1900 became 169 million by 1905 and rose to 324 million in 1910 (see Table 11). Reports of merger negotiations in London were confirmed in Buenos Aires in 1906, when the four companies formed in 1887–88—Gran Nacional, Capital, Nueva, and Metropolitana—requested municipal approval for consolidation.[55] Rumors that an international combine, based in London, Berlin, or Brussels, sought to control the city's transportation system continued to circulate.[56] In 1907 the Anglo-Argentine secured permission to use tracks of the Buenos Aires y Belgrano. The following year the Anglo-Argentine followed up the arrangement by absorbing not only the Buenos Aires y Belgrano, but also the Eléctricos de Buenos Aires, which had built a trolley line to Belgrano, and the Belgo-Argentino, which had initiated construction in 1906.[57] With this merger the last fifteen-centavo fare—that of the Belgrano line—disappeared, and ten centavos became the standard rate for all streetcars. As had happened earlier, the reduction brought an immediate increase in traffic, estimated at 4500 passengers daily, on the Belgrano line.[58] By 1909 the Anglo-Argentine assumed a virtual monopoly over the system when it acquired the combined lines of Gran Nacional, Capital, Nueva, and Metropolitana.[59] This British-financed company now controlled approximately 80 per cent of the streetcar track within the Federal District and carried nearly 85 per cent of the passenger traffic. The only independents were the Lacroze lines and two small companies, one serving the port area and the other the suburb of Barracas and the town of Adrogué beyond the Federal District to the southwest.

The impact of electrification and consolidation from 1902 to 1909 can best be seen in the ten-centavo fare that became standard in 1908. With rising wage levels from 1905 to 1912, this fare represented nearly 4 per cent of a peon's daily earnings, or 2 per cent of the wages made by a skilled construction worker.* Although half-fare "worker cars"—referred to as *cucarachas*, or cockroaches, because of their filthy, worn-out appearance—circulated infre-

* These calculations are made on the basis of 1.25 gold pesos for a peon's daily wage and 2.25 gold pesos for a skilled construction worker's (see Table 7).

quently, two trips per day at regular fare now fell within the budgets of most of the city's blue-collar laborers.[60] Inexpensive and rapid transportation enabled workers to move to outlying suburbs and secure cheaper housing than they could find in the downtown area. As a result, built-up urban areas reached out for four to eight blocks on each side of streetcar tentacles that stretched to the limits of the Federal District.[61]

After 1900, the mass of the porteños began to benefit from the availability of small individual lots and homes. Workingmen could now afford this new "luxury" because of the greatly reduced fare and the improved service of the streetcar, as well as the cheap lands and credit facilities offered by auctioneers and building companies. One- to three-room houses on the outskirts, either owned or rented, now housed many porteño laborers. The Central City and surrounding zones suffered no loss of population, for the constant influx of immigrants more than filled the conventillos, apartments, and rooming houses. But for the workingman, upward mobility clearly lay via residence, and, often, ownership of a plot, in the suburbs.

The buildings that emerged in this outward spread of the city ran the gamut from squatter hovels to mansions, but small houses multiplied most rapidly. Population in the western half of the Federal District increased more than threefold between 1904 and 1914 —from 106,000 to 456,000 inhabitants—while the city's over-all population rose from 951,000 to 1,575,000. In this same period the number of houses in the western half increased from 16,110 to 57,394. By 1914, 86 per cent had six rooms or less; 52 per cent had three rooms or less.[62]

During the boom years from 1905 to 1912 acquisition of a small lot and a modest house came within the reach of the skilled laborer, artisan, or white-collar worker in Buenos Aires. Lots thirty feet by 120 feet sold for the equivalent of 200 to 500 gold pesos, and a one-room house could be built for another 200 gold pesos.[63] If all conditions could be met—frugality, good health, full employment, and, above all, a wife and teen-aged children who worked—a savings of five or six gold pesos a month could put lot and house in a man's hands within six to ten years. Some took advantage of auctioneer offers and occupied their plots immediately after the down payment. They then laboriously set to work, on Sundays and holidays, building a one-room shack—a procedure always fraught with the danger of losing everything if payments on the lot could not be met. Others saved until they could buy the lot outright. Many, of course, satisfied themselves with rental, assured that even by that step they had improved their status over their conventillo days.

In the open fields of the city's outskirts, developers and surveyors applied the same elongated rectangular lot that had given form to the patio-style residence of the wealthy in the gran aldea. Even the antiquated measure of ten varas, a standard frontage in downtown lots, was used in many outlying areas. But because of modest resources, the construction of the individual workingman's house was modified somewhat from that used in the interior-patio design. Whether built for speculation and rental by a developer, or constructed by the owner himself, these houses followed a typical pattern.

A mud brick wall marked the boundaries of the property—undoubtedly continuing the effort to enclose and protect the family from outsiders, a notable characteristic of the patio-style home. The lot, approximately thirty feet wide, extended back for a depth four or five times the width of the frontage. As much as possible of the patio-style construction was conserved. A shallow well was sunk at the back of the property, and a garden, fruit trees, and perhaps a few rabbits or chickens occupied the rear half of the lot. Near the house was a latrine and a shed for charcoal or wood. The house, which had one or two rooms, was set back at least forty feet from the street—fifteen feet to allow for sidewalk and another twenty-five to permit subsequent addition of rooms to the front of the building. Usually the house occupied the entire width of the lot, although occasionally there would be a narrow passage running along one of the boundary walls to give access to the rear garden area. In a one-room house, the entire space—roughly twelve by fifteen feet—served as kitchen, living room, and sleeping quarters for the family. As family earnings increased, the building would be expanded: the room became a kitchen and living area and a second, third, and even fourth room would be added as bedrooms. Finally, as a Brazilian visitor noted, ". . . sometimes fifteen years after acquiring the lot, with his daughters attending normal school and as-

37. A typical worker dwelling of one or two rooms on the outskirts of the city. (*Caras y Caretas*, Dec. 29, 1906.)

piring to a bourgeois status, this rising member of society added a *sala*, or living room."[64] In the end, the owner would have a five- or six-room house, with a front room opening directly on the sidewalk or, at most, set back a few feet from a front gate.

The city's outskirts also contained housing for the less fortunate or less provident; these were often remote from transportation and located in squatter settlements that had occupied marginal lands since colonial times. The graphic name *cinta negra*, or black belt, had not yet been coined, but in 1896 the *Revista Municipal* described this environment of temporary shacks:

> The Arroyo Maldonado, the swampy lands [south] of Flores, the municipal slaughterhouse, the Riachuelo, La Boca, the lagoons of the port surround the city like a chain; the links are the marshes, mudholes, pools of stagnant water, and garbage dumps, reinforced by a rosary of factories, plants and other industrial establishments which have no way of throwing off their wastes without endangering the hygiene and health of the city.[65]

Several years later the *Boletín del Departamento Nacional del Trabajo* noted that the poor had expanded into these undesirable lands:

> To the South and West in the low-lying lands of Barracas, San Cristóbal, Flores, Vélez Sársfield, and San Carlos, and in the North in the frequently-flooded areas of San Bernardo, Palermo, Arroyo Maldonado, along Darwin and Álvarez Thomas, and in the lowlands of Belgrano and Saavedra there have sprung up in the last few

38. Temporary shacks in the port area, around 1910. (Archivo General de la Nación.)

years numerous centers of population and buildings which with rare exceptions totally lack running water, sewage disposal, paving, drainage, or lighting.[66]

Inhabitants of the Barrio de las Ranas, located alongside the municipal garbage dump, lived in six-foot-high shacks made of odd lumber and galvanized iron sheets that rented for as much as nine gold pesos a month.*[67] Buildings made of flattened oil cans provided even flimsier shelter. Similar housing appeared on landfill of the

---

* A newspaper reporter vividly described his impression of sitting down with a family of nine in their one-room hovel to a meal consisting of a jar of water and a bowl of discarded bread and bones freshly garnered from the dump; see *La Prensa*, May 10, 1903, p. 4.

recently completed port area and in the Bajo de Belgrano, an area of low-lying land located along the estuary between the city's two major racetracks.

Electrification of the streetcar system not only brought settlement to the urban outskirts, it also changed the way urban land was sold. During the 1870s a buyer paid for land in cash, or, occasionally, in mortgage bonds from the provincial bank. In either case, those without resources could not enter the market, so only the well-to-do bought land. The boom of the 1880s broadened the market somewhat, as the occasional advertisement directed to the poor suggests. But credit facilities—represented by *cédulas,* or mortgage bonds, of the provincial bank and the national mortgage bank (Banco Hipotecario Nacional, founded in 1886) or by the mortgages extended by numerous private banks and companies—still were restricted to large operations, preferably in rural holdings, by those with resources and influence. Even for the moderately well-off, credit facilities were anything but liberal. A typical advertisement of 1888 hailed an important auction of thirty lots near Plaza Constitución: "within reach of everyone . . . with extremely generous terms not usually extended, in order that anyone can secure a lot." The "extremely generous terms" consisted of one-quarter of the sale price in cash, one-quarter in three months, one-quarter in six months, and the balance by the ninth month.[68]

Credit for the purchase of land or a house remained beyond the reach of most people until the end of the century. In 1898, and again in 1904, changes in the national mortgage bank for the first time permitted loans up to 50 per cent of land value plus the price of the house to be constructed.[69] For the small borrower, however, this type of assistance remained out of reach. In order to secure a loan at government banks, where the interest was lower (usually around 8 per cent), one needed both influence and wealth. The market rate ranged between 10 and 18 per cent, usually close to 18 per cent.[70] High closing costs and taxes pushed such credit beyond the grasp of laborers and clerks. Taxes on a one-year mortgage, for example, nearly equaled those on outright sale of the property.[71] Untangling the legal and official red tape on a 1000-peso mortgage invariably required as much time and often cost as much as negotiating a 10,000-peso loan.[72] Construction taxes likewise were assessed so that the small house paid, in proportion to its value, four to five times more than larger residences did; in percentage terms, the elegant chalet or palacio paid the lowest of all.

Around 1900 this bleak credit picture for the small borrower changed, in large measure because of increasing stability of the Argentine peso. Some arrangements were purely extortionate. At least thirty loan offices operated in the city, and they gave advances to government employees at standard interest rates of 18 per cent, which was recovered by garnisheeing salaries. If an employee who earned 200 pesos a month wanted a loan of 1000 pesos, he signed an I.O.U. for 2000 pesos with a due date of the following day. The loan company then presented this receipt in court where the judge issued a withholding order of 50 pesos per month against the man's salary.[73]

The credit most extensively used by the small buyer came, however, from the subdividers and developers of large urban holdings. These entrepreneurs tapped a wholly untouched market, with procedures described in 1904 as follows:

> It is well known that for the last six or eight years the custom of subdividing huge landholdings in the Federal District and selling them in public auction on the basis of twenty, thirty, forty, and even sixty monthly payments has been growing up. By this means a vast number of lots have been sold, in large measure to individuals with little capital, most of them workers, who at the expense of food and sleep have met the small monthly installments. . . . Lands which had not been worth fifty centavos a square yard thus have been sold for one and a half and even two pesos the square yard.[74]

By 1902 newspapers featured half-page advertisements of sales that guaranteed immediate occupancy of a lot on the basis of forty, sixty, or eighty monthly payments, with a down payment of the first two or three months' installments. One offer underlined an eighty-month plan with the following appeal: "Workers: Leave your conventillo and buy a lot in Floresta [an area to the west of Flores] or in any other healthy environment, if you want to ensure the well-being of your children and see them content and happy."[75] A typical auction held west of Flores rapidly sold 100 lots, each with a ten-yard frontage and depths of thirty-six to forty-six yards, for an average of little more than one peso per

39. An advertisement for a land auction. (*La Prensa*, May 7, 1904, p. 12.)

square yard payable over eighty months. Added attractions included a public school within four blocks, paved roads only 500 yards away, and a near-by electric streetcar.[76] A 1904 advertisement hailed "The Great Auction of the Day for the Poor." The turgid prose continued:

> With a little more than the down payment, one can begin to build a house with one or more rooms; thus the buyer can occupy his lot immediately after the auction and live in the house he is building. At the end of sixty months of paying ten to fifteen pesos a month—in other words what it costs to rent the smallest conventillo room in the center—he will become an owner. In a sense he is merely paying rent in order to be the owner of the land and of the house he is building.[77]

During 1905 these auctions increased; the pages devoted to advertisements and announcements in the major newspapers rose from a daily average of two or three pages to eight pages. By 1906 sales of 500 and 600 lots per auction had become common. Auctioneers not only offered free train or streetcar tickets to the site of the auction, circus tents under which to take shelter in rain or shine, and seats on which to recline during the bidding; they also threw in such attractions as free lunches and sometimes a pile of 10,000 bricks per lot.[78] Of course, just as there had been speculators and auctioneers who placed a few streetcar rails near the sale site in order to give the impression of imminent construction of a line, so sharp operators continued to make illusory claims and promises. The exaggerated claims of advertisements, such as "Only a step from the station," or "This important town boasts two rail lines, a church, municipal council, schools, hotel, and commercial establishments, etc.," became the object of biting satire, as can be seen in cartoons from 1909 on the next pages.

Another important source of credit for workingmen after 1900 came from the newly established building and loan companies. The Buenos Aires Building Society held periodic lotteries; a cash prize or loan to winners made mortgage conditions very attractive for the lucky few.[79] The Banco del Bien Raíz provided 500-peso loans on the basis of monthly payments of 5.25 pesos extending over a ten-year amortization period; one-eighth of the principal had to be deposited with the bank before one could secure this type of loan.[80] One of the earliest companies, El Hogar Argentino, established in 1899, offered its members shares bearing 11 per cent interest which could be purchased on installments as low as one peso per month, as well as mortgages of 1000 pesos repayable in ten to fifteen years. La Propiedad, organized in 1905, provided savings booklets to record members' deposits of five pesos a month as the means of building toward a capital of 1000 pesos, and it offered mortgages of 1000 pesos which were repayable in ten-peso monthly quotas.[81] La Constructora Nacional, also founded in 1905, invited members to apply for building loans in units of 500 pesos for which the monthly payments were two pesos for approximately ten years. A lottery system determined the order of allocation of mortgages to members.[82] City employees enjoyed an added advantage when, in 1905, the council authorized them to draw on the municipal retirement fund for small real estate loans.[83]

—A un paso de la estación.

40. The cartoons on these pages satirized the overblown claims about the "excellent" locations of building sites in the suburbs. For example, the above cartoon ridicules the location of lots "in the most aristocratic faubourg of the future." (*Caras y Caretas*, March 13, 1909.)

Public credit agencies continued to have little to do with urban real estate or with the small borrower. Of the mortgages issued by the Banco Hipotecario Nacional from 1903 to 1908, 90 per cent went to rural properties.[84] During the first half of 1910—at the height of the urban real-estate boom—this bank made only fifty-seven loans within the city in the 1000- to 2000-peso category. Although the bank's interest rates were favorable, the procedure for small loans remained inordinately costly and time-consuming.[85] In 1910–11 the Congress overhauled the bank's statutes in order to encourage loans of less than 6000 pesos. Even so, an official publication had to admit the bank's failure to reach this market:

— Este importante pueblo cuenta con dos líneas férreas, iglesia, municipalidad, escuelas, hotel, casas de comercio, etc., etc., etc.

—La ubicación de los lotes, en el más aristocrático faubourg del porvenir...

> . . . experience demonstrates that the general building loans, ex-
> tended up to 50 per cent of assessed property value, have been ex-
> tremely successful and have contributed to the growth of cities
> throughout the country. Not the same can be said for the small
> loans, extended up to 60 per cent of the property's value, for they
> have not been generally accepted. The average employee or worker
> in our country prefers to acquire his house by means of monthly
> installments and to guarantee that credit with the value of his prop-
> erty.[86]

Government authorities proved equally uninterested in housing projects for workers. The philosophy expressed toward an 1874 housing project, which had been intended as an alternative to the increasing number of conventillos, predominated in official circles: "Since the general attitude has already developed that the government should not enter business itself, the project will be announced but its execution will be left up to private initiative."[87] The spectacular profits that accompanied conventillo construction could not be expected from this venture, and it was only through the generosity of a wealthy landowner that one unit did reach completion.[88] Similar attitudes discouraged implementation of suggestions in the 1880s for "model conventillos," experimental homes for workers, and city-financed housing projects.[89] One municipal venture in 1887 bore modest fruit—twenty houses built on land which had been occupied by a municipal slaughterhouse, just west of the Recoleta cemetery. For a while the city rented these four-room units, equipped with kitchens, toilets, and running water, to worker families. Deterioration and neglect soon set in, and by 1891 it was noted that "the cleanliness and upkeep [of these buildings], both inside and out, leave much to be desired."[90] The crisis of 1890 ended even these limited efforts.

Despite increasing publicity about European cooperative and municipal housing projects after 1900, public agencies continued to show little interest in worker housing.[91] A Chamber of Deputies committee neatly sidestepped the issue when bills for the construction of one- and two-room worker houses were introduced in 1904 and 1905. In place of these projects the committee proposed that the municipality issue two million pesos in bonds for worker housing. Congress approved that measure without debate.[92]

The municipality responded unenthusiastically. The public

works and finance division had already raised objections to the construction projects in Congress, and a report from city authorities to the Ministry of Interior indicated that such legislation was totally unnecessary. According to this report, the city enjoyed excellent public health conditions and the conventillos provided very satisfactory worker housing. Furthermore, the municipality, forced to provide services to the many new suburbs that had sprung up under the stimulus of the electrified streetcar system, had no money for anything except the most urgent necessities.[93] As an alternative, the municipal council proposed a contest to select the best design for worker houses and a five-year tax relief for all buildings built according to the winning architectural plans.[94]

In mid-1907 the municipal council got around to approving the bond issue that had been authorized by Congress two years earlier, and the Intendente publicized plans to acquire land on which to build small worker houses. These would be rented for eighteen gold pesos per month, and the tenants would become owners after a period of nine to twelve years.[95] Since a skilled construction worker at this time received from forty to fifty gold pesos a month, this housing seemed beyond the grasp of most blue-collar laborers. At the end of 1907 a cornerstone for the project was laid, just west of Parque Patricios, site of the former garbage dump on the south side. The press dutifully recorded that the President of Argentina and the Intendente mixed with workers at the festivities and handed out commemorative medals along with the sandwiches and cakes.[96]

Despite the grandiose phrases that accompanied this occasion, nothing happened at first. A new Intendente promised to carry out the project, but he encountered serious difficulty in floating the necessary two-million-peso loan. A donation of land—a rare act of individual charity among wealthy porteños—provided more building sites in the Parque Patricios area, but no funds.[97] The local banking house of Tornquist & Co. finally took over the loan, and in 1910 the municipality dedicated a group of sixty-four houses and initiated construction of an adjacent 100-house project.[98] Objections to government management, however, soon caused the administration of the housing to be turned over to a ladies' charitable society, Sociedad Protectora del Obrero.[99]

Another source of funds promised to support worker housing in 1911. The Jockey Club had begun to make huge profits on its race-track, and it needed worthwhile projects in which to invest. The membership had been less than enthusiastic about building and do-nating to the city a large downtown avenue. The suggestion of sup-porting worker housing was better received, and legislation in 1910 authorized the club to turn over one million pesos each year from its Thursday afternoon races to underwrite low-cost housing loans.[100]

Both Congress and the municipal council, nevertheless, seemed to have more of a taste for projection than for implementation. Many of the proposals that emerged just before the depression of 1913-14 verged on pure fantasy. One project, thought up in 1913, called for construction of worker-housing units throughout the country, based on a 120-million-gold-peso loan.[101] In the same spirit, the Intendente of Buenos Aires proposed a contract to put up 10,000 five-room houses over five years. Sale of these houses to municipal employees at a monthly payment of twenty-five gold pesos, or a cash payment of nearly 4000 gold pesos, would have limited the housing to well-paid bureaucrats.[102] Juan F. Cafferata in 1912 introduced in Congress the only successful measure—creation of the Comisión Nacional de Casas Baratas, which was supported by a 1-million-peso loan. The bill became law in 1915.[103]

Private ventures to build worker housing generally met with more success than those financed and administered by government agencies. During the 1880s the Banco Constructor de la Plata com-pleted nearly 150 worker houses on Montes de Oca, on the city's south side.[104] Despite the general absence of cooperative movements in Buenos Aires, or in Argentina as a whole, several housing coop-eratives flourished after 1900. La Paternal opened a worker coop-erative near the Chacarita cemetery in 1903.[105] By 1907 La Casa Popular Propia had completed over 300 one- and two-room houses in Caballito, to the east of Flores.[106] El Hogar Obrero, formed by Socialist party leaders in 1905, began to lend small amounts for house construction on lands owned by its members and by 1913 had completed 192 houses.[107] In addition, a number of construction companies specialized in building worker housing. The most im-portant included the Constructora Nacional and the Sociedad de

Edificación y Ahorro "La Propiedad," incorporated in 1905; the Edificadora Económica, in 1906; and the Banco Familiar and El Hogar Para Todos, in 1907.[108] A few manufacturing companies, such as the Fábrica Nacional de Calzados, located on Corrientes near the Chacarita cemetery, offered small loans to workers in order to stimulate the growth of settlements around their factories. Railroad companies—notably the Western and the Southern—built small houses for their employees near stations just outside the Federal District on terms that led to ownership after payment of several years' rent.[109] Even the charitable society of Saint Vincent de Paul became involved in worker housing when it opened a home for working girls in Barracas in 1906; it subsequently laid plans for 100 worker homes near Parque Patricios.[110]

But housing projects for workers, whether government or private, contributed little to the city's housing needs. Most construction for non-elite groups continued to come from the credit facilities afforded by auctioneers and loan companies. Some workers built their own homes, but the vast majority arranged for construction, on an individual basis, with a small contractor or building company.

The outward sprawl which the electrification of streetcars facilitated gave the city its configuration as a metropolis. In the 1870s, the city—except for the villages of La Boca and Barracas to the south—ended at Entre Ríos/Callao, a mile from the Plaza de Mayo. The expansion of train and horse-drawn streetcar lines during the 1880s and 1890s pushed the city outward another mile to Jujuy/Centro América (Pueyrredón) and extended fingers of continuous settlement to Flores in the west, Chacarita in the northwest, and Belgrano in the north. But it was the electric streetcar that served as the prime builder of the numerous suburbs which filled in the Federal District during the first decade of the twentieth century.

Growth of these new suburbs provoked one Spanish visitor to comment in 1904 that Buenos Aires "was not a city, but a combination of adjoining cities."[111] The development of suburbs signaled a new era for the city. For the wealthy and for the professional groups, the Plaza de Mayo still constituted the city's center. For the immigrants in the conventillos, the Central City and its

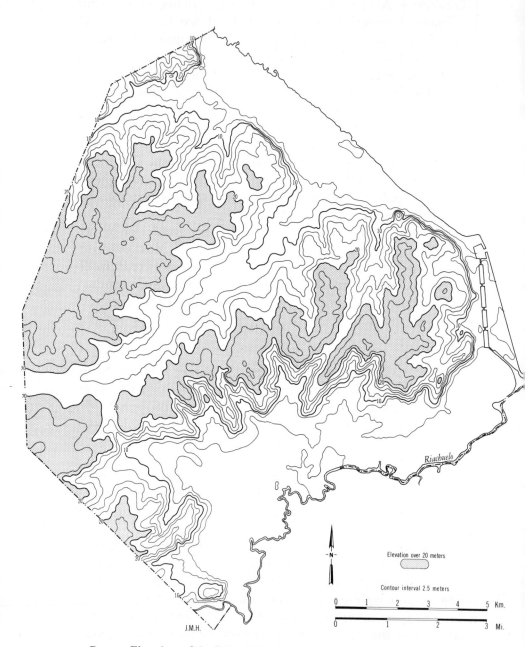

11. Contour Elevations of the Federal District.

immediate environs remained their place of residence and work. But more and more people now established their homes in the suburbs. By 1910 only 10 per cent of the city's 1,230,000 inhabitants lived in the Central City. If one adds population in the immediately adjoining census districts that constituted contiguous built-up zones, as well as the districts of La Boca and Barracas, the figure increases to 39 per cent.* Although two other major centers of population, Flores and Belgrano, fall within the remaining 61 per cent, one can say that by 1910 at least half of the porteño population lived in suburbs of the Federal District.[112]

Each suburb developed its own individual character, depending on its elevation, transportation facilities, and land-use patterns. The configuration of the land's surface, although not obvious in the apparently flat terrain of the city and surrounding plains, provided a crucial factor in orienting transportation routes. These almost imperceptible undulations also added differing climatic and environmental conditions that affected settlement and land use.

The southern edge of the city, along the Riachuelo, lay eight to twelve feet above sea level and consequently was exposed to periodic flooding (see Map 11). A similar low-lying area made a narrow indentation along the Maldonado, a stream on the city's north side, but generally the northern part of the city ranged between thirty and sixty feet in elevation. One ridge ran west from the Plaza de Mayo and formed the route of the street Rivadavia and of the Western Railroad through Flores. Another accounted for most of the northwestern area of the Federal District lying between Villa Devoto and Belgrano.

Well-to-do foreign residents, especially the British, early noticed the importance of slightly higher elevations. As a result, they tended to build on the edge of a low bluff along the estuary north of the city, in order to catch summer breezes and avoid winter's disagreeable humidity. Wealthy porteños began to seek higher ground after the 1871 yellow fever epidemic, and they established summer homes in Flores and Belgrano. The railroad lines, followed by streetcars, endowed the city's two principal ridges and the gen-

* These calculations are based on the population reported in the 1909 municipal census (see Table 1) for Districts 13 and 14 (Central City), 10, 11, 12, and 20 (immediately adjoining the Central City), and 3 and 4 (Barracas and La Boca).

erally rising ground to the northwest with good transportation facilities.

This thrust reinforced the city's links to its hinterland, since, by the late nineteenth century, the western and northwestern routes connected the port of Buenos Aires with the most populated and developed areas of Argentina. The region south of the city had first emerged as a sheep-raising zone in the mid-nineteenth century; by 1900 it had become an important cattle zone. But neither of these activities required large populations or any substantial movement of goods and passengers.

A more complete picture of the formation of suburbs through interaction of trains and streetcars emerges from comparing maps of the two systems (see Map 8, p. 94, and Map 10). Outside the central area, trains had carried settlement beyond Flores to Floresta and Liniers on the Western line, beyond Chacarita to Villa Devoto, Villa del Parque, and Villa Catalinas (or Urquiza) on the Pacific and Buenos Aires-Rosario lines, and beyond Belgrano to Coghlan, Villa Saavedra, and Núñez on the Poblador and Northern/Central lines. By 1910 the streetcars had reinforced the western thrust with lines not only to Floresta but also to Nueva Chicago and to the newly developed zone of Villa Santa Rita (or General Mitre). The greatest impact, however, came in the areas to and beyond the Chacarita cemetery. Villa Crespo, Villa Malcolm, and Villa Alvear had all taken shape in the 1890s, and they became solidly built-up zones shortly after 1900. Beyond Chacarita, three nuclei—Villa Ortúzar, Villa Mazzini, and Villa Modelo—developed rapidly along new streetcar lines built after 1904. Toward and beyond Belgrano, streetcar lines that reached as far as Núñez by 1910 added cheaper and often more convenient transport facilities to those already provided by the railroads.

During the period of rapid growth, land use and settlement patterns that resulted from considerations of terrain and transportation gave rise to sharp distinctions between the south and the north sides of the city. For a time in the 1870s enough prestigious families lived south of the Plaza de Mayo to draw attention to the area's needs and secure municipal action. But by the 1880s, the development of port works, streetcar lines, and beautification projects had created overwhelming support for the north.

For a decade the south side fought back, but against impossible odds. In October 1882, for example, 300 landlords and merchants organized a protest. They delivered a petition to President Roca, complaining about the lack of attention paid to municipal problems in the southern districts.[113] The movement immediately blossomed into the "Club Buenos Aires," a political movement aimed at defending those local interests and securing more representation for the south on the municipal council. One of the leaders, Francisco A. Tamini, who subsequently won a seat on the council, noted: "Of the present councilmen, fifteen belong to the northern section of the city and only five to the south."[114] Tamini, along with Juan Antonio Boeri, waged a valiant struggle in the council against the city's vigorous Intendente, Torcuato de Alvear, who clearly favored development of the north side. As a protest against the adornment of the northern zone at a time when so many of the south's streets remained impassable, Tamini announced he would not attend the official opening of the water fountains and park near the Recoleta cemetery.[115] On another occasion he sought to shame the council with a description of a particularly notorious pothole, at the intersection of Entre Ríos and Cochabamba, where for months a long pole with a white flag had warned all passing carriages and carts of the dangers of toppling into this bottomless pit.[116] In 1884 Tamini tried unsuccessfully to stop the paving of the street of Arenales and other streets around the Plaza 6 de Junio (later Plaza Vicente López)—areas that were just beginning to attract well-to-do families—until paving of the main southern thoroughfare of Caseros had been completed.[117] In similar fashion, Boeri opposed the Intendente's proposal to widen Avenida Alvear, in order to facilitate the circulation of carriages, until Bolívar and Caseros were at least rendered passable.[118]

But economic and financial power as well as political control of the council had passed into the hands of men associated with northward expansion. Throughout the 1880s there was a steady stream of complaints against unhealthy conditions, bad paving, poor lighting, and the absence of parks and plazas, suggesting continued inaction by the municipality. Slowly the south slipped behind the north and even the west in facilities, services, land values, and prestige. By 1890 an image had emerged of shacks, slaughterhouses, garbage dumps, swampy open fields, and muddy rutted streets. The fact that some wealthy families still built palatial residences in Barracas or that clusters of well-off professional and merchant families still lived in Monserrat or, farther west, in San Carlos did not counteract the general impression of poverty.

As the city pressed outward, other differentiations between suburbs emerged. Villa Devoto, somewhat in the same fashion as Flores and Belgrano, was initially a zone of quintas for wealthy porteño families. Bank speculation (in 1889) in this type of real estate, the relatively high elevation—fifty feet—and the convenient station of the recently completed Pacific Railroad all favored Villa Devoto's rapid growth as a prestigious suburb. The slow development of streetcar lines in this outlying area tended to discourage those without resources from settling there.[119] Similarly, Villa del Parque and Coghlan, where the streetcar penetrated slowly, were settled by professional and the better-paid white-collar groups who traveled each day to the vicinity of the Plaza de Mayo and could afford railroad transportation. As the streetcars reached out to these suburbs in the years just before World War I, the same adjustment that had already taken place in Flores, Belgrano, and other suburbs first served by the train could be observed: the more affluent groups clustered close to the railroad station or around a plaza near the station, while the newer and poorer elements spread out along unpaved, unlighted streets eight to twelve blocks from the center of the suburb. On the other hand, suburbs that developed on the basis of streetcar lines tended to have a preponderance of clerical and skilled workers. Such was the settlement pattern of Villa Crespo, Villa Malcolm, and Villa Alvear on the Lacroze line to the Chacarita cemetery, and beyond Chacarita to Villas Ortúzar, Mazzini, and Modelo (see Map 10).

The location of industrial establishments in Buenos Aires, unlike that in many cities, merely reinforced the land use patterns already determined by terrain and transportation. In large measure, small artisan plants dominated the porteño industrial scene, at least until the 1930s. As noted by that acute French observer, Émile Daireaux, in the 1880s:

> Large-scale industry, requiring sizable numbers of workers in huge plants, does not exist here, and consequently there is no industrial

working class or worker problem. That is not to say there are not workers, artisans, manual laborers, and apprentices; those who work by the skill of their hands are in fact very numerous. . . . The distinctive characteristic of the worker, however, is to be isolated, more of an artisan than an industrial worker, a kind of small entrepreneur associated with, more than he is in charge of, several assistants whom he treats as equals.[120]

In small shops—often merely a room in a home—these artisans, aided by members of the family and by four or five employees, devoted themselves to the manufacture of cigarettes, candies, furniture, glassware, pottery, shoes, sandals, lamps, baskets, mattresses, noodles, soap, jewelry, liqueurs, hats, and saddles, or to bookbinding, sheet-metal work, or printing. These industries depended on the skills, tools, and small amounts of capital brought into Argentina by individual immigrants, and while some flourished and grew into large enterprises the great majority remained small, most employing less than ten workers. Since none of these activities required a great deal of space or needed complex marketing or transportation facilities, no tendency developed to group them in a particular location. One could find a representative mixture of these shops in any district of the city. Many even tended to remain close to the downtown area, leading *La Prensa* to complain in 1897:

Since 1867 when the last ordinance on industrial establishments was adopted, a huge number of manufacturing industries have sprung up in the most central part of the city, and although small at the outset these plants have enlarged their installations until they are not only a nuisance but also a danger for security and public health.[121]

Large plants that could be characterized as "industrial" prior to 1910 engaged primarily in processing food and agricultural products—these were breweries, distilleries, flour mills, meat-packing and leather-tanning establishments, and sawmills. A few artisan shops—because of the entrepreneurial abilities of their owners or unusual economic opportunities—grew into sizable operations, especially in the manufacture of shoes, hats, liqueurs, and candies. These larger factories, employing 100 workers or more, showed some tendency to move outward in search of cheaper land and also, after 1900, to converge on the city's south side. The famous biscuit and cracker company of Bagley moved three times, first north to-

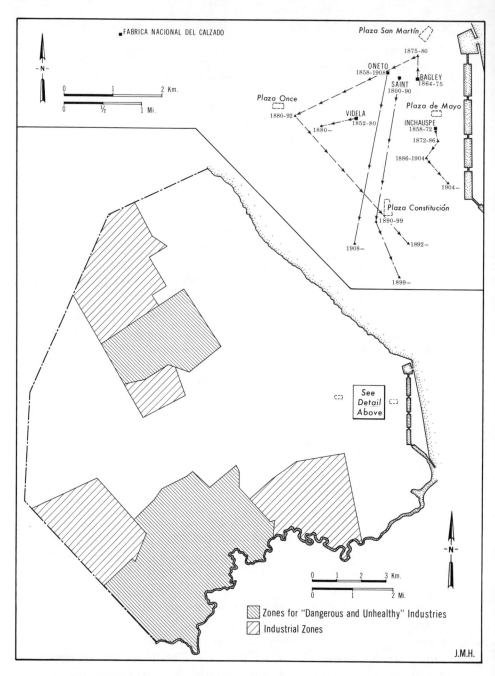

FABRICA NACIONAL DEL CALZADO

Plaza San Martín

1875-80

ONETO
1858-1908

BAGLEY
1864-75

SAINT
1800-90

Plaza Once
1880-92

VIDELA
1852-80

Plaza de Mayo

INCHAUSPE
1858-72

1872-86

1880—

1886-1904

1904—

Plaza Constitución
1890-99

1892—

1908—

1899—

See
Detail
Above

-N-

0   1   2 Km.

0   ½   1 Mi.

-N-

0   1   2   3 Km.

0   1   2 Mi.

Zones for "Dangerous and Unhealthy" Industries

Industrial Zones

J.M.H.

12. Outward Movement of Selected Industrial Establishments and Formation of Industrial Zones, 1914.

ward the Plaza San Martín, then west to the vicinity of Plaza Once, and finally south to Plaza Constitución. Inchauspe in liqueurs, Oneto in flour, and Saint in chocolates also moved south, while Videla in shoes and the Fábrica Nacional del Calzado chose locations to the west of the downtown area (see Map 12).

Gradually, public pressure developed for the removal of particularly noisome activities from heavily populated areas. At first the authorities had attempted proscriptions, prodding "unhealthy, dangerous, and annoying" industries away from the Plaza de Mayo: in 1873 leather-tanning operations were pushed thirty blocks distant; in 1884 the distance for brick factories increased from twenty to forty blocks.[122] In 1897, when two major fires in short succession destroyed the Central Railroad Station and a large downtown wholesale house, demands increased for the removal of explosive or inflammable materials from the downtown center as well as for controls over the location of industries.[123] After 1900, the heavy reliance on soft coal imported from Cardiff and Glasgow to make steam and electrical power caused more agitation to push factories outward. Jorge Newbery, an Argentine engineer and director for lighting and electric power for the city, suggested in 1906 and again in 1907 that factories be concentrated on the city's south side and that future sites be limited to specific areas.[124] Even so, the *Revista Municipal* in 1909 complained: "In the heart of the city large factories of all varieties continue to function, and in spite of municipal regulations they constitute a danger and a nuisance to the inhabitants."[125]

In 1914, the municipal council finally approved regulations that established two zones for "dangerous and unhealthy" industries, one covering the southwest corner of the Federal District and the other located west of the Chacarita cemetery (see Map 12). In addition, the ordinance provided for four "industrial zones"— around the municipal slaughterhouses at Nueva Chicago, in a large area west of Barracas, at the suburb of Villa Urquiza, and in a section between Villa Santa Rita and Villa del Parque—where large industries could operate. At the same time the regulations stipulated that any industry that did not constitute a nuisance for a neighborhood—namely, most small artisan establishments—could be carried on anywhere in the Federal District.[126]

Records of land sales from 1904 to 1914 show the economic differences imposed by terrain, transportation, and land use. A few
general trends can be traced, although they are imprecise because
of the large size of census districts and fluctuations in the number
and type of transactions. Land immediately north of the Plaza de
Mayo in Census District 14 sold, on an average, for nearly twice
that south of the plaza in District 13 (see Table 13). As one moved
from the downtown area toward the outskirts the higher values
continued to appear on the north and west sides of the city. Particularly notable were the number of times that land prices multiplied between 1904 and 1912—the climax of the early twentieth-
century boom years. The north and west grew most rapidly. For
Belgrano the factor stood at 14.4, highest of the Federal District.
Adjacent Palermo registered an increase of 10.5, while land in
Flores multiplied 10.6 times in value. North of the Plaza de Mayo,
land in District 14 increased 7.5 times in value, the same factor as
for Vélez Sársfield, on the southwestern outskirts, and San Bernardo, in the northwest.

Ethnicity appeared as a characteristic in the suburbs, although
it was muted. Foreign-born groups seem to have clustered primarily in the downtown areas, with notable percentages of Spaniards in Districts 12, 13, and 14, French in Districts 14 and 20, Russian Jews in Districts 9 and 11, and Italians in Districts 4 and 10
(see Table 1). The newly arrived immigrant, often lacking language and other facilities of the host culture and qualified primarily for unskilled manual labor, found it desirable to remain
downtown, within a compact enclave of his fellow countrymen
and near to employment. In the suburbs, most foreign-born groups
tended to appear in percentages slightly below their city-wide
averages or in some cases were noticeably absent. Spaniards, for example, did not participate significantly in the northwestern expansion, and there were virtually no Russian Jews on the outskirts.

The native-born Argentines predominated in the suburbs. The
largest native-born group were not those whose parents or grandparents had been born in Argentina, but rather those who had been
born in Buenos Aires to European immigrants. These first-generation Argentines provided a notable Argentine-born cast to Vélez
Sársfield in the southwest, to Flores and San Carlos Sud in the west,

and to the whole northwestern sector—Districts 16 through 19 (see Table 1).

The Italians—an exception among the foreign-born groups—also participated in the move toward the suburbs. In Districts 7 through 10, which led to Flores in the west, as well as in Districts 15, 17, and 18, in the northwest, Italian-born percentages were considerably higher than the 23 per cent recorded for the city as a whole. In addition, a study of property held by Italians reinforces the conclusion that they were the most aggressive and successful in moving outward to become shopkeepers and owners of small plots of land. In 1909, throughout the city, they ranked a close second to Argentines as property holders; in that year they comprised 26 per cent of the total number of owners. The highest percentages of Italian ownership occurred on the outskirts: 52 per cent of all property owners in San Bernardino; 49 per cent in Palermo; 45 per cent in Vélez Sársfield; 44 per cent in Las Heras; and 38 per cent in Belgrano.[127]

Terrain, transportation, and land use served to differentiate suburbs, but running throughout the outward expansion of the city toward the suburbs was the common experience and unifying theme of the barrio, or local neighborhood. Although nowhere precisely defined or recorded as a unit of measurement, the barrio, along with its smallest component, the cuadra, was integral to the city's formation.*

The barrio and the cuadra were developed principally through a sense of attachment and social contact between inhabitants. The facing sides of a block-long section of street formed the cuadra. In heavily built-up zones the barrio might consist of a single cuadra, while in outlying, sparsely inhabited areas it might include as many as a dozen cuadras. Furthermore, the barrio changed shape with the

---

* The term "barrio" is used in Argentina to mean both the local neighborhood described here and the larger unit referred to in this work as a "suburb." For examples of barrios in the sense of suburbs, see *Manual de los 45 barrios porteños* (Buenos Aires, n.d.); Miguel D. Etchebarne, "Antología de los barrios: II," *La Nación*, Mar. 29, 1959, Sunday Supplement; and Ordenanza No. 23,698, June 25, 1968, *Boletín Municipal de la Ciudad de Buenos Aires*, No. 13,336, pp. 7428–30, which lists 46 areas as the official barrios of the city. At the beginning of the twentieth century there were between 2000 and 3000 local-neighborhood barrios in the city.

41. A typical porteño cuadra, around 1910. (Archivo General de la Nación.)

addition of new homes and stores, with the development of new economic activities or transportation facilities, and with the moving in or out of families. Only occasionally, as in an outlying area, could one draw boundaries around a barrio. Yet the inhabitants themselves were aware of the barrio's small sphere and the smaller, more precise limits of the cuadra. Unspoken yet unmistakable lines existed beyond which personal links and contacts did not extend. In what grocery or bakery did you shop? What school did the children attend, and to what Mass did the women go? Why did mothers let their children play around the corner of one block but prohibit them from going to the next? What café drew men for an evening of cards or dice? Where did you greet a face at the doorway with a nod and salutation and where did you pass on in silence? Why did you grieve with a bereaved family in an adjacent street but know nothing of a death a block in the other direction? What curious or even hostile looks met the stranger who might pause or stop within this neighborhood? Such the often intangible elements that made reality of the barrio and the cuadra.*

* Settlements on the urban outskirts provided an environment in which features of barrio and the cuadra could be identified. Personal experiences with and local reminiscences of these still-existent phenomena in Buenos Aires add further dimen-

The number of inhabitants in a barrio might vary from a few hundred to over 1000 persons. One isolated barrio, Los Olivos, located at the outskirts of Barracas on the city's southern edge, had thirty scattered houses on the 1895 topographical map of the city. To these families, who numbered 150 to 200 persons, must be added the twenty Italian truck-gardening families who were considered part of the neighborhood, which brings the population to 300 persons.[128] In settled zones, a barrio would contain around 500 persons, while the cuadra usually numbered between fifty and 100. Some ethnic ghettoes—especially those of Russian Jews and Syrians, or turcos—held over 1000 persons in a single barrio or cuadra.

Certain institutions added dimensions to the barrio, although they did not serve to delimit its boundaries. In Los Olivos one woman, as a private venture, provided schooling through the fourth-grade level in her home. Young children thus remained close at hand for chores and errands and did not have to wade through the winter's knee-deep mud to the nearest public school, ten blocks away.[129] For most, schooling stopped at that level or before. In more developed districts, an elementary school drew children from a number of barrios. Even then, however, the school tended to reinforce the associations within the barrio: children walked to school together and continued the contacts they had first developed in play along the barrio's streets. In like manner, the Catholic Church might include within a single parish 50 to 100 barrios. Nevertheless, the chatting and salutations at Mass took place between neighbors from the same barrio and thus strengthened the spirit of association, the sense of belonging to the smaller rather than the larger unit.

Local neighborhood stores added social as well as economic unity to a barrio. The four corners of nearly every block in Buenos Aires housed small shops, businesses, or artisan establishments. The retail and food trade, and, consequently, the employment of thousands of porteño families, remained linked to a distribution system by which hardly any home in the built-up area was more than two

---

sions. These, supplemented by manuscript census returns for 1869 and 1895, enable me to sketch the principal features of the barrio and the cuadra and to suggest the important role played by these largely forgotten institutions in the city's development.

blocks from a butcher shop, a bakery, and an *almacén*, or grocery store. The people of a barrio tended to patronize a particular butcher, baker, and grocer, and the spheres of influence of these establishments helped to delimit the barrio.

To the sense of familiarity and belonging that grew up in daily visits to such shops, and the accompanying exchange of gossip or pleasantries with neighbors, was added a significant economic bond. Neighborhood shops made most sales on credit. A storekeeper entered notations of purchases on a scrap of paper or in his note-book, and customers settled accounts at weekly or monthly inter-vals. Patronage and credit thus remained closely linked; once you were a regular customer of a corner store, you might grumble at the periodical settlement of the bill or haggle over prices, but it took a conflict of major proportions to make you shift your alle-giance and shopping elsewhere. In outlying areas the role of the almacén proved even more important. Often this institution was the first to be established in a developing zone. New residents turned to the almacén not only for credit on food and household supplies, but also for help and advice on a myriad of matters—for building materials, for construction suggestions, for an opportu-nity to read a newspaper, for mail, for conversation about common problems and local events. In such barrios, the almacén became the social, economic, political, and intellectual center of the com-munity. In more developed areas you would have access to other gathering places—most often a local café—to exchange ideas and to visit with neighbors, but the almacén was still the heart of the barrio.

Since business and artisan shops remained scattered throughout the city, a large proportion of the working force found employ-ment in their homes or within a few blocks of home. Many locally made or locally assembled consumer items—clothes, shoes, and household goods in general—were prepared and sold in neighbor-hood outlets. Imported commodities and foodstuffs passed through the same small retail outlets in each barrio. About one-third of em-ployed men worked within their own barrio. Only women from blue-collar or manual laboring families worked, but of those who did, as many as two-thirds earned wages at home as seamstresses and laundresses. As a result the barrio achieved the added sense of

42. Focal point of the barrio—a porteño almacén, around 1910. (Archivo General de la Nación.)

identity that grew out of the fact that a sizable proportion of its adult population was employed within its confines.

Although inhabitants of a barrio often had similar occupations and social status, considerable heterogeneity existed. The dominant occupational group residing in the barrio set the tone of house fronts, sidewalks, paving, and stores. But a barrio heavily populated by manual laborers from the docks and construction sites also had its storekeepers, artisans, small businessmen, and perhaps even a few men from the professions. Likewise, a moderately well-off barrio in Belgrano might have masons and peons living in a cuadra where government employees, office managers, and lawyers also lived.

It was even more difficult to identify ethnic or nationality clusters than it was to determine uniform occupational or social status within barrios. Except for the groupings of immigrants from a certain country that sometimes emerged in downtown conventillos, most barrios contained varying mixtures of the largest nationality groups—Argentine, Italian, Spanish, and French. Several families of a single nationality frequently lived next to each other, and within the smaller unit of the cuadra one foreign group or its first-generation descendants might predominate. But ghetto-like units rarely appeared.

The sense of neighborhood, either in barrio or in cuadra, brought a village atmosphere to the burgeoning metropolis, whose population topped the million mark around 1905. This was the barrio's most important contribution to the mass of the porteño population.

The well-to-do and professional groups grasped the reality of the city and the nation. For them the downtown core represented the city and served as their economic and social focus. But for the vast majority of porteños, it was the neighborhood that gave meaning to their lives. A man belonged to a particular cuadra or barrio and only secondarily and in minor degree to a suburb, a parish, or the city.

One must not, however, mistake the sense of association found in shopping at the same almacén, greeting neighbors on the street or at Mass, or playing a game of dice at a local café for close personal interaction between inhabitants. Much of the patio design, as well as the spirit of enclosing the family, was carried to the suburbs in the brick walls that bordered the elongated lots. Families looked to their own members to solve problems, survive hardships, or advance in social and economic position. Rarely was the outside world welcomed within the sanctuary of the home. Neighbors might watch comings and goings across the street, or chat in the doorway about the weather, a recent birth, or the state of health of family members. A funeral might bring close neighbors into the sala, or front room, for mourning. Otherwise, only relatives entered and visited inside the house. Social contacts had to develop and flourish outside: male associations took place at work or at the café; women visited at their doorways or in the shops; children squabbled, ran, and played in the street. Even courting remained strictly outside the home, and it was usually limited to doorstep conversation or a few moments stolen at Mass or the almacén. Once the young man entered the girl's home for a visit he became a member of the family—*comprometido*, or engaged.

As a result, the air of neighborliness found in the barrio or cuadra carried with it little spirit of cooperation or intimacy. Neighbors rarely associated with each other at this level for any sort of community action. On rare occasions, an active leader stirred the larger area of a suburb into cooperative ventures. In 1907, for example, the inhabitants of Coghlan got together and hired peons to plant trees along their streets. To the south, in Nueva Pompeya, a vociferous *comisario*, or district police chief, mobilized the workingmen of the area to carry pleas for sanitation measures to the municipality.[130] Similarly, local political clubs, like the Club de Buenos Aires, first established to support the sectional interests of the south in 1882, began after 1900 to emerge in outlying areas in *sociedades de fomento,* or development societies. Invariably, the initiative in these larger areas of the suburb or the parish came from an owner of an almacén, a comisario, or a priest motivated either by personal ambition or by the broad interests of his district. Likewise, after 1900 ephemeral weekly or fortnightly newspapers developed to speak for large districts. These sheets, which had earlier been established in the well-defined areas of La Boca, Flores, and Belgrano, now spread outward, as with *La Unión* in Barracas in 1900, *La Nueva Era* and *La Luz* in the southwestern portion of the city in 1902, and *El Popular* in the outskirts of Belgrano in 1903.

In 1910 most porteños continued to view the barrio—not the suburb or the parish—as the principal focus for their lives outside the home. By the first decade of the twentieth century the barrio had reached the height of its psychological, social, and economic importance. In the vast and expanding reaches of Buenos Aires there were innumerable barrios and cuadras, often possessing imprecise and changing boundaries and loyalties. The neighborhood workshop, grocery store, butcher shop, bakery, and café played important roles in the lives of the inhabitants. Local gossip, children's play, and elementary schooling still provided contact and satisfaction. You could stroll along shade-covered and mud-rutted streets within a few blocks of any of the city's thoroughfares and feel far removed from the metropolis.

But change had begun to affect the barrio even at the height of its influence. Although it retains much importance to this day, the city supplemented the barrio after 1910. New forces—broadened education, an increased variety of occupations, improved transport, large downtown stores, and popular entertainment—drew people out of the barrio. With the fare on streetcars at ten centavos, the common man ranged afield in search of work. On occasion, he took his family outside the barrio. Laborers began to stroll the downtown avenues, but only when they were dressed in their best clothes. Huge sums spent in bets on horse races and other forms of gambling, gradual improvement of the porteño parks, audiences drawn to circuses, musical reviews, theatrical farces, lectures, and the increasingly popular Sunday pastime of marches and demonstrations—all suggested that the barrio was losing some of its hold on the lives of the people.

6

Social Structure
and Cultural Themes

According to contemporary accounts, in 1870 the social structure of Buenos Aires had two main divisions: *gente decente*, the upper class, those who by ancestry, education, and wealth had prestige and power within the community; and *gente de pueblo*, the common people, the workingmen, those who depended on society rather than directing it. The sevenfold increase in population and the substantial changes in urban environment had not basically altered that structure by 1910. More strata had emerged, but the two major divisions or categories remained.

Throughout this period, ancestry and family constituted principal criteria of the gente decente. This upper class thus recruited its membership largely from its own ranks. Because of financial disaster or personal mishap, individuals and even families occasionally slipped down into the common people. New blood also periodically entered, most commonly through acquisition of wealth, as a result of secondary and university education, or by advantageous marriage.

Education, occupation, and income tended to depend upon one's family connections. The son or daughter of gente decente received the appropriate education or training. For the man, this meant university education in one of the professions, assumption of a military or clerical post, or experience alongside his father, uncle, or cousin

43. A well-to-do porteño family relaxing at their quinta in the 1880s. (Archivo General de la Nación.)

in ranching, banking, or exporting. The woman was expected to become accomplished in needlework, learn how to manage servants and a household, and perhaps become proficient in music or a foreign language.

Occupations for men—women of gente decente did not normally seek employment—involved non-manual work, required substantial education or capital, and implied independent action and decision-making. Cattlemen, businessmen, professional men, and university and secondary students generally belonged to the gente decente.[1]

Gente decente also had to have enough income to maintain servants, rent or own an individual house, and provide their families with appropriate clothing, food, education, and environment. But this minimum necessarily flowed from considerations of ancestry, education, and occupation. Although wealth gained in importance as a measure of elite status, particularly during the economic booms of 1884–89 and 1905–12, it did not serve as the principal dividing line between the two major social categories. As a result, precise measurements of wealth or income had less relevance than they did in many other societies. It was more desirable to belong to a family of modest means but proud ancestry than to be a nobody who had made a fortune through some lucky venture. Likewise, the fortune that a Basque sheepherder of the 1840s might have made on land and flocks acquired respectability only in the hands of his grandchildren.

Gente de pueblo included all other people, roughly 95 per cent of the city's population between 1870 and 1910 (see Table 14). Because of their number, gente de pueblo were divided into many strata; these strata, in turn, determined their status according to the same criteria—family, education, occupation, income—as the gente decente.

Family served as the most decisive factor in placing people. While an expanding economy and the increasing number of employment opportunities afforded some upward mobility, most children remained in the stratum of their fathers and mothers. Education was usually limited to the six grades of primary school; for those in the lower levels, formal education ended after the first or second grade. They learned their skills by working at a trade or in a shop with parents or relatives, or through serving as apprentices or clerks.

During the period of rapid urban growth, occupation and income became increasingly important as the means to differentiate strata.[2] White-collar workers—office employees, clerks, primary school teachers, bookkeepers, draftsmen, telegraph operators—and those who directed others and had some capital, notably storekeepers, stood at the top of the social ladder. Their earnings might equal or only slightly exceed those of skilled laborers, but they often had completed six years of primary schooling and might even have gone on to a year or two of colegio, or secondary school. In housing, clothing, and living conditions, they closely imitated the gente decente, and it was from this stratum that new additions to the upper class most often came.

Skilled artisans and laborers who worked at a trade, had their own tools and equipment, and possessed some economic independence were also gente de pueblo. Income sharply differentiated the environment and prospects of a master shoemaker, with his machines and apprentices, from those of a recently arrived immigrant who pieced together bits of leather in a corner of his conventillo room. Butchers ran the gamut from the thriving proprietor of a corner store in a wealthy neighborhood to the ragged assistant who labored in some stall of a downtown market. A carpenter or mason might be merely a member of a construction gang or he might have reached the status of an independent contractor. Although little possibility existed for an artisan to vault into the gente decente, children of the most prosperous and established tradesmen on rare occasions made the leap as dentists, public accountants, or engineers. More frequently, they acquired the education to move into the white-collar stratum.

Ranged below the artisans were large numbers of men in semi-skilled occupations that involved dependent employee status, little training, or few tools and equipment—apprentices, railroad workers, streetcar operators, peddlers, charcoal vendors, milkmen, deliverymen, gardeners. Income—and, consequently, housing and living conditions—varied little between or within these occupations. Advancement usually came on the basis of outstanding individual ability—the humble peddler who raised himself to shopkeeper, or the apprentice who persevered to become a master mechanic.

Day laborers, soldiers and sailors, and servants formed the bottom layer of the occupational pyramid.[3] Recently arrived immigrants

44. Near the bottom of the social scale—scavengers digging through the municipal garbage dump. (Archivo General de la Nación.)

most frequently filled the menial occupations of coachmen, cooks, waiters, domestics, and doormen, or they joined the pool of unskilled manual laborers on the docks, construction sites, and streets of the city. Many were illiterate or had at most a year or two of primary schooling. To this work they brought no skills, no special training, no education. Wages were generally higher than those paid in European cities, but the cost of living was high and the immigrants had to make do with crowded conventillos, ragged clothes, and the cheapest quality of food. For these groups upward mobility could be won by frugality, hard work, and, above all, good luck. The self-made man who lifted himself from stevedore to bank president did not exist in Buenos Aires. The most successful was the adolescent immigrant who acquired some skills and savings as a day laborer, married and raised a family in a downtown conventillo, and then, by combining his earnings with those of wife and children, managed to buy a plot and build a home on the outskirts. His sons usually followed in his footsteps as day laborers or semiskilled workers, while his daughters aspired to be little more

45. Washerwomen at the port of Buenos Aires, around 1880. (Archivo General de la Nación.)

than laundresses or seamstresses. Only the grandchildren got enough education or training to allow them to move upward a notch or two in social stratum.

Because of the role of the family in determining status, the social structure had both continuity and stability. Rapid physical growth and change in the city little affected that structure. As long as the economy continued to expand—as it did by leaps and bounds because of agricultural exports and the influx of foreign immigrants and capital in the late nineteenth century—the range of economic and financial opportunities for both gente decente and gente de pueblo continued to increase. It was thus possible to achieve limited upward mobility. Furthermore, management of the commercial and administrative structures of both city and nation functioned well with a centralized, elite bureaucracy. Although Argentina was no longer only a "land of cows," as it had been described in the first half of the nineteenth century, the exploitation of large estates for the products of the soil, the exchange of agricultural commodities for manufactured goods, and the development of a transportation and communications system to support these trade patterns thrived on the use of many hands and control by relatively few chiefs. The influx of immigrants, the increase of skilled and clerical labor, and the development of small household manufacturing, along with the visible trappings of a progressive economy and government—paved streets, a literate populace, streetcars, adequate food, telephones, elections—created little demand for change in the existing social structure.

The self-perception that each of the two major categories held of itself further reinforced this stability. The gente decente clearly saw themselves as those who controlled Argentina. They perceived Argentina as a nation, and they knew that they held economic and political power over both city and nation. From their ranks came the city's business and political leaders as well as the national elite. Residential, business, and social contact within or close to the downtown core helped to draw the gente decente together. Common colegio and university training added another bond. Most important, despite the increasing numbers of gente decente, blood and marriage played as great a role in the metropolis as it had in the gran aldea. The overwhelming importance of family antecedents resulted, almost by definition, in extended family ties among most of the gente decente. As a result, they formed a large but united family that shared common goals and values.

The gente de pueblo, on the other hand, had become increasingly stratified, often divided by interests and ambitions as well as by income. Indeed, their only common bond was that they did not belong to the gente decente. Even so, the upper strata of the gente de pueblo yearned to join the gente decente, religiously mimicked its standards, and occasionally saw one of their number succeed in making the leap.

Rather than creating solidarity or a sense of common interests, the increasing distinctions in occupation and income among gente de pueblo served to emphasize individualism or, at most, alignments among particular strata. Dispersed residential and employment patterns further reinforced these trends. Had ghettoes of ethnic and religious groups or housing by occupational groups been more developed in Buenos Aires, the workingman might have been more inclined toward group solidarity. The conventillo, however, primarily served new arrivals to the city. Once acclimated, these inhabitants or their children headed for the suburbs. Although larger manufacturing operations had shown a tendency to locate on the city's south side, no substantial body of workers had been drawn together within factories or worker settlements. Small plants, artisan shops, stores, and businesses were to be found in every suburb. Such dispersion hardly fostered unity, communication, or interrelationships between workingmen. For many, residential loyalty to the cuadra or barrio or—in the case of some foreigners—ethnic loyalty to a particular nationality group superseded any sense of common worker interests.[4]

The beckoning of opportunities also postponed expression of class or group interests, just as it limited pressures on the social structure. Upward mobility—as demonstrated in the movement toward the suburbs or the security sought in ownership of a plot of land—required tremendous financial sacrifice and effort. Children of gente de pueblo, instead of gaining an education that might have put pressure on the limited number of positions available for the gente decente, entered the labor force at an early age in order to add to family income. At the same time, the faint chance of moving upward from one stratum to the next, or even the improbable dream of crossing over into the gente decente, stimulated workers to try to succeed within the existing system rather than pushing them toward group reaction or rebellion.

Although occupational classifications from the censuses cannot precisely define this social structure, these materials are the only source on which we can base general conclusions about the composition and size of the two major categories. Unfortunately, each census classification embraced a number of distinct strata, especially those of differing income and education, and this makes impossible an analysis of individual strata. But two sub-groups of gente de pueblo can be distinguished: one, the manual laborers, the other, the blue-collar and white-collar workers. Although a three-class model—upper, middle, lower—does not accurately describe the porteño society until after 1910, these two sub-groups provide the basis for the subsequent development of lower and middle classes, just as the gente decente equates with the upper class.[5]

The resultant profile of the social structure rests on compilation by occupation of all employed males fourteen years of age and older (see Table 14). The male, as the principal provider, generally established the family's status. Inclusion of females does not alter this profile, since women in late-nineteenth-century porteño society did not work outside their homes unless the family's financial position absolutely required it. Employed females, consequently, came almost wholly from families at the very bottom of the social ladder, where they worked as house servants, cooks, washerwomen, and seamstresses.*[6]

The occupational breakdown suggests that between 1869 and 1914, 4 to 5 per cent of the employed male population belonged to the gente decente. At the other end of the social structure, the proportion of manual laborers gradually declined from one-third to one-quarter of the total. The large sub-group of blue-collar and white-collar workers meanwhile increased from 60 to 70 per cent of employed males.

This occupational profile, when divided according to native- and foreign-born elements, demonstrates that, while immigrants provided the bulk of the laborers, they constituted no threat to a social structure dominated by the gente decente (see Table 15). The native-born clearly predominated among the gente decente, with percentages ranging from a low of 69 per cent in 1895 to a high of 81 per cent in 1914. Foreigners who entered Argentina as managers, directors, or technicians usually had sufficient antecedents in family, education, or wealth to belong to the gente decente, and, consequently, they were interested in supporting the existing social

---

* The 1887 municipal census, the first to distinguish sex in occupational lists, recorded no women in upper-class or gente-decente occupations save for 42 ranchers. Primary school teaching, although not really an upper-class occupation, provided the only moderately respectable occupation above that of servant: in 1887, 583 girls were enrolled in formal school training and 789 were teaching primary school. In contrast, there were 29,570 women employed as washerwomen, ironing women, or domestics. By 1914, despite the addition of a few more women to upper-class occupations, this situation had not changed appreciably. In that year, 517 could qualify in gente-decente professions (103 ranchers, 4 impresarios, 3 lawyers, 89 doctors and dentists, 13 chemists and doctors of letters, 51 writers and journalists, 7 appraisers, and 247 university and secondary school teachers). The 3988 listed as students undoubtedly included a large number of fourteen-year-olds who were completing the final (sixth) year of primary school or who had embarked on normal school training. Another 5848 were classified as primary school teachers. At the same time, nearly 93,000 women were domestic servants or washerwomen.

46. Workhorses for Argentine development—newly arrived immigrants at the port, November 1904. (Archivo General de la Nación.)

structure. Immigrants, on the other hand, predominated among the gente de pueblo. Approximately 80 per cent of the unskilled labor force and two-thirds of the blue-collar and white-collar group were foreign-born. By 1914 the Italian and Spanish immigrants who entered the system at the bottom outnumbered native-born as menial laborers by a ratio of 6:1. Among blue-collar and white-collar workers, the proportion of foreigners to natives had gradually declined, from 4:1 in 1887 to 2:1 by 1914, largely because the sons of immigrants were included in the ranks of the native-born.

Although the occupational profile of the porteño social structure oversimplifies a complex and stratified situation, it focuses on two aspects that played important roles in the cultural themes* of the city. A small, closely knit, native-born upper class dominated and controlled the social structure, while immigrants and their children largely made up the widely diversified and dependent labor-

---

* The term "cultural themes" is used in this work to mean the set of learned beliefs and values shared by the members of a society.

ing category. This contributed to continuity and stability during a period of rapid urban growth. A porteño of the gran aldea transplanted to the Buenos Aires of 1910 would have been amazed by the physical transformation of his city—port, avenues, suburbs. But he would have found much that seemed familiar to him in its society. Massive immigration of Europeans laid the basis for eventual social change, but it was change that would occur later, during the lifetimes of their grandchildren and great-grandchildren.

Many of the city's cultural themes had existed since colonial days, and their roots extended to the interaction of Iberian, Roman, and Moorish heritages in medieval Spain. The scorn the upper class held toward manual labor; the high regard accorded the lawyer, priest, or anyone devoted to the study of humanistic subjects; the central position of the family; the emphasis placed on the individual, the person, in all human relationships; the continuous and open display of manliness and virility; the admiration expressed for the roguish or clever man—all of these had helped push Spain toward its world preeminence in the sixteenth and seventeenth centuries, and all still flourished in many areas of its former empire. Peculiarities of the porteño environment, along with the reinforcement of certain values by Italian and Spanish immigrants, gave local form to these characteristics. But, despite the influx of other nationalities and religions, the gente decente as well as those who imitated them continued to subscribe to these cultural themes in the metropolis of 1910. Indeed, the principal cultural contribution of the late-nineteenth-century economic expansion and massive immigration, in addition to reinforcing or moulding these values to their porteño surroundings, seems to have been limited to a spirit of materialism and a concern with progress.

The attitude that only the untrained and uneducated masses occupied themselves with rude physical labor sprang in large measure from the Spanish heritage, which always had placed the gown and sword far above the hammer, spade, and anvil. In the Argentine environment this trait took on further significance. The area around Buenos Aires had not been endowed with any sizable or sedentary Indian settlements. Despite the importation of some blacks as slaves, a large proportion of the Hispanic and mestizo population had to perform manual tasks. Toil thus continued to separate the masses from the gente decente. A peculiarity of this attitude emerged, however, out of Buenos Aires' early exploitation and exportation of hides and tallow from the wild herds of horses and cattle. First the herds and then the land on which they grazed acquired value, and the man who controlled the land became wealthy and powerful. The prestige attached to the horseman in Spain's military tradition transferred itself to the rude work of the hunt or the roundup. Throughout the nineteenth century the rural laborer who performed his work on horseback ranked far above those who herded sheep, plowed fields, harvested crops, or dug postholes and ditches. Similarly, manual work involving horses and cattle was accepted and expected of gente decente: an estanciero should be able to outperform his peons in breaking a wild horse or throwing a cow.

Scorn for any manual labor not performed on horseback was strong among the Argentine-born masses. During the nineteenth century, in the writings of both foreign observers and Argentine critics, "criollo" became synonymous with shiftlessness and laziness. As horsemen, criollos, who had been active in the repeated civil wars and in the extension of the cattle frontier into the pampas, demonstrated as much endurance and fortitude as the sixteenth-century Spanish conquistador had before them. But other types of manual labor moved them to no feats. Little wonder Argentine statesmen despaired of the criollo and turned to the European immigrant to cultivate the fields, build the railroads, and carry out the myriad manual tasks associated with a burgeoning economy.

Attitudes toward manual labor fostered by Argentina's early economic development produced a major distinction between gente decente and gente de pueblo.* Boundaries between the two major categories were clearly marked, as suggested by distinctions that remained in force even in the annual release of energy and emotions during Carnival, the several days of celebrations preceding Lent. Water might be thrown at anyone; the lawyer might disguise himself as a beggar; the prostitute might appear as a princess. At the leading public ball in the Colón Theater, to which all could come,

* Use of the hands by the educated and wealthy, except in artistic pursuits, remains unusual in Argentina to this day. A doctor or university professor prefers not to carry parcels in the street; an engineer or architect will have an assistant do those portions of his work which are considered to be beneath his status; a lawyer rarely washes and polishes his car or weeds his flower garden.

there were no differences in the price of admission and no ushers or
signs to direct the revelers. Yet no one erred as to which part of
the theater he or she was supposed to go. The working masses
poured helter-skelter onto the main floor, where they engaged
in riotous clowning and can-cans, while the gente decente went to
the balconies and salons for genteel fun.[7] In the same spirit, it
seemed logical for a projected concession for public baths presented
to the municipal council in 1889 to include one set of baths set
aside for the "working classes."[8] This merely continued the practice that had been used in the gran aldea when the estuary's mud
flats in front of the city served as public baths: stretches of the
bank known to everyone were allocated according to sex and then
further divided between gente decente and gente de pueblo. Such
"special" status can be seen in a newspaper account from 1902,
which reported that several laborers had been denied admission to
the visitors' gallery at the Congress building. The comments underlined the need to hide any association with manual labor, since the
well-dressed man could go anywhere without being challenged:
"His elegance is the only title that he needs."[9]

The common man therefore attempted whenever possible to disguise the fact that he was a laborer. As a Spanish visitor observed
in 1904, "Even though there are many workers, they wear no special or distinguishing garb as in our cities."[10] The concern with
dress as the means to hide links with manual occupations appeared
graphically in the contrast between recently arrived immigrants
and properly attired pedestrians near the Plaza de Mayo who had
already begun to climb the social ladder. Likewise, "worker cars"
—coupled in the early morning and late afternoon to regular streetcars and costing half the fare—often went nearly empty. Even when
the seats were occupied, passengers sported coats and ties instead of
workingmen's garb.*

Complementing the disdain for manual labor was the admiration
and status given those with advanced education. Within the Spanish
empire, three powerful groups—the Church, the university, and the

---

* Similarly, in the 1940s and 1950s the Peronists attempted to dignify manual labor,
but they encountered subtle resistance among construction workers, who arrived at
and left their jobs dressed in coats and ties, their work pants and blouses neatly
tucked away in briefcases.

47. Well-dressed pedestrians near the Plaza de Mayo. This is Avenida de Mayo at the corner of Perú. (Archivo General de la Nación.)

royal bureaucracy—had established the importance of university training and the law degree for the elite. The cult of "doctor"—the title given lawyers upon completion of the standard five-year course in the university—lived on in Latin American countries, accepted by all as the capstone of intellectual achievement. In addition, advanced education served as the principal means by which new blood occasionally entered the gente decente.

These attitudes toward education helped to maintain an elitist and rigid educational structure oriented toward humanistic studies throughout the country's period of rapid economic growth. Determined efforts by Argentina's schoolteacher President, Domingo F. Sarmiento (1868–74), introduced some United States practices at the elementary level, imported several dozen schoolmistresses from the United States, and broadened the base of those who attended a few years of primary school. But despite the ambitious plans voiced by many statesmen and educators to reproduce the North American public school system in Argentina, rudimentary literacy—not social advancement for the bulk of the population—appeared to be the primary result. Most children completed only a few grades or attended school during only a small part of the year. The predominant view among gente decente, succinctly expressed by one Congressman, held that children of worker families needed no more than a basic knowledge of reading, since "The child is in school—and in a very healthy one—when he is in the workshop and has a tool in his hand."[11]

In 1907 less than 2000 children, out of a primary-school-age population of 232,000 in the city, completed the final year of primary school. The pyramid of attendance by grade is even more revealing: 46,000 in first grade, 19,000 in second, 11,000 in third, 7000 in fourth, 3000 in fifth, and 1900 in sixth.[12] Two years later the number of students in the first grade totaled 48,000, while those in the sixth numbered 2200.[13] Thus, approximately 5 per cent of those who began first grade completed primary school. By 1914 the official census returns painted a more optimistic picture: out of the 230,000 school-age children in the city, approximately 83 per cent registered for school and 62 per cent attended on a more or less regular basis.[14] But completion of primary school still remained beyond the reach of most porteño children, in major degree because their families could not forego their earning power until they reached fourteen. Furthermore, unless one continued on to the secondary or normal school—uncommon steps that already placed one at the very top of the gente de pueblo or on the verge of joining the gente decente—the acquisition of a skill or trade proved far more useful than an education which, by the fourth-grade level, began to prepare one principally for the colegio and the university.

The gente decente's goal of achieving rudimentary literacy for the mass of the population by broadening attendance in the lower grades of elementary school neatly complemented their continued monopoly of secondary and university education. As the Minister of Education said in 1892, the colegio and the university must be directed toward forming "the highest intellectual class, the enlightened groups, the leaders of society."[15] This education remained oriented toward the classics, the humanities, and philosophy, and it emphasized theoretical discussion rather than applied experimentation. Even medical students learned anatomy from texts, not from dissection, and future engineers rarely got any practical training until after they had received their degree.

The narrowing of the educational pyramid toward a small elite apex was not as marked at the secondary and university levels as it was in the primary schools. Nevertheless, in 1909 the city's secondary schools that offered at least five years of instruction had 1961 students enrolled in the first year of studies and only 642 in the fifth year. In that same year the Medical School of the University matriculated 469 students in the first-year class, but had only 212 in the final year. The School of Engineering and Exact Sciences recorded a first-year group of 231, but only 30 in the final year of course work.[16]

The structure of advanced education—never noted for its flexibility and adaptability in any society—proved remarkably rigid and uncompromising in Argentina. Despite persistent undercurrents of discontent with incompetent and absentee professors, antiquated texts and lectures, high fees, and lack of discipline, system, or relevance in studies, no attempt at reform emerged from the educational hierarchy itself. Comments made in 1872 and 1873, "There is no teaching and no learning [in the University]," or "[The University] serves only to grind out a profusion of titles without attention to the needs of and capabilities of the students," reechoed with strange familiarity when Congress intermittently studied reform proposals amid sporadic but violent demonstrations in the Law and Medical schools from 1903 to 1906.[17] In 1904, during debate on a reform project, one Congressman summarized the conflict between the old and the new in terms highly relevant to the changing conditions:

> On one side there is the implementation of the new scientific approach demanded by the students; on the other is the University which, despite having lived through a century of intense reform and change, has always looked toward the past.
> On one side one can see students anxious to absorb the new knowledge; on the other, one finds sincere professors, good fathers to their families, correct and respectable as gentlemen and individ-

uals, but unable to respond to the intellectual demands of the present and, as a result, to the future needs of our national talent.[18]

But the older, more traditional groups yielded control slowly. Not until 1918 did pressure from students and politicians enable the leaders of a reform movement to seize control of the University of Córdoba. From this movement emerged substantial reforms in the administration of Argentine and other Latin American universities, principally the establishment of tripartite rule by students, faculty, and alumni. Even then, however, the traditional orientation that emphasized theoretical and humanistic approaches to learning changed only gradually.

On the porteño scene the influence of traditional humanistic training also emerged in attitudes toward technical education. Engineering as a field of study had first developed within the Faculty of Exact Sciences in 1866, but university degrees in other fields useful to a burgeoning economy came slowly: a Faculty of Economic Sciences began operation within the University in 1914; an Institute of Advanced Commercial Studies joined the University in 1911; and in 1918 the specialized degree in industrial engineering was added to the offerings of the Faculty of Natural and Exact Sciences. In 1910 the University of Buenos Aires' 4650 students still heavily favored traditional professional careers: medical sciences and law stood at the top, with 2500 and 1100, respectively; natural and exact sciences followed with 600; philosophy and letters had 250; and agronomy and veterinary science brought up the rear—in this agriculture-oriented economy—with 200.[19]

At the secondary level, technical studies faced similar handicaps of low prestige. There existed, in effect, no middle ground in the Argentine educational system. The gente decente benefited from the elitist educational structure that prepared their children for "leadership." Parents from lower strata who by dint of savings and sacrifice pushed a child into colegio training had no desire to settle for "trade school" education. Significantly, the first project for technical training, advanced in 1882, was designed to be established in the city's orphan asylum. Its initiator assured his colleagues that such training would be complemented with indoctrination "dealing with the morals that Governments are obligated to instill in the lower strata of society."[20] The general response in Congress was that this type of technical education cost too much and that, thanks to European immigrants, the country had enough artisans anyway.[21]

At the end of the nineteenth century an industrial school, under government protection, finally emerged. Its first director underlined the need it was to fill: "Even though it is easy for factories to train their workers, the same is not true with their directors, foremen, and plant managers."[22] Yet by 1908 the country's single industrial school had only 450 students enrolled in three basic courses —industrial training, industrial drawing, and chauffeuring.[23] Increased support for this school died in congressional committee in 1908, and when reintroduced in 1911 it was vetoed.[24]

By 1910 attitudes toward technical education apparently had not changed, as indicated by one Congressman's apologetic introduction of a bill to institute training at the elementary and secondary levels in order to prepare mechanics, electricians, chemists, and construction foremen:

> I am not a believer in turning our youth away from literary and liberal careers and we should continue to support this sort of preparation which in due course will lead to the lofty doctoral education, but meanwhile we should also give serious organization to technical training, enabling a good portion of the youth to take up useful and practical activities.[25]

This and similar measures never even reached the floor of Congress for debate, and the law or medical degree remained the capstone of traditional university training revered by most, even though such limited higher education was totally inadequate to deal with the rapid economic growth being experienced by both the city and the nation.[26]

Another major cultural theme, the dominant position of the family, received powerful reinforcement from Italian and Spanish immigration. It also constituted a powerful element for stability in porteño society. Not only did the family serve as a principal determinant of status within the social structure, it also bound together gente decente through ties of blood and marriage. Such families extended far beyond the nuclear group of man, wife, and children; they included unmarried brothers and sisters, parents, married children, and, occasionally, grandparents, cousins, nephews, and nieces. Each household had an average of four to five employed males.[27] The rise in the number of employed men of gente decente, from 3400 in 1869 to 20,000 in 1909, suggests that this class had grown from about 800 to about 5000 families in forty years—still a small enough group that family and personal links could unite them.

At all levels of the society the family—especially in its extended form—served to provide for its members' welfare. The municipality and the Church supported asylums and hospitals for the indigent, aged, and sick—but these were places of last resort, for those who had no family. The extended family thus assumed responsibility for all members. Families of the gente decente were often large —they might include a widowed son who had returned to his parents' home with several small children, a sister who had no grown children of her own to turn to, or unmarried daughters who had no alternative but to live out spinsterhood within their parents' home. There were many such spinsters in 1869, when families frequently had four, five, or six single daughters who had reached the virtually unmarriageable age of twenty-five.* Among gente de pueblo the extended family, although not as large, also afforded security in times of illness or unemployment. The work of many hands—children of nine or ten who earned a few pennies as bootblacks or street vendors, sisters and daughters who took in washing or sewing, brothers and cousins who worked as manual laborers—frequently helped put carrots and potatoes in the puchero or made it possible for the family to save toward a plot of land on the outskirts. Admittedly, the obligations of the extended family also could place a drain on resources, and such families occasionally had

* Although the published statistics of 1869 do not divide occupation by sex or nationality, one can probe beneath the apparently favorable balance of 40,000 single men and 22,500 single women in the city in that year and observe that 76 per cent of these men were foreign-born, while, in the sixteen to thirty age group, Argentine-born women, married, widowed, and single, outnumbered Argentine-born men by two to one. Undoubtedly the large number of males, especially of young porteño upper-class men, drawn off to fight in the Paraguayan War (1865-70) contributed substantially to the imbalance. This considerably reduced the field for girls of the gente decente, who, given the humble origins of most immigrants, had to find husbands among the native-born of their own class. These conclusions are borne out by a study of the families examined in note 27, p. 297.

their savings wiped out by the indigence, illness, or unemployment of its members.

Emphasis on the individual and on the personal seemed to threaten the cohesiveness and stability that the family brought to the porteño scene. This predilection for the individual, however, involved highly complex Spanish traits, made even more intricate by the local environment and by immigrant groups.

On the one hand, personalism signified the establishment of bonds of loyalty or duty on the basis of personal relationships, either real or sensed. In the political sphere, these attitudes had underwritten *caudillismo*—the power of the local chieftain to dominate and lead his followers. In return for support and obedience, the caudillo afforded his followers protection, employment, and often, a dominant father symbol. In addition to their political implications, personal links and individual contacts gave meaning not only to the bonds of friendship, but also to many social actions. To a great degree, links established by *simpatía*, or congeniality, by bribery, by fear, or by power tied porteños to companions at work, to storekeepers, to friends and neighbors, to the local policeman, and to the politician.

On the other hand, individualism represented the freedom of the person to express, at least within himself, his own sentiments. Spanish literature and art repeatedly paid homage to this freedom, which could not be cut off by imprisonment or by outside sanctions or restrictions. Indeed, the outward expression of freedom or individuality often was not the most important part of this individual liberty—a subtlety which other cultures found hard to comprehend. Such values, regardless of outward or inward expression, encouraged a man to develop his own independent approach to his environment and to express it whenever the strictures of family, government, or outside forces permitted. Thus, despite outward manifestations of concern with legalism and legal procedures, the Spaniard often rejected the establishment of rational standards that ruled the individual's will. As a result, men frequently lacked internal norms that would govern in the absence of outside enforcement. In Argentina this came to mean that as long as some symbol of authority did not expressly prevent an action, that action was permissible. In everyday life, these attitudes gave sanction to the customs inspector who overlooked an obviously smuggled item, the passenger who lit up a cigar in the no-smoking compartment, the professor who failed to show up for a lecture. The emphasis on individualism also encouraged vociferous and explosive defense of one's position unless adequate authority or force were present: consider the frequent arguments on streetcars between passengers and conductors, the reluctance to yield the narrow sidewalk to another person, the furious recriminations of carriage drivers at intersections.

Another strand of individualism and personalism emerged in the spirit of egalitarianism evident in Buenos Aires. In medieval Spain this attitude had been voiced as equality of all *hidalgos*, or gentlemen, below the king. Despite the many strata in porteño social structure, public attitudes, as can be seen in the numerous popular *sainetes*, or one-act plays, supported the view that no one man was innately superior to another. Often, however, the sainetes suggested that advancement came not so much by means of drudgery, economy, or use of one's hands as by one's luck and wits. While in reality career and future remained irrevocably bound to one's family origins, such egalitarianism postulated that anyone might rise to the highest level of society.

An equally complex theme in Buenos Aires developed out of the Spanish, Italian, and criollo concepts of masculinity and virility. Undoubtedly, Argentina's gaucho heritage had an important influence on porteños. The idealized version of the gaucho that emerged in ballads, poems, plays, and novels written by men of the city in the late nineteenth century placed major emphasis on reckless, defiant courage.[28] This swaggering ideal reached its culmination with the gaucho who sauntered into a group, carelessly dragging the ends of his poncho on the ground so as to brush the boots or spurs of bystanders and thus invite a knife fight to the death. Other overtones of manliness also sprang from this heritage. The legendary gaucho, although he might venerate his mother, viewed other women primarily as objects of physical desire. Sentiments or attachments represented unacceptable weaknesses or softness in a virile world.

Most porteños had to limit themselves to vicarious enjoyment of the gaucho's legendary defiance. Nevertheless many gente decente in the late nineteenth century carried revolvers, and most workers wore a knife. As a result, the outward show of manliness, strongly supported by Spanish and Italian traditions, occasionally led to bloodshed. More acceptable in urban surroundings was the expectation that men, in addition to being good fathers and providers, should demonstrate virility by pursuing unattached females, visiting prostitutes, and deprecating love as a deep, emotional feeling.

The *compadrito*, or neighborhood tough, who flourished in the suburbs of Buenos Aires in the last years of the nineteenth century brought together many of the Spanish, criollo, and Italian values on masculinity. Like the gaucho, the compadrito eventually was depicted in a literature that accentuated and occasionally distorted the colorful aspects of his personality.[29] In the real world, the compadrito belonged to the gente de pueblo. Usually he had no police record, although he showed little reverence for law and regulation. Invariably, he was native-born—although often of immigrant parents—and stressed the criollo accent and vocabulary into which some of the gaucho's intonation and phrases had been absorbed.* His trademarks were high-heeled boots, a silk handkerchief knotted at the neck, and a slouch hat. Exaggeration in dress or mannerisms made him stand out among his companions. But unless someone responded to his insolent stare or to his aggressive parade of masculinity, he was harmless.

The rise of the compadrito was closely entwined with the origins of another porteño phenomenon—the tango. This dance had evolved in the final decades of the century, in the city's outlying districts, or *arrabales*, where it totally lacked respectability or social acceptance. Around 1900 the tango jumped the Atlantic to Paris, where it promptly acquired fame and prestige.[30] Its return to Buenos Aires a decade later launched it as a national symbol. But in the music of its earlier era—the harsh, insistent tones, the strutting but precise steps, the rhythmic flow, the absence of words—and in its performance with other men or with prostitutes, the tango gave the compadrito a perfect stage on which to parade his postures and attitudes.

---

* As such, the compadrito's argot should not be associated with the language of the underworld, nor with the slang dialect of *lunfardo*, which developed in Buenos Aires in the late nineteenth century.

At the other end of the social ladder, and at nearly the same time, emerged the compadrito's counterpart—the *niño bien,* or upper-class sport. In the golden age of the 1880s, these sons of the porteño elite sowed their wild oats in theaters on Victoria and Rivadavia, in bars along Corrientes and Esmeralda, and, farther from the center, at restaurants such as Hansen's in Palermo. Known in that era as the *indiada,* or Indian horde, these boys, who were in their late teens and early twenties, became notorious for their provocation of passersby, for pranks, and for wild parties. Police authorities feared to interfere, knowing full well that from these youngsters would spring the political elite of tomorrow, while society in general tended to look upon their antics as outbursts of youthful exuberance. But since the niño bien exhibited much of the same arrogance and aggressiveness as the compadrito, there were frequent, bloody clashes between bands of these two groups in cafés, houses of prostitution, and restaurants. Such violence finally brought more effective police action, and by 1910 newspapers could find little more to report than the periodic annoyance of patrons of sidewalk cafés by niños bien who recklessly drove around downtown streets in that new toy of the rich—the automobile.

One porteño characteristic that flowered in the late nineteenth century emerged from the interaction of widely divergent backgrounds: the picaresque tradition of medieval Spain, the legendary cunning of the gaucho, and the self-conscious defensiveness of the immigrants' children. European immigrants posed no threat to gente decente. But the criollo laborer faced inundation from a stream of hardworking, ambitious, and penurious foreigners. The incorporation of first-generation Argentines into blue-collar and white-collar occupations caused the percentage of foreign-born listed in the census to decline slightly, from 79 per cent in 1887 to 65 per cent in 1914. Foreigners assumed even greater preponderance in manual occupations: they made up 86 per cent of this subgroup (see Table 15). In light of the long-standing criollo disdain of manual labor, few employers—especially if they themselves came from immigrant backgrounds—hid their preference for reliable, sober, and hard-working Europeans. In all the lower strata of society, the criollo had good reason to envy and distrust the immigrant. Although the violence that occasionally struck at the immigrant in the Argentine countryside rarely afflicted the numerically predominant foreign element in Buenos Aires, the native-born gente de pueblo expressed hostility toward immigrants that ranged from jealousy to scorn.

Viveza criolla, or native cunning, constituted the principal weapon in the arsenal of the native-born.[31] Viveza described the ability to advance one's own position or cause at the expense of others without physical exertion. The rash of confidence men who struck the city toward the end of the century merely pushed viveza to extremes unthought of by the average criollo. But as long as the target remained the immigrant, few objections were raised. What made viveza criolla a peculiarity of the porteño makeup was not the ability of the clever or the crooked—as in any major city—to take advantage of the gullible and naïve, but the general acceptance and even admiration of that ability. Such exploits received audience and applause, and the overt approval extended carried no sense of shame or secrecy. "What viveza!" meant praise, not condemnation.

The criollo also subjected the immigrant to ridicule. Although Argentine authorities insisted, especially after 1900, that all schoolchildren be exposed to the symbols of flag, independence, and Argentine greatness, the taunts and jibes aimed at the foreigner served even more effectively to condition acceptance of local customs. Epithets of *gringo*, *gallego*, or *ruso* might bounce off immigrants' ears, but they sank their shafts deeply into the children of immigrants. Gringo, a word usually associated with Italians, implied a stereotype of a plodding, penurious drudge incapable of enjoying pleasure. Gallego, a Spaniard, meant an inoffensive, stupid workhorse. Ruso, referring to the sizable Russian-Jewish immigration, expressed anti-Semitism along with the stereotype of strangely dressed and dirty peasants. These and similar jeers encouraged the children to mould themselves on what they saw as criollo model in speech, customs, and attitudes and to reject the language and ways of their parents. If the father mutilated Spanish with his Galician or Genoese phrases and accent, the son would roar with laughter at music-hall parodies of the clumsy immigrant; he himself would convincingly slur the local slang—which, ironically, incorporated French and Italian phrases. If the father proudly wore a beret, enjoyed an afternoon at the bocce court with his cronies, or hungered for paella, the son sought, in dress, amusements, and food, to avoid anything that might identify him as a foreigner. If the *viejo*, or "old man," toiled on the docks and avoided hard liquor in order to put a few pesos in his mattress or bank account at the end of the month, the son often showed his disdain for manual work and placed his faith in the stroke of luck or the assist from a friend. The scorn heaped on the clumsiness, ineptitude, or stupidity of the gringo, gallego, or immigrant in general eventually grew into a nearly psychotic fear of ridicule in the porteño personality. Derision and mockery served to bring social conformity at all levels within the city.

The late-nineteenth-century economic growth and the massive influx of European immigrants and foreign capital stimulated the development of one cultural trait—materialism—that owed little to the country's Hispanic heritage. In the gran aldea the gap between gente decente and gente de pueblo had been measured more in terms of family, education, and occupation than in terms of wealth. Ostentation and luxury had meant little in the enclosed patio style of life. But prosperity revolutionized this environment. The dream of *hacer la América*—to succeed in the New World—moved the Piedmontese farmer, the Neapolitan stevedore, the Ligurian store clerk, the Asturian butcher, and the Basque sheepherder across the Atlantic. Porteños, encouraged by major economic booms from 1884 to 1889 and from 1905 to 1912, became a highly materialistic people. Expectation of gain—not only through daily wages, but through profits from stores and shops, stock speculations, cattle ranches, and land sales—generated frenetic activity. A Spanish observer in 1910 noted this mood: "The city is forever remaking and altering itself and everyone seems to live in a constant state of alert as if at war, stimulated by the preoccupation of enriching himself as quickly as possible."[32]

The surge of materialism soon appeared openly among the gente decente. By 1910 wealth could make up for serious deficiencies in lineage and education. The emphasis on materialism found reflection in changing housing styles. The villas, chalets, *petits hotels*, and palacios not only required more land than the interior patios

48. A gathering of the porteño elite at the Palermo racetrack, around 1900. (Archivo General de la Nación.)

in which generations of Argentines had been reared; they also offered the rich better opportunities to parade their wealth before the world. Fortunes inflated by the rising value of land allowed many wealthy men to build mansions, often several mansions: palacios, complete with trees and gardens, on their cattle ranches; palacios on elegant residential streets such as Santa Fe and Avenida Alvear; and chalets on the riverbank toward San Isidro.

Sumptuous feasts and splendid parties began to replace the enclosed and guarded family style of the 1870s. Houses of the elite sustained an ever gaudier social whirl: the ideal was, as one diarist noted, "A real house for parties, apparently expressly built and furnished for that purpose."[33] A New Year's Eve dance in 1904 at the Tornquist quinta in Belgrano featured a repast for 1000 guests; they dined under the trees at tables set with exquisite linens, crystal, silver, and china, and they sipped the best of French wines and champagnes.[34] The golden wedding anniversary of the Guerricos in 1906 titillated even a blasé porteño society. Hundreds of workmen transformed the garden of this residence near Plaza San Martín into one vast salon, fully equipped with gas heating, electric lights, and running water. Twelve hundred guests, including the President, sat down to a feast which started off with tiny woodcocks stuffed with paté de foie gras and chestnuts and was climaxed by the invariable Moët Chandon with dessert.[35] In dress, art collections, furniture, table service, and carriages, the Argentine elite were determined to equal or outdo the wealthy of Europe.[36]

The gente decente also demonstrated increasing concern with the trappings of material progress for their city. By 1910 porteños prided themselves on having built the Paris of South America. They confidently viewed their city as the leading metropolis of the Americas, principally because it so much resembled European urban centers.

At the same time, materialism helped to change attitudes toward how one achieved success. The *coima*, or bribe, was virtually unknown in Buenos Aires before 1880. But during the economic boom of the 1880s, coima became an accepted way of doing business, and a bribe, deftly palmed off, got you past a doorman, sped your petition through a municipal office, permitted you to retrieve goods from the customhouse, and allowed you to avoid numerous delays or annoyances. Although sums might become larger and the method of payment more complicated, bribes also gained support for railroad concessions in Congress and secured favorable decisions in federal courts. One estimate, made in 1904, suggested that each year the equivalent of one-quarter of the national budget was spent on bribes in Buenos Aires alone.[37]

The spirit of materialism spawned similar attitudes among the gente de pueblo. As ostentatiously displayed wealth moved further from the grasp of this social category, the long shot or gamble became an attractive substitute for hard work and sacrifice. Increasingly, success was credited to one's influential friends rather than to one's own efforts. At the beginning of the twentieth century, newspapers and government officials began to express concern at one symptom of this—the tremendous surge of gambling on lotteries, horse races, and other sports. In the 1890s—a period when the Argentine economy was anything but flourishing—the porteño public invested nearly half a billion pesos in gambling, an amount that was approximately equivalent to one-fifth of the value of the country's total exports for the decade.[38]

Despite the intense concern with achieving the appearances of material progress, the gente decente saw no need to change the existing economic, political, and social structures or to preoccupy themselves with integration of the foreign-born population or stimulation of industrial development. The world economy proved kind to Argentina from 1880 until World War I. As a result, Argentines confidently expected that the demand for agricultural products and the continued supply of European immigrants and capital would guarantee stability and maintain rising prosperity.

In their search for material progress the gente decente developed ambivalent views toward the foreigner and the foreign. Progress depended on foreigners and foreign elements. French literature, Italian opera, German science, English industry, and United States public education, along with foreign managers, bankers, technicians, artisans, and merchants, were warmly received in the city. On the other hand, immigrants themselves never escaped the role of the outsider—they were distrusted and envied by the lower strata, while the gente decente viewed them as satisfactory laborers who served but did not belong. The French observer, Émile Daireaux, touched on this crucial porteño attitude when he wrote, in the 1880s,

> The foreigner on his side deeply feels his condition as a stranger even when he has resided for years in this land, a condition which keeps him in a state of inferiority that no one will admit or openly suggest but that is nonetheless very real.[39]

The gente decente thus advocated immigration while at the same time carefully protecting the political structure from immigrant interference. The overwhelming preponderance of foreign-born over Argentine males in Buenos Aires in 1869—52,000 to 13,000 between the ages of fifteen and fifty-nine—did not challenge the political system and resulted in only an occasional demonstration by the largest and most recently established immigrant group, the Italians. In February 1870, Italian residents held noisy demonstrations for several days, protesting insults directed against their com-

munity by a local porteño newspaper.[40] A secret Italian society in
La Boca reportedly attacked policemen on several occasions in
1874; for a time thereafter the police seem to have singled out Italians as troublemakers.[41] In 1875 a Masonic-sponsored demonstration protesting government return of property to the Jesuit Order
enlisted the enthusiasm of a number of recently arrived, rabidly
anti-clerical Italians. After being harangued by leading porteño
politicians at the Plaza de Mayo, the crowd became aroused. Before police could disperse the demonstrators, the Jesuit colegio had
been sacked and burned, scores of persons had been hurt, and a
dozen men, including a few priests, lay dead.[42] The next year, police authorities nervously stood by while 5000 cheering Italians
greeted the arrival of a new diplomatic representative from Italy;
the immigrants seized that occasion to demonstrate against police
brutality.[43] But these gatherings did not indicate that there was foreign interference in internal Argentine politics.

Argentine authorities saw to it that the foreign element remained
isolated from the periodic civil conflicts within the city. For a moment in 1873, during sharp divisions between *mitristas* and *alsinis-
tas*—followers, respectively, of Bartolomé Mitre and Adolfo Alsina—the mitristas reputedly mounted a drive to naturalize foreigners in order to secure their votes. When faced with the evident
danger of embroiling the enormous foreign element in the struggle,
they abandoned the attempt.[44] Several years later, on the eve of the
brief civil war that led to the federalization of the city, the alsinis-
tas reinforced the neutrality of the foreign communities by dis-
missing all foreigners from the city's police force.[45]

By the late 1870s the foreign communities had abandoned demonstrations as a route of protest, and they had turned instead to
making expressions of solidarity with Argentina. In 1878, at the
centennial celebrations of the birth of Argentina's independence
leader, José de San Martín, between 8000 and 10,000 Italians paraded through the city's streets and porteño newspapers hailed the
numerous Italian societies, marching bands, flags, and banners
which had taken up a length of twelve city blocks in the parade.[46]
Two years later, at the centennial of Bernardino Rivadavia's birth,
20,000 foreigners joined in the parade; on this occasion their banners and societies far outnumbered those of the Argentines—in

part, at least, because the latter were busily preparing for civil conflict over federalization of the city.[47] In 1882, 60,000 persons turned out to commemorate the death of Giuseppe Garibaldi—who was well remembered in the Río de la Plata area for his role in the defense of Montevideo during the Uruguayan civil war of the 1840s, as well as for his more renowned career in Italy—with a massive meeting in the Plaza de Mayo.[48]

Foreign immigration to Argentina increased sharply during the 1880s, and some began to urge that immigrants should become Argentine citizens. After the 1880 civil war one newspaper commentator suggested, "The foreign element is basically conservative and once it has joined in public deliberations it will bring an end to the turbulence which has afflicted us."[49] A committee of the Club Industrial, forerunner of the Unión Industrial Argentina, the leading organization of the city's business and manufacturing interests, recommended legislation to make citizenship easier to acquire. In 1882 a bill requiring any foreigner employed in government service to take out citizenship papers was placed before the Chamber of Deputies, but a congressional committee reported it out unfavorably on the grounds that such discrimination was both unnecessary and unconstitutional, and the Chamber rejected the measure, 20 to 12.[50]

The extreme liberality of the Argentine Constitution toward the foreigner admirably served the gente decente's interest in keeping the immigrant out of the body politic. The foreigner, because of his many privileges as a resident alien, felt no pressure to become a citizen. As an alien he could work or conduct business on an equal footing with the native-born Argentine. He could move around the country, marry, and own property as freely as any citizen could. Within the city of Buenos Aires he could even vote in municipal elections. The advantages of an appeal to one's consular or diplomatic agent against local injustices declined sharply after the unification of all the provinces in 1862 provided Argentina with a national government sensitive to any challenge to its sovereignty.[51] Nonetheless, the foreign male continued to escape duty in the national guard and, after 1902, universal military service.

An undercurrent of hostility and obstructionism frustrated those few foreigners who might have wanted to adopt Argentine citizenship. Powerful social pressures existed against naturalization. In the words of Émile Daireaux:

> The citizen of the Spanish American republic is too patriotic and has developed such a cult of worship toward his homeland and the idea of patriotism that he cannot forgive a foreigner who gives up his own country of origin. There is no homage which he receives more coldly than that of the foreigner who surrenders his citizenship in order to take out that of the new country. Of all the hierarchical ideas which democracy may be able to suppress or weaken and which divide criollo from foreigner, this is probably the strongest and for a long time it will maintain a distance between the artisan and worker [in other words, the foreigner] and those who employ them.[52]

In addition, despite apparently simple naturalization proceedings —according to the 1869 naturalization law, a petition filed with a federal judge after two years' residence in the country—red tape, or *trámites*, ensnarled and stopped most applications. The lower echelons of bureaucracy, especially the police, constituted an effective obstacle to Argentine citizenship. In the countryside, the paper work that had to be executed in a distant provincial capital, along with the long trip required to appear before a federal judge, frustrated most potential citizens. But in the city equally effective barriers developed. When a resident alien applied for citizenship, the judge instructed him to appear at police headquarters. After the applicant had completed a long questionnaire, the police called him back repeatedly to central headquarters or to the local district office for questioning. Delay followed on delay and, as occurred in one case studied by *La Prensa* in 1903, the employer also was called in for questioning. Thereupon one of the investigators advised the applicant to drop the whole procedure, since he was better off as a foreigner anyway.[53] According to comments made by a Socialist Congressman, this method still worked effectively in 1914, even though the Sáenz Peña law of secret ballot and universal male suffrage had two years earlier placed a higher premium on the acquisition of citizenship and the right to vote:

> The naturalization process which emerges from the Constitution and from the citizenship law of 1869 is a liberal one, aimed at facilitating the rapid incorporation of the foreigner. But in its place has been substituted another process, tortuous, illegal, long, and expen-

sive. . . . The police, in line with practices followed by federal judges and supported in confidential instructions from the executive branch, have acquired tremendous control and influence over the naturalization of foreigners.[54]

Regardless of oratory stressing the need to integrate the immigrant, no serious efforts were made to change procedures that effectively kept him from participating in the political system. Numerous proposals were made in Congress to simplify acquisition of citizenship—appearance before a justice of the peace instead of a federal judge, specific declaration required of resident aliens to maintain foreign citizenship, automatic conferral of Argentine citizenship on anyone who voted or held a government position.[55] None of these bills even reached the floor of Congress for debate. In fact, in 1902 the Argentine authorities gave yet another concession to encourage foreigners to maintain their original citizenship: the many aliens employed in the national and municipal bureaucracy were specifically exempted from the provision of the universal military service law that obliged all government employees to serve.[56]

Statistics on naturalization confirm that foreigners either did not desire or could not acquire Argentine citizenship. The 1895 census registered only 715 foreign-born men as naturalized citizens, out of the 206,000 foreign-born men in the city—a mere 0.35 per cent.[57] Partly in response to pressures from the Socialist party, which supported naturalization of foreigners, the total of naturalized citizens in the city rose markedly after 1900, to 5000 in 1904, 8000 in 1909, and 18,000 in 1914—representing 2, 2.5, and 4 per cent, respectively, of the foreign-born male population.[58] Even these relatively low figures seem inflated in light of statistics cited in the Chamber of Deputies in 1913—there were only 2384 naturalized citizens in the city, of whom nearly 1000 were sailors on coasting vessels and another sizable number were policemen and mailmen, who had been strongly urged to secure citizenship in order to hold their jobs.[59] The Argentine authorities themselves admitted, in a published volume of the 1914 census, that the percentage of naturalized males to foreign-born males for all of Argentina—2.25 per cent—stood in stark contrast to the United States' 1910 figure—46 per cent.[60]

In Argentina naturalization became submerged, especially after 1900, in a larger issue which concerned many groups—the establishment of a strong spirit of nationalism. At the end of the century, a number of new social clubs for gente de pueblo began to take shape, with the objective of encouraging criollo values, music, and dances. The names of these *centros criollos* stressed Argentina's gaucho heritage—La Pampa, El Matorral, Los Rastreadores, La Criolla, Hijos del Desierto.[61]

The gente decente also sensed the need to affirm their "Argentinism." In late 1901, Argentina and Chile once again, as they had in 1898, verged on the brink of war over boundaries, and the young men of the porteño elite responded with the formation of the Liga Patriótica Nacional, or National Patriotic League. In addition to urging rifle practice and providing facilities for drill and shooting for its members, the new organization supported naturalization of foreigners and opened a public subscription to acquire a cruiser for the navy. The movement spread rapidly through the city and into the provinces, and by mid-January a mass meeting of its members in Buenos Aires formally adopted statutes dedicated to strengthening Argentine patriotism throughout the country.[62]

Although this group was never called upon to defend Argentina's boundaries, some of the initial enthusiasm continued to flare up in counter-demonstrations against Socialist and Anarchist parades after 1904 and during the centennial celebrations of Argentine independence in 1910. Expressions of patriotism occasionally took strange forms. In early May of 1910 a band of at least 1000 youths, many from well-known porteño families, attacked and burned the circus tents which Frank Brown, a long-established entrepreneur, had just set up on a vacant lot along Florida. To many porteños, circus acts did not seem a sufficiently dignified way of celebrating the nation's birth. Even serious journals such as the *Revista Municipal* voiced approval of this violence:

> Buenos Aires has left behind its infantile adulation of the clown's gyrations or its childish pleasure at the leaps of an acrobat; a fundamental warning springs from this protest against its restoration— that it is never possible to turn back the clock or reestablish the characteristics of the past.[63]

In fostering nationalism, the gente decente aimed at instilling patriotism and "Argentinism" in the children of the city's large alien population. As more and more children entered private schools maintained by the foreign communities, serious dangers to Argentina's integrity as a nation seemed to be developing. The Argentine school system responded by changing its curricular focus. The nation's history and geography—previously considered to be part of world history—became separate subjects in the 1880s. In 1888 Argentine history, previously allotted two hours a week in the final year of secondary school, was taught for six hours each week in the first and second grades of primary school, and it was continued as part of the curriculum during the entire six years of primary education.[64] But during the 1880s and 1890s these measures did not affect private schools. Congress proved reluctant to move beyond the vague powers over primary schools given the Consejo Nacional de Educación, or National Education Council, by the famous educational law, No. 1420, of 1884—a law whose main effect has been to remove the influence of the Church from the educational system. Indeed, when a bill which required that all primary instruction be given in the Spanish language finally reached the floor of Congress in 1896, it was defeated, 19 to 34, amidst vociferous accusations that it represented a chauvinistic attack on European heritage and culture.[65]

After 1900, the renewed influx of Europeans, the threat of war with Chile, and continued friction with Brazil caused the Consejo Nacional de Educación to turn its attention to more effective controls over foreign community schools. The perils of the so-called "foreign" schools were described in a detailed report made by the Consejo's new and aggressive president, José María Ramos Mejía, in 1908:

> The Italian, German, French, and English schools [in Argentina], supported by their respective governments, have been in most cases exact replicas of educational institutions in those countries and were characterized by a marked loyalty to those foreign states. . . . Argentine history, geography, and civics, as well as other subjects established as the minimum mandatory curriculum were given a very secondary position and almost placed in ridicule; quite the contrary occurred with the history and geography of the nation to which the school belonged. . . .

With telling accuracy, Ramos Mejía concluded:

> Only the Argentine teacher or one closely linked to this country will teach our history with enthusiasm. . . . The school is the only

instrument by which duty to and love of the fatherland can be instilled in the hearts of our schoolchildren at an early age.[66]

In its effort to control the private schools, the Consejo finally seized on a clause in the 1884 law which required all private schools to certify teachers with the national government. Before the start of the 1909 academic year, all such primary schools were to register their teachers with the Consejo. Whenever teachers lacked the appropriate degrees or titles, they had to establish their credentials by examination. Only Argentine citizens could teach Argentine history, geography, and civics. Spanish instruction had to be given by a native speaker of the language. The curriculum had to contain basically the same subjects as did that of the public schools. Early each year, before the start of classes, the academic schedule and the list of textbooks to be used had to be submitted to the Consejo. The decree also singled out for particular attention the two Argentine independence days, May 25 and July 9: special celebrations and lessons were to be held, and a branch of the Consejo was to give detailed instruction on the observance of those days to the directors and teachers of all private schools.[67] These regulations effectively carried forward the spirit of indoctrination set forth in the previous year, when the Consejo had ordered revision of all school textbooks in order to inculcate national values by placing proper emphasis on Argentina's heroes, especially José de San Martín.

When the Consejo's instructions were implemented in 1909, a ceremony of allegiance that formerly had been restricted to new conscripts entering military service became a major school event. This *Jura de la Bandera*, or Oath to the Flag, was held for the first time in schools throughout the city and in several public plazas on July 8, the eve of one of the independence days.[68] In 1910 the focus shifted to May 25—perhaps because the centennial celebrations of that year honored that date—with a parade of 20,000 children in front of the Congress buildings and with other festivities, speeches, and processions throughout the city.[69] Thereafter, the Jura de la Bandera, sworn to by thousands of children dressed in their best clothes, became a regular institution in the festivities of May 25.[70]

Patriotic education received further reinforcement from daily

49. The parade of schoolchildren along the Avenida de Mayo, May 25, 1910. (Archivo General de la Nación.)

homage to the flag, training that brought children to their feet at the mention of San Martín's name, and catechistic recitation of formulas such as the following:

Q. How do you esteem yourself in relation to your compatriots?
A. I consider myself bound to them by a sentiment which unites us.
Q. And what is that?
A. The sentiment that the Argentine Republic is the finest country on earth.
Q. What are the duties of a good citizen?
A. First of all, to love his country.
Q. Even before his parents?
A. Before all.[71]

This nationalistic emphasis on primary education emerged from the fact that the great majority of schoolchildren in the city attended only the first year or two of school; in the words of a Spanish visitor, "the school conceived of itself as the center of education for patriotism; in it, with deliberate and persistent effort, is to be formed the spirit of the nation."[72] This same observer also concluded, "one can, with some exaggeration, reach the conclusion that the whole purpose of the school is to prepare the children for the May celebrations."[73]

Thus, at the same time that Argentine leaders were effectively excluding immigrants from political participation, they saw to it that all children born in the country became Argentines in spirit and attitude as well as in legal status. In these efforts, the authorities received considerable support from the city's social structure as well as from the cultural traits of the Argentine people.

On the economic front, however, Argentine leaders found little cause to intervene—either in the late-nineteenth-century flowering of the pampas or in the development of an export-oriented agricultural system. The very success of the city's dedication to commerce and bureaucracy discouraged any change in economic and financial arrangements, and no pressures emerged to stimulate industrialization, encourage import substitution, or prod merchants and landowners to invest in factories. While agriculture and commerce expanded rapidly, most industry remained scattered throughout the city in workshops that utilized the skills, tools, and small amounts of capital introduced by European craftsmen. Argentina's few large industrial establishments developed only in those areas that were related to agriculture and export—flour mills, meatpacking houses, and tanneries, as well as some plants that processed food for local consumption.

Argentine statesmen, economists, and businessmen all seem to have agreed that the country's future lay in the growth of its agriculture. Early in his second term President Roca, in his annual message to Congress, enunciated a basic philosophy of the national government:

> This country should make every effort to increase and improve the quantity, quality, and price of those products which already have ready acceptance in foreign markets; at the same time it must

abstain from protecting those ephemeral industries which are truly inferior and which can only damage the country's principal and basic industries—livestock and crop farming—that have such a great future ahead of them.[74]

Examples drawn from the area of tariff policy illustrate the prevalent attitude that exchange of agricultural products for imported manufactured goods was both good business and common sense.[75] After 1890 the otherwise reform-minded *La Prensa* assumed the stance that protection for industry was counterproductive to the country's interests and that Argentina's future lay in increasing its agricultural production and exports. Likewise, the first Socialist deputies in Congress feared that protectionism would drive up prices, and thus they voiced distrust of industry and opposition to tariffs. Porteños, especially gente decente, who were accustomed to the wide variety of European manufactured goods that could be purchased easily and cheaply, showed little inclination to pay added costs in order to stimulate and build up local industries. The guiding principle in tariff protection remained that which was expressed by Ponciano Vivano in the Chamber of Deputies in 1898:

> I accept the need to protect those major industries which all countries find necessary or desirable to develop in order to complement their independence or to protect themselves militarily; but under no condition can I accept that because we make nails we have to pay four or five times their value, or for a collar which should be bought for fifty centavos we are charged one peso.[76]

The chief purpose of tariff legislation throughout the nineteenth century was to secure revenues, not to provide protection. Customhouse receipts financed between 80 and 90 per cent of all government expenditures. Buenos Aires' position as the country's major port and principal customhouse had enabled the city and province to act as the center of government throughout the disturbed first half of the nineteenth century. Expenditures connected with the outbreak of the Paraguayan War in 1865 forced tariffs up to 18 per cent ad valorem on imports and 6 per cent on exports, and this rise was followed by further increases of 5 per cent and 2 per cent, respectively. In 1870, at the war's end, Congress established a basic 20 per cent levy on everything but alcoholic beverages and tobacco, which were taxed 25 per cent. Any protective features, however, were largely annulled by special categories of "10 per cent" and "free" for items judged useful and necessary to Argentina's economic development.

Because of the concern for revenues, the Congress patched together a series of tariff provisions late each session, in hot, humid December or January, when Congressmen were only too anxious to leave Buenos Aires. Most often, tariffs were levied on imports considered essential to or demanded by large portions of the population, especially food items. Since individual needs for such items remained relatively inelastic, the lower strata of society bore a share in financing national budgets totally out of proportion to their incomes. At the same time, whether or not the country had the necessary raw materials to manufacture or process its own consumer goods seemed irrelevant to legislators. Tariffs on flour, sugar, wine, crackers, beer, or shoes might accidentally include protective features. But equally high rates were assessed on items not produced in the country yet used in large quantities by gente de pueblo, such as coffee, kerosene, and olive oil. Even at the height of the depression in 1891, when the fall in the value of the paper peso meant that tariffs on food and other items heavily used by the common man reached levels of 100 and 200 per cent, Congress refused to reduce duties for fear of further unbalancing the budget.[77] A doubling of the duty on kerosene for 1898, although at first blocked by a tie vote in the Chamber of Deputies, finally received approval on the basis of fiscal need.[78] After another increase in tariff schedules in 1902, and despite stabilization of the peso, a special study revealed that the tax on petroleum products amounted to 100 per cent, on rice 75 per cent, on codfish 33 per cent, on olive oil 36 per cent, and on construction materials, such as nails and galvanized iron, 50 to 75 per cent.[79]

A few expressions in favor of protection of industry were made from time to time by newspapers, in business circles, and on the floor of Congress. In 1875 Carlos Pellegrini introduced the idea of protective tariffs into Congress for the first time. Save for proposals that would directly affect Argentina's agricultural production, such suggestions fell on deaf ears. Legislation supported the flour-milling industry as an adjunct of the country's increasing wheat production and levied a tax of approximately 40 per cent on imported flour.[80] In 1883, as a result of increased sugarcane production in Tucumán and improved railroad transportation to the northwest provinces, protection was extended to the coarser grades of sugar. Shortly thereafter, wines received similar protection—an acknowledgment of the importance of the vineyards in San Juan and Mendoza and the railroad links between these western provinces and Buenos Aires. In 1891, despite high food costs for the common man, Congress raised the tariff on rice in order to help Tucumán producers—a much needed barrier, since freight on a ton of rice from Tucumán to Buenos Aires amounted to forty pesos, while shipping a ton from Bremen to Buenos Aires cost only fifteen pesos.[81] Similar supports went to Argentina's struggling tobacco and *yerba mate* producers to protect them from the competition of imports from Paraguay. The intermittent and totally ineffectual protection extended to the cotton textile industry was justified primarily on the ground that it might promote the growing of cotton in Argentina.[82]

Frequent changes in rates and the absence of any policy beyond the search for revenues further frustrated inclinations toward industrialization. Characteristic were levies placed on exports of scrap iron, which affected the supply of several foundries in Buenos Aires. In 1891, for the first time, a five-peso tax per ton was imposed on exported scrap; the tariff rose to twenty-five pesos in 1893 and was removed completely in 1897; in 1898 it was restored at five pesos.[83] Similarly inconsistent tariff measures discouraged needed capital investment in such important fields as chemicals, metallurgy, and textiles, which produced by 1913 only 38 per cent, 33 per cent, and 23 per cent, respectively, of Argentina's needs.[84]

As the tariff patchwork became more complicated, the government authorities struggled unsuccessfully to establish some rationale beyond the immediate need for revenues. In 1894 a presidential commission sought to "rationalize" existing schedules, but its recommendations never won congressional approval. Increasingly, Congressmen showed themselves wary of tampering with the structure. In 1898 the subcommittee on tariffs, with a few minor changes, merely rubber-stamped the tariffs of the preceding year. In 1899 the subcommittee expressed regrets at its failure to undertake examination of commercial treaties or the complex revision proposed by one of its members; it gave as reasons the dangers of upsetting the fiscal system and becoming too involved in disputes between the commercial and industrial communities.[85] In bewildering succession, commissions from the Ministry of Finance in 1902, from Congress in 1903, from the Ministry of Interior in 1904, and from the President's office in 1905 attempted to work out the problems inherent in tariff legislation, and in 1907 and 1910 the executive submitted a specific proposal to tighten up the laws—all to no avail.

The attitude that industrialization was not good business during these years of rising exports and imports produced still other effects. Not only was technological education neglected in Buenos Aires, but inventiveness also received little encouragement or reward. The first patent law of 1864 afforded no protection. Congress never revised this law during the country's period of rapid growth, and in 1907 it buried a projected reform, suggested by the executive branch, in subcommittee.[86] Despite the innovativeness and creativity of thousands of small artisan shops and household industries, inquisitive minds received little official encouragement. In 1904 the patents registered in Argentina numbered one-third of those in Mexico—an underdeveloped country in Argentine eyes—and only 1 per cent of those in the United States.[87]

Industry and commerce struggled with similar flaws in the country's first trademark law, which dated from 1876. After repeatedly failing to revise the law's penalties and enforcement provisions, which stood as open invitations for evasion, Congress finally made some minor changes in 1900.[88] Pleas and projects from the executive branch brought no response; the statement made in 1910 that "among us, industry today totally lacks legal protection" summarized the painful truth.[89] The handicaps that local technology struggled under received acknowledgment in a proposal, from the executive branch to Congress in 1913, that prizes be awarded annually by the Ministry of Education for the best published works in science and literature. The preface to this proposal read: "It is a well-known fact that intellectual productivity does not keep pace with our national development, creating a striking contrast to the economic growth and prosperity which has reached truly amazing proportions."[90]

The city's social structure, along with its cultural values, did provide elements of stability in an otherwise rapidly changing environment. These elements well complemented world economic conditions, which fostered Argentina's agriculture and the city's commerce. The social structure proved adaptable to the city's physical growth and the country's economic expansion. Although a man's position strongly depended on his family background, education, occupation, and income, he did have opportunities to move up or down the social ladder. While conformity and continuity remained important features of upper-class values, there was no rigid caste system preventing the incorporation of new talents. Economic expansion meanwhile encouraged the creation of increasing numbers of non-elite strata, along with differentiation between levels that further satisfied desires for social mobility.

The Argentine culture, derived in large measure from the Spanish, and reformulated in the local environment through the influence of massive Italian and Spanish immigration, served to bring further stability to porteño society. The disdain for manual labor, the respect of humanistic education, and the exalted position of the family helped to maintain elitist control of politics, finance, and education. At the same time, the emphasis on qualities of personalism, virility, and cleverness permitted considerable self-expression and individuality, while the new spirit of materialism significantly expanded the range of differences between social strata and emphasized the outward manifestations of wealth and progress.

None of these structures or values encouraged Argentines or porteños to make any major changes in their economy or the society. Immigrants were welcome to develop the country economically, but not to participate in its political evolution. The upper class supervised the educational system, both to ensure elitist direction of society and to propagate values of nationalism and conformity. And the success of the country's agriculture and commerce inhibited any tendency to diversify or industrialize the economy.

In such surroundings, important human resources lay dormant until trade conditions forced a readjustment in patterns of development. World depression and World War II finally exposed the shortcomings in the city's orientation. What had been common sense and good business in 1910 proved disastrous after 1930. It was then that the city and the nation turned toward a new period of change from which neither has yet emerged.

✻7✻

The Commercial-Bureaucratic City

The particular experiences of Buenos Aires during its period of most rapid demographic growth and physical expansion stimulate comparisons and contrasts with other urban centers. Buenos Aires developed as the nation's primate city, providing commercial and administrative services to an expanding agricultural economy. Argentina possessed rich agricultural potential, but lacked industries, capital, and a labor force adequate for self-sustaining growth. Europe possessed the industrial goods, the human and financial resources, and the need for food supplies to stimulate Argentina's initial spurt of economic growth. In the long run, however, Argentina's economic prosperity came to depend heavily on external supplies of labor and capital as well as on external markets for her agricultural products, an unhealthy state of dependency.

These conditions of agricultural production and external dependency, taken within the context of exploitation of the Argentine pampas in the late nineteenth century, spawned the type of urban growth that is characterized as "commercial-bureaucratic," in which urban economic activity remains concentrated in commerce and government or in closely related, subordinated fields.[1] In Buenos Aires, the commercial-bureaucratic orientation tended to accentuate certain ecological and social patterns:

1. Social and residential focus of the elite within a small downtown core;
2. Settlement of immigrant manual laborers in downtown slums, close to employment;
3. Geographical mobility of acculturated blue-collar and white-collar groups, who moved toward the outskirts in search of the security of landownership;
4. Vitality of local neighborhoods as the social and economic foci for non-elite groups;
5. Small, closely knit upper class dominating other dependent strata which were differentiated by family, education, occupation, and income;
6. Continuity and stability in education, society, and economy, fostered within the Argentine environment by a culture with Spanish roots reinforced by heavy European immigration.

Once these patterns developed, they tended to reinforce the commercial-bureaucratic orientation of the city, as well as its political and economic hold over the hinterland. In the Argentine context, at least, the strength of the commercial-bureaucratic factor added to the difficulties that the city and the country experienced in breaking out of the web of dependency and advancing into an industrialized economy. Only further inquiry and investigation can answer in what fashion these patterns may evolve or how they may reappear in other urban situations.

During the years from 1870 to 1910, the city's and the nation's upper class remained part of the downtown core. Many, however, moved from the vicinity immediately south of the Plaza de Mayo to an area several blocks north of the plaza. This move took place because of the incorporation of new members and because of changing architectural styles which stressed exuberance, outward display, and more floor space than the enclosed one-story edifice built around interior patios. The financial and social center for the upper class also remained centered just north of the plaza, in the small area of 100 blocks that even in the 1970s constitutes the central business district of the city.

In part, this focus on the center sprang from the Spanish tradition that placed those with wealth and power close to the principal plaza. But it received significant reinforcement from the commercial-bureaucratic orientation in which the management of merchandising, finance, and government lends itself to centralization. Furthermore, the small, compact upper class enjoyed conveniences and close contacts by having its places of work, residence, and play in the same location. Interrelationships fostered by proximity, frequent contacts, and common focus in turn encouraged the continued emphasis of commercial-bureaucratic activities by this class and perpetuated the pattern of residential, occupational, and social emphasis on the downtown core.

Newly arrived laborers likewise congregated in the downtown area. Deterioration of residences once occupied by the upper class afforded crowded but cheap housing for the massive immigration of manual laborers from Europe. This tendency to congregate at the city's center enabled the newcomer to adapt gradually to new surroundings while, by joining with other recent arrivals, he maintained the security of familiar language, compatriots, and environment. The commercial-bureaucratic orientation, with its emphasis on transportation and construction, also required large supplies of manual laborers at the city's center. Newcomers most frequently qualified for precisely these unskilled or semiskilled jobs, and they saved money and time by living in tenements within walking distance of work. The demand for manual labor encouraged a steady stream of new immigrants and, occasionally, migrants. The very ease by which this labor pool could be replenished tended, however, to continue Argentina's reliance on manual labor as well as its dependence on outside sources for labor.

The recently arrived immigrant might have no alternative to taking unskilled manual labor and living in a tenement residence at the core, while, obviously, the upper class enjoyed substantial advantages from its focus on the city's center. But the mass of the porteño population sought to move outward from the center. The blue-collar and white-collar workers—63 to 73 per cent of the total employed male population—sought security and upward mobility in individual house lots and homes. The search for better living conditions, cheaper land, and lower rents—all made possible by the development of the streetcar system—rapidly pushed this group toward the outskirts.

The predominance given commerce and bureaucracy discouraged the spread of large-scale industrialization beyond that related to the country's agricultural production. At the same time, the commercial-bureaucratic focus permitted considerable individual initiative and mobility among such diverse groups as shopkeepers, butchers, mechanics, carpenters, clerks, and office workers. The outward spread thus absorbed the energies of the working population while satisfying their desires for security and mobility. Dispersed population also generated an increasing employment in merchandising, construction, and services which further confirmed the commercial-bureaucratic orientation.

This heterogeneous, sprawling settlement made the local neighborhood the logical focus for psychological, social, and economic attachments. The neighborhood frequently served as the place of work and recreation as well as the residence of the common man. In addition, it provided a sense of belonging through the village atmosphere of small shops, stores, and homes. Just as the recently arrived immigrants turned to the conventillo, and the wealthy to the environs of the Plaza de Mayo, for familiar and reassuring contacts, so most other porteños relied on the barrio or cuadra to give form to their lives. By successfully protecting its inhabitants from the metropolis, and by providing attachments, amusements, and amenities in tiny units scattered throughout the city, the local neighborhoods helped postpone the integration of many porteños into a citywide economy and society. It also helped perpetuate their reliance on the small retail outlets, artisan shops, and home industries.

Commerce and bureaucracy fostered development of a small upper class closely interrelated by family ties. This class had a near monopoly on higher education, and it dominated the managerial and professional occupations. Below it ranged numerous strata which were differentiated by family background, opportunities for training and using skills, occupational standing, and property and income levels. The people in each stratum tended to imitate and aspire to the status of those immediately above them. Some degree of mobility existed, and the upper class occasionally recruited new members from white-collar groups on the basis of education and ability. Since recent arrivals had less opportunity for advancement, the proportion of foreign-born increased as one descended

the social scale; in 1914 only 19 per cent of the upper class, as contrasted with 86 per cent of the unskilled manual laborers, were foreign-born. Because of the importance of family origins, the self-
made man remained unknown in Buenos Aires, and any climb
upward required several generations. Limited upward mobility and
extensive stratification helped, however, to postpone or avoid class
alignments or social conflicts and, along with the self-interest of the
gente decente, contributed to the perpetuation of a stable social
structure linked to bureaucracy and commerce.

The cultural themes involved in porteño development evolved
largely from the Iberian heritage and received subsequent reinforcement from massive Spanish and Italian immigration. These,
along with the city's commercial-bureaucratic emphasis, created a
society which held manual labor in contempt and accorded prestige to humanistic training, emphasized the central role of the family and the importance of the individual, and admired both virility
and roguishness. At the same time, new concerns with materialism
and progress helped stimulate ostentation among the wealthy and
efforts at economic advancement among the rest of the population.

These various cultural attributes also served to accentuate continuity and stability. Foreign technology and ideas fostered material progress, not structural change of the society or economy.
Immigrants contributed labor, but they remained outside of the
political structure. Primary education instilled nationalism—along
with support for the existing system. Economic policy did nothing
to stimulate industrialization or alter Argentine dependence on foreign capital. The city's culture thus reinforced the commercial-
bureaucratic orientation precisely because that orientation was so
successful.

Argentina enjoyed a Cinderella success during the late nineteenth and early twentieth centuries. But the productivity of the
pampas redounded to porteño benefit, not to the growth of the
hinterland. Indeed, economic prosperity, combined with the success of the commercial-bureaucratic orientation, helped ensure that
Argentina remain locked into agricultural production and dependence on Europe.

This system, which had developed out of an agricultural economy, was self-reinforcing, not self-sustaining. Agricultural profits encouraged railroad building and port works. Railroads advanced the frontiers of cultivation and stock raising. Commercial growth stimulated urban construction. And city expansion furthered immigration. But the system depended almost entirely on external factors: on world demands for agricultural products and on constant supplies of foreign capital and labor. Few of the multiplier effects of mercantile and industrial growth experienced in Great Britain and the United States operated effectively in Buenos Aires.[2] Labor and land, rather than capital, expanded production. Local capital, which might have been available for investment in industries or in activities that in turn would generate demands and stimulate further investment, was drained away in luxury consumption of imports by the upper classes, in savings sent by the immigrants to their families in Europe, and in the purchase of urban real estate.[3] Further, a large percentage of the labor force in Buenos Aires remained in the tertiary, or service, sector, where its contribution was limited by low productivity and underemployment.

Despite attempts at state planning, subsidization of industry, and regional diversification which have been made since 1930, the commercial-bureaucratic heritage has proved hard to overcome. The city of Buenos Aires still shows its effects. Settlement patterns in the Federal District have not changed much since 1910. The central business district provides commercial, financial, administrative, cultural, and amusement services for the upper and upper-middle classes in the same small area. Conventillos survive downtown, while shanty towns, or *villas miserias,* ring the outskirts. Increasingly, the wealthy have moved out to the northern riverbank beyond the Federal District, although many still cluster in Barrio Norte. Industry has concentrated on the south side and beyond the Federal District to the west and south, but small plants and workshops remain scattered throughout the city, even close to the Plaza de Mayo. The barrio has lost considerable psychological and economic significance, since work, school, and play now push the inhabitants outward; but for several million porteños it still serves as the basic framework for their daily life. The city, with its overwhelming commercial, administrative, and now industrial dominance, has drawn talents, resources, and products to itself. This success has exacted a price in strained railroads and congested port facilities. The head continued to rest on an extended but under-developed body, while new economic zones or other urban areas appeared slowly or assumed secondary roles. Even industry, which since 1930 has been accepted as one of Argentina's needs, has re-ceived limited inputs of capital and technology. Despite the growth of Buenos Aires as a metropolis, the city's social structure and mores have changed slowly. Many blue-collar and white-collar workers have emerged to form important parts of a middle class. But this class lacks unity or direction, and its members continue to imitate the upper class. Meanwhile, the political authorities fear the lower classes and seek through repression to stifle their new de-mands and appetites. Attitudes toward manual labor, social distinc-tions, and materialism recall those of the late nineteenth century, while social and educational patterns reflect much of the values of an earlier age.

The Buenos Aires experience, springing out of the country's ag-ricultural economy and external dependence, has been repeated in other Argentine cities to a marked degree. In the late nineteenth century, the population began to move from the countryside to-ward the towns and cities. The urban-rural ratio (based on 2000 as the smallest urban unit) changed from 25:75 per cent in 1869 to 53:47 per cent by 1914. Whether the cities were port centers, such as Rosario or Bahía Blanca (population 223,000 and 44,000, respec-tively), provincial capitals turned railroad terminuses, such as Cór-doba, Tucumán, or Mendoza (135,000, 91,000, and 59,000), ad-ministrative capitals and provincial trade centers, such as Salta or Catamarca (28,000 and 13,000), or small rail and local trade cen-ters, such as Río Cuarto or Junín (30,000 and 21,000)—they all by 1914 shared strikingly similar demographic, physical, and ecologi-cal patterns. Each city received migrants and raw materials from its immediate area and transmitted them, along with capital, toward the coast, primarily toward Buenos Aires. Each had its small elite of landowners, merchants, bureaucrats, and professionals. In each the residences and activities of the elite centered on the plaza, while non-elite groups spread outward in search of cheaper lands. The commercial-bureaucratic system dominated the secondary cities and made them way stations for channeling goods, services, mi-grants, and capital toward Buenos Aires.

The timing and, indeed, the initial prosperity of Buenos Aires' rapid growth from 1870 to 1910 contributed to the problems that the nation faces today. Buenos Aires entered the twentieth century as a cosmopolitan metropolis, already drawing resources from the provinces and benefits from its position between the pampas and Europe. The city's monopoly of human resources, its social structure, and its lack of an industrial base owed much to the way the Argentine economy had developed around the exploitation of the pampas. Economic success available to the upper classes, and, in more limited fashion, to the common man, brought an air of complacency that hung over Buenos Aires for several decades.

The promise of continued expansion that porteño growth had forecast began to dissipate, however, by 1930. A static per capita gross national product, a sterile political conflict, and the people's apparent loss of faith in their future exposed the handicaps of agricultural production and external dependency for the nation and of commercial-bureaucratic orientation for the cities. The nation as a whole had not received an adequate share of the gains from the spectacular growth of its cities, especially from that of its capital and principal port. That city's orientation during its late-nineteenth-century period of rapid expansion had left Argentina ill-prepared for changing patterns of world trade, for industrialization, or for popular rule.[4]

The commercial-bureaucratic urban growth of Buenos Aires poses a number of questions for comparative study.[5] Under what conditions does agricultural productivity, combined with dependence on foreign markets, external capital, and immigration, generate self-sustaining growth or self-perpetuating dependency? What other types of urban growth can be associated with agricultural production and economic dependency? What ecological and social patterns emerge within cities that have grown rapidly by dominating, commercially and politically, a rich agricultural hinterland? How do these patterns differ from or resemble those found in cities that have evolved through other functions or in other cultural milieus?

In the Argentine experience, the features of agricultural production and external dependency and the commercial-bureaucratic orientation appear closely related. Furthermore, the commercial-bureaucratic orientation apparently encouraged certain patterns of urban development which in turn supported the porteños' continued dedication to commerce and bureaucracy. To what degree these relationships can be established as causal, and what validity may be given to the commercial-bureaucratic characteristic as a type of urban growth are questions that provide challenges to comparative urban research. The evidence may reveal interesting aspects of dependency and urban development within developing nations. The present book must limit itself, however, to suggesting that such relationships do exist, and advancing the commercial-bureaucratic city as the type of urban experience which resulted from patterns of growth at Buenos Aires from 1870 to 1910.

Statistical Tables

For the convenience of those interested in measuring urban and economic change, certain quantifiable aspects of the city's development have been collected in the following appendix. References to these tables appear at appropriate places in the text itself. Map 3, p. 20, and note 1 of Chapter 4 will assist the reader in locating census districts or areas used in tables 1, 2, 4, 5, and 13.

Table 1. Ethnic composition of the Federal District by Census Districts, 1909.

District and Name	Total Pop. (in 000s)	Arg.	Ital.	Span.	Fr.	Russ.	Amer.	Other
Federal District as a whole	1,232	54.5	22.5	14.2	2.1	1.1	2.9	2.7
1. Vélez Sársfield	48	58.6	21.7	12.1	1.5	0.8	3.1	2.2
2. San Cristóbal Sud	54	58.3	20.8	15.1	1.1	0.4	2.8	1.5
3. Santa Lucía	95	52.9	19.3	19.2	2.1	0.4	2.9	3.2
4. San Juan Evangelista	65	53.8	31.1	8.3	0.7	0.6	2.6	2.9
5. Flores	47	64.8	15.8	12.2	1.8	0.5	3.1	1.8
6. San Carlos Sud	61	60.2	23.9	10.1	1.6	0.1	3.0	1.1
7. San Carlos Norte	51	58.9	24.7	9.8	1.9	0.6	2.9	1.2
8. San Cristóbal Norte	78	56.5	27.1	10.6	1.2	0.4	2.9	1.3
9. Balvanera Oeste	73	52.0	25.6	13.3	1.9	3.0	2.8	1.4
10. Balvanera Sud	46	53.0	29.1	11.8	1.5	1.3	2.2	1.1
11. Balvanera Norte	39	49.7	19.4	11.4	2.4	11.0	2.6	3.5
12. Concepción	68	50.4	18.2	24.1	1.7	0.3	3.2	2.1
13. Monserrat	68	49.1	9.6	32.4	3.1	0.3	3.0	2.5
14. San Nicolás	57	39.0	19.1	23.4	6.2	3.2	3.2	5.9
15. San Bernardo	48	55.0	28.2	9.2	1.5	1.0	2.9	2.2
16. Belgrano	52	56.9	21.3	10.7	2.5	0.6	3.7	4.3
17. Palermo	49	60.0	24.7	7.9	1.4	0.3	2.6	3.1
18. Las Heras	103	59.5	25.7	7.7	1.5	0.4	2.6	2.6
19. Pilar	75	57.5	23.4	11.3	2.2	0.7	2.9	2.0
20. Socorro	46	47.4	18.4	19.6	4.9	0.5	2.9	6.3
Riverine incl. Martín García	9	17.1	29.3	11.2	0.4	0.1	0.4	41.5

Source: Censo general de población, edificación, comercio e industrias de la ciudad de Buenos Aires . . . de 1909, I, 3-17.

Table 2. Total housing by census districts, with percentage of houses with three rooms or less, 1904, 1909, 1914.

	1904		1909		1914	
	No.	% less	No.	% less	No.	% less
District and Name	Houses	4 rms.	Houses	4 rms.	Houses	4 rms.
Federal District						
as a whole	82,540	39.0	111,135	20.0	131,742	32.8
1. Vélez Sársfield	2,463	70.0	7,594	59.8	13,868	67.3
2. San Cristóbal Sud	3,736	61.0	4,913	21.2*	5,354	40.2
3. Santa Lucía	6,271	33.1	6,926	25.2	6,501	21.7
4. San Juan						
Evangelista	3,241	26.9	3,592	12.2	3,710	11.7
5. Flores	3,539	47.7	6,850	35.1	9,871	39.8
6. San Carlos Sud	4,138	60.5	6,398	8.5*	6,994	27.9
7. San Carlos Norte	3,879	53.1	5,489	31.7	6,156	29.0
8. San Cristóbal						
Norte	5,460	28.5	5,979	14.4	5,298	13.4
9. Balvanera Oeste	5,020	38.7	5,463	11.4	5,220	11.3
10. Balvanera Sud	2,618	19.9	2,245	15.2	2,416	9.2
11. Balvanera Norte	2,716	15.2	2,933	21.9	2,545	6.8
12. Concepción	4,177	15.8	4,404	4.4	3,920	8.0
13. Monserrat	4,307	13.0	3,960	3.0	3,313	5.7
14. San Nicolás	4,133	13.7	4,288	2.5	3,750	7.3
15. San Bernardo	2,319	78.9	7,099	11.9*	13,312	60.3
16. Belgrano	4,886	55.0	7,972	16.5*	12,137	46.5
17. Palermo	2,903	66.2	6,014	22.3	8,206	34.2
18. Las Heras	7,276	57.4	9,012	20.4	10,121	24.5
19. Pilar	6,086	27.5	6,613	10.3	6,164	9.7
20. Socorro	3,372	12.1	3,391	12.2	2,886	4.9

* Although all entries for housing in 1909 show a considerable discrepancy from 1904 and 1914, these particular entries appear to contain substantial error.
Sources: Censo general . . . de la ciudad de Buenos Aires . . . de 1904, pp. 105, 109; *Censo general . . . de la ciudad de Buenos Aires . . . de 1909*, I, 171, 173; *Tercer censo nacional . . . 1914*, X, 485-95.

Table 3. Control of the Argentine railroad system by major British companies, 1910.

Railroad	% Length of track	% Loco- motives	% Pas- sengers	% Total freight	% Total employees	% Total capital	% Total revenues	% Net revenues
Southern	18.0	17.7	34.1	20.6	20.6	19.9	21.5	24.4
Central Argentine	15.4	18.6	27.6	21.8	25.0	17.9	24.1	24.2
Western	8.5	10.2	13.8	10.3	9.3	10.8	10.7	11.9
Buenos Aires Pacific	8.6	14.8	8.9	9.4	9.1	12.2	12.9	15.1
Total of "Big Four"	50.5	61.3	84.4	62.1	64.0	60.8	69.2	75.6
N = Total for all railroads	27,713 km	3,079	59,850,000	33,074,000	111,161	1,100*	111.4*	45.5*

* Million gold pesos.
Sources: Tercer censo nacional . . . 1914, X, 408–19.

Table 4. Population and buildings in the Central City, 1869, 1887, 1895, 1904, 1909, 1914.
(Districts 1–6 in 1869, 1887, and 1895; Districts 13–14 in 1904, 1909, and 1914)

Year	Total population	% City's total population	Total foreign-born	% Foreign-born in city	% Foreign-born in Central City	Foreign-born in Central City as % of total foreign-born	Total bldgs.	% City's total bldgs.	Bldgs. over 2 stories	% City's bldgs. over 2 stories
1869	83,460	46.9	43,548	49.6	52.2	49.4	8058	41.2	162	89.5
1887	108,326	25.0	64,578	52.8	59.6	29.2	6938	20.5	352	74.6
1895	110,676	16.7	65,872	52.0	59.5	18.5	6937	12.7	567	62.2
1904	129,722	13.6	71,500	45.0	55.1	16.7	8440	10.2	867	63.7
1909	125,671	10.2	69,772	45.6	55.5	12.4	8248	7.4	1535	47.2
1914	137,662	8.7	87,659	49.4	63.7	11.3	7063	5.4	1678	31.2

Sources: Primer censo nacional, 1869, pp. 46, 80–81; *Censo general . . . de la ciudad de Buenos Aires . . . de 1887,* II, 32–33, 109; *Segundo censo nacional, 1895,* II, 6, and III, 3; *Censo general . . . de la ciudad de Buenos Aires . . . de 1904,* pp. 4–6, 105, 107; *Censo general . . . de la ciudad de Buenos Aires . . . de 1909,* I, 11–12, 17, 171–7; *Tercer censo nacional, 1914,* II, 3, and X, 485.

Table 5. Conventillos in the Central City, 1887 and 1904.

	Total no. conventillos	% Total conventillos	No. inhabi-tants in conventillos	% Total pop. Central City	% Total conventillo pop.
1887 (Districts 1–6)	877	30.9	35,227	32.5	30.3
1904 (Districts 13–14)	647	26.3	34,790	26.8	25.2

Sources: Censo general . . . de la ciudad de Buenos Aires . . . de 1887, II, 30; *Censo general . . . de la ciudad de Buenos Aires . . . de 1904*, pp. 6, 125.

Table 6. Total and foreign-born employed population in selected occupations, 1869, 1895, and 1914.

Occupations	1869 [177,787; 1]*		1895 [663,854; 3.7]*			1914 [1,575,814; 8.7]*		
	Total employed	% Total employed	Total employed	% Total employed	% Foreign-born	Total employed	% Total employed	% Foreign-born
All occupations	98,723	100.0	305,124	100.0	72.3	792,361	100.0	64.7
Masons, albañiles	3258	3.3	11,304	3.7	89.8	25,986	3.3	84.9
Carpenters, carpinteros	3061	3.1	9444	3.1	86.8	17,370	2.2	81.0
Painters, pintores	804	0.8	4286	1.4	79.8	10,808	1.4	59.8
Seamstresses, costureras, modistas	7291	7.4	18,241	6.0	60.2	38,445	4.9	50.7
Tailors, sastres	1127	1.1	4626	1.5	92.9	12,347	1.6	87.4
Shoemakers, zapateros	2945	3.0	10,418	3.4	89.5	13,905	1.8	76.3
Blacksmiths, herreros	1301	1.3	4195	1.4	85.8	10,204	1.3	66.0
Butchers, carniceros	653	0.7	1945	0.6	74.0	3498	0.4	53.3
Bakers, panaderos	1198	1.2	3374	1.1	89.1	6107	0.8	88.5
Mechanics, mecánicos, maquinistas	342	0.3	4387	1.4	84.4	13,712	1.7	66.9
Servants, domésticos, mucamos, sirvientes, cocineros, niñeras	13,769	13.9	32,140	10.5	66.5	88,227	11.1	66.3
Washerwomen, lavanderas, planchadoras	5744	5.8	10,542	3.5	65.9	14,427	1.8	64.5
Cartmen, carreros	2214	2.2	5530	1.8	76.1	6443	0.8	73.0
Day laborers, peones, jornaleros	10,200	10.3	28,463	9.3	86.5	82,506	10.4	90.8

* Total population, followed by ratio to 1869 population. Note that 1869 census does not record foreign-born employees as a separate category.
Sources: Primer censo nacional, 1869, pp. 64–75; Segundo censo nacional, 1895, II, 47–50; Tercer censo nacional, 1914, IV, 201–12.

Table 7. Daily wages for day laborers and skilled construction workers in gold pesos, 1870–1910.

Year	Day laborer	Skilled construction worker	Source
1871	1.20	4.00	(4)
1873	0.75–1.00	2.50	(8)
1880	0.75	1.50	(3)
1885	1.00	1.90–2.10	(3)
1890–91	0.60	1.20	(1), (2), (3)
1892	0.30–0.50	0.75–1.00	(1), (10)
1894		0.90	(1)
1896	0.50–0.60	1.10–1.20	(1)
1897	0.50	0.85–1.00	(5)
1901	0.55	1.10–1.50	(6)
1907	1.00–1.50	2.00–2.50	(7)
1909	1.00–1.40	2.00–3.50	(7)
1910	1.20–1.50	2.10–2.70	(7), (9)

Note: Equivalents of paper currency to the gold peso calculated from values, "Cotización del oro," *Tercer censo nacional, 1914,* X, 395–96.

Sources:

1. William I. Buchanan, "La moneda y la vida en la República Argentina," *Revista de Derecho, Historia y Letras,* I, 2, Dec. 1898, pp. 211–13.
2. "Report on Immigration," by Herbert, July 4, 1891, attached to Pakenham to Salisbury, July 21, 1891, FO 6, Vol. 418, No. 30.
3. Jacinto Oddone, *Historia del socialismo argentino* (2 vols., Buenos Aires, 1934), I, 75–78.
4. Phipps, "Report on the Condition of the Industrial Classes," attached to Macdonnell to Granville, July 15, 1871, FO 6, Vol. 304, No. 79.
5. Adrián Patroni, *Los trabajadores en la Argentina* (Buenos Aires, 1898), pp. 113–14.
6. "Los obreros y el trabajo," *La Prensa,* series of forty articles, Aug. to Nov. 1901.
7. "Condiciones del trabajo en la ciudad de Buenos Aires," *Boletín del Departamento Nacional del Trabajo,* 1907, No. 3, 319–44, 347–59; 1909, No. 10, 326–51, No. 11, 476–502; 1910, No. 12, 5–22, No. 14, 528–31.
8. St. John to Granville, March 6, 1873, FO 6, Vol. 314, No. 5.
9. F. Stach, "Estudio sobre salarios y horarios de los obreros y empleados en los diferentes trabajos de la Capital Federal y en el resto de la República Argentina," *Boletín del Museo Social Argentino,* 1913, III, 44–49, 193–200.
10. M. F. Wodon, *Les états de la Plata au point de vue de l'emigration et de la colonisation* (Paris, 1892), pp. 116–27.

Table 8. Ethnic and occupational composition of conventillos in Census District 1, 1869.

Address	Total population	Adults 14+	Foreign-born adults	Argentine-born adults	Children 13−	Argentine-born children	% Predominant ethnic group of adult population	Employed males	Blue-collar, White-collar	Unskilled manual labor	Employed females
Corrientes 68	162	132	128	4	30	?	37.9 French	108	61	47	7
25 de Mayo 262	60	40	28	12	20	18	37.5 Spanish	22	3	19	14
Córdoba 16	62	33	22	11	29	25	63.6 Italian	16	6	10	15
Tucumán 17	56	38	36	2	18	?	86.8 Italian	21	2	19	6
25 de Mayo 19	75	54	47	7	21	15	44.4 Italian	30	16	14	9
Tucumán 26	109	53	51	2	56	44	54.7 Italian	28	16	12	17
San Martín 256/58	81	53	52	1	28	26	92.5 Italian	22	11	11	27
Temple 46	102	77	74	3	25	23	72.7 Italian	27	15	12	16
Totals	707	480	438	42	227	?		274	130	144	111

Sources: Archivo General de la Nación, Censo Nacional de 1869, Ciudad de Buenos Aires, 1ª Sección, Tomo 1º, Ciriaco Cuitiño; Tomo 2º, Jorge María Bouquet, Eulogio N. Bustos, Florencio B. Mármol, Juan Castañeda; Tomo 3º, Ángel Gregorio Carranza.

Table 9. Number, rooms, inhabitants, and rents of conventillos, 1870–1910.

Year	Number of conventillos	No. inhabitants	No. rooms	Monthly rental, gold pesos
1871[1,2]	700–800	10,500–14,000		4–8
1877[3]	1779			
1878[4]	1770	51,915	24,023	
1880[5,6]	1800–2100	55,337		
1882[7]	2074			
1883[7,8]	1870	64,600–65,400	25,645	
1885[1]				7–9
1887[9]	2835	116,167		
1890[1,10]	2249	94,723	37,603	8–10
1892[11]	1963			
1893[12]	1689			
1901[13]				8–10
1904[14]	2462	138,188	43,873	
1905[13]				9–11
1907[13,15]	2500	150,000		
1911[16]				12–14

Sources:
1. *La Prensa*, Sept. 8, 1901, p. 4.
2. *La Prensa*, Feb. 2, 1871, p. 1.
3. *Memoria de la Municipalidad*, 1877, I, 143–5.
4. *Memoria de la Municipalidad*, 1879, I, 27.
5. *Memoria de la Municipalidad*, 1880, pp. 120–26.
6. *La Prensa*, Aug. 5, 1880, p. 2.
7. *Memoria de la Municipalidad*, 1883, pp. 402–6.
8. *La Prensa*, Nov. 18, 1883, p. 1.
9. *Censo general . . . de la ciudad de Buenos Aires . . . de 1887*, II, 30.
10. *Anuario estadístico de la ciudad de Buenos Aires*, 1891, pp. 433–43.
11. *Memoria de la Municipalidad*, 1890–92, pp. 361–62.
12. *Memoria de la Municipalidad*, 1893–94, pp. 716–27.
13. *Boletín del Departamento Nacional del Trabajo*, 1907, No. 3, p. 479.
14. *Censo general . . . de la ciudad de Buenos Aires . . . de 1904*, pp. 128, 132.
15. Spalding, Jr., "Cuando los inquilinos hacen huelga . . . ," p. 38.
16. *Boletín del Departamento Nacional del Trabajo*, 1912, No. 21, pp. 452–53.

Table 10. Streetcar companies, with number of trips and passengers carried, 1873, 1874, 1877, 1882.

	1873		1874		1877		1882	
Company	Trips	Passen-gers	Trips	Passen-gers	Trips	Passen-gers	Trips	Passen-gers
Ciudad de Buenos Aires	179,637	5,161,074	265,075	5,855,536	265,865	5,512,576	318,057	7,480,279
Anglo-Argen-tine							213,941	3,608,938
Central Argentino	54,716* 60,491	1,807,570* 2,221,041	64,846 58,910	2,072,303 1,470,177	74,440 79,732	1,583,623 1,491,581	111,292 (becomes Anglo-Argentine)	4,003,561
A Belgrano Nacional	37,302† 65,879	770,444† 1,146,607	85,642 86,642	1,747,661 1,476,999	87,268 105,832	1,396,260 1,513,919	98,722 (becomes Anglo-Argentine)	1,892,145
Boca y Barracas	39,745*	1,043,926*	48,783	901,259	49,404	877,107	42,721	1,261,467

* Figures for April to December.
† Figures for June to December.
Sources: *Registro estadístico de la provincia de Buenos Aires*, 1873, pp. 323–24, 1874, pp. 345–46, 1877, pp. 388–89.
Memoria del presidente de la comisión municipal . . . *1882*, pp. 562–63.

Table 11. Streetcars: mileage, number of trips, and passengers carried,
1873–1910.

Year	Mileage	Total No. of trips, in 000s	Total No. passengers, in 000s
1873	13	438	12,151
1874	16	610	13,504
1875	—	620	13,744
1876	—	649	12,663
1877	—	653	10,979
1878	—	670	12,668
1879	—	621	10,996
1880	—	—	13,618
1881	—	—	15,161
1882	93	779	18,446
1883	93	793	20,057
1884	94	827	22,832
1885	94	885	27,236
1886	83	980	30,922
1887	94	1006	36,228
1888	133	1123	41,627
1889	123	1325	49,013
1890	155	1672	56,141
1891	173	1739	57,799
1892	179	1793	67,161
1893	200	1979	73,906
1894	222	2024	76,994
1895	239	2216	84,992
1896	237	2588	92,080
1897	240	2823	100,062
1898	246	3212	105,965
1899*	278	3634	116,448
1900	281	3738	122,887
1901	282	3814	125,525
1902	295	3840	126,232
1903	303	3779	133,719
1904	315	3944	148,279
1905	302	4069	168,942
1906	298	4645	200,700
1907	344	4372	225,041
1908	473	4700	255,074
1909	403	4760	281,712
1910	405	5017	323,791

* Beginning in 1899, electric-powered streetcars were included.
Sources: Anuario estadístico de la Ciudad de Buenos Aires, 1891, pp. 228–29, for
1873–91. Thereafter taken from appropriate section of the annual publication,
Anuario estadístico de la Ciudad de Buenos Aires, 1892 to 1911.

Table 12. Percentages of passenger traffic carried by electric and horse-drawn streetcars, Buenos Aires, 1899–1907.

Company	1899 Horse	1899 Electric	1900 Horse	1900 Electric	1901 Horse	1901 Electric	1902 Horse	1902 Electric	1903 Horse	1903 Electric	1904 Horse	1904 Electric	1905 Horse	1905 Electric	1906 Horse	1906 Electric	1907 Horse	1907 Electric
Ciudad de Buenos Aires	29	—	27	—	27		26		22		20		(absorbed by Anglo-Argentine)					
Anglo-Argentine	25	—	23	—	21		19	3	4	22		30	14	34	3	43	—	46
Buenos Aires y Belgrano	5	4	2	8		11		11		11		11		10		9		9
Lacroze	5	—	6	—	7		7		7		7		7		7		3	5
Gran Nacional	13	8	14	—	14		14		14		13		10	4	2	15	—	18
Capital	1	—	—	10		12		12		12		11		10		11	—	10
Nueva	6	—	5	—	3		4		3		3		1		(absorbed by Gran Nacional)		
Metropolitano	4		4		4		3		3		1	2		6		6		5
Tramway Eléctricos de Buenos Aires	—			1		1		1		2		2		4		4		4
Total % Horse-drawn	88		81		76		73		53		44		32		12		3	
Total % Electric		12		19		24		27		47		56		68		88		97
N = millions of passengers	116.4		122.9		125.6		126.2		133.7		148.3		168.9		200.7		225.0	

Source: Anuario estadístico de la Ciudad de Buenos Aires, 1899–1907.

Table 13. Average price per square meter in land sales by census districts in the Federal District, 1904–1914 (in pesos moneda nacional).

District and Name	1904	1906	1908	1910	1912	1914	Factor of Increase, 1904 to 1912
1. Vélez Sársfield	1.3	1.6	1.8	5.4	9.8	10.5	7.5
2. San Cristóbal Sud	8.1	7.3	12.1	25.8	21.1	17.2	2.6
3. Santa Lucía	14.8	35.2	52.7	55.8	99.1	85.5	6.7
4. San Juan Evangelista	23.4	40.6	39.4	51.3	73.6	48.9	3.1
5. Flores	3.9	5.0	13.3	23.9	40.0	39.6	10.6
6. San Carlos Sud	9.1	9.3	23.8	39.9	63.9	65.0	7.0
7. San Carlos Norte	11.9	21.8	27.0	43.6	69.7	65.7	5.9
8. San Cristóbal Norte	29.8	34.4	47.2	82.6	103.8	76.8	3.5
9. Balvanera Oeste	29.4	31.8	75.4	111.5	123.2	117.0	4.2
10. Balvanera Sud	51.0	67.5	87.4	121.9	203.0	150.1	4.0
11. Balvanera Norte	61.5	99.7	103.1	194.6	285.8	260.0	4.6
12. Concepción	42.3	77.8	74.6	129.4	159.2	128.8	3.8
13. Monserrat	100.5	129.1	179.9	292.3	381.7	236.7	3.8
14. San Nicolás	133.3	232.0	226.8	442.0	998.5	446.5	7.5
15. San Bernardo	1.6	2.4	2.9	8.7	12.0	10.9	7.5
16. Belgrano	1.6	5.7	6.8	14.3	23.1	21.0	14.4
17. Palermo	5.5	9.5	14.4	31.7	57.6	35.0	10.5
18. Las Heras	12.8	21.3	31.2	61.1	104.5	80.7	8.2
19. Pilar	40.2	60.3	37.5	144.5	249.6	172.7	6.2
20. Socorro	91.3	149.4	196.4	269.1	469.6	375.0	5.1

Source: Calculated from *Transferencia de inmuebles, de acuerdo a los certificados expedidos por la Administración de Contribución Territorial, Patentes y Sellos* (Buenos Aires, 1915).

Table 14. Percentages of total employed males, fourteen years of age and over, distributed by occupational structure, 1869, 1887, 1895, 1904, 1909, 1914.

Category	1869[1]	1887[2]	1895	1905	1909	1914
Gente decente or upper class[3]	4.9	4.8	4.9	5.0	4.5	4.5
Blue-collar and white-collar[3]	63.1	65.7	68.3	71.5	74.7	73.8
Manual labor[3]	32.0	29.5	26.8	23.5	20.8	21.7
	100.0	100.0	100.0	100.0	100.0	100.0
N = Total employed	98,700	157,300	234,100	312,700	462,400	597,800

1. Figures for 1869 include all employed persons, since no distinction is made between males and females.
2. In addition to those registered as employed by the census, a total of 3132 individuals enrolled in colegios and the university has been included in N and in gente decente categories. Since this figure is not divided between foreign-born and Argentine-born persons in the census, the percentage of foreign-born students to all students reported in the 1895 census, 12.4%, has been applied to give 2744 Argentine-born and 388 foreign born students in 1887.
3. See notes 1, 2, and 3, pp. 295–96, for a description of these categories and the principal occupational groups contained within each.
Sources: Calculations based on *Censo general de la ciudad de Buenos Aires de 1887*, II, 43–47; 541–42; *de 1904*, 55–63; *de 1909*, I, 53–60; *Censo nacional de 1869*, 64–75; *de 1895*, II, 47–50; *de 1914*, IV, 201–12.

Table 15. Foreign-born males as percentage of total employed male population, fourteen years of age and over, 1887, 1895, 1904, 1909, 1914.

Category	1887	1895	1904	1909	1914
Gente decente, or upper class[1]	31	36	24	30	19
Blue-collar and white-collar[1]	79	77	68	64	66
Manual labor[1]	78	81	74	67	86

1. See notes 1, 2, and 3, pp. 295–96, for a description of these categories and the principal occupational groups contained within each.
Source: See Table 14. No percentages are given for 1869, since that national census did not distinguish between Argentine-born and foreign-born in the employment figures. The N for each individual percentage is the absolute figure that could be calculated for that entry in Table 14.

Notes

Preface

1. For a discussion of national themes, with incidental attention to the city of Buenos Aires, see James R. Scobie, *Argentina: A City and a Nation* (2d ed.; New York, 1971).
2. As an extension of this work, I have begun to analyze the ethnic, occupational, and demographic composition of the population at the block level from manuscript census returns of 1869 and 1895 that are available in the Archivo General de la Nación, Buenos Aires.

Chapter 1

1. Horacio C. E. Giberti, *Historia económica de la ganadería argentina* (Buenos Aires, 1954), p. 15.
2. Nicolás Besio Moreno, *Buenos Aires, puerto del Río de la Plata, capital de la Argentina: Estudio crítico de su población, 1536-1936* (Buenos Aires, 1939), pp. 375-91.
3. Zulma L. Recchini de Lattes and Alfredo E. Lattes, *Migraciones en la Argentina: Estudio de las migraciones internas e internacionales, basado en datos censales, 1869-1960* (Buenos Aires, 1969), pp. 88-89.

Chapter 2

1. Carlos Ibarguren, *La historia que he vivido* (Buenos Aires, 1955), pp. 185-86.
2. An incomplete but indicative list of travelers' accounts of visits made between 1906 and 1916 includes Angel P. Bonetti, *De la República Argentina y sus*

detractores (2d ed.; Buenos Aires, 1910); Mario Brant, *Viagem a Buenos Aires* (Rio de Janeiro, 1917); James B. Bryce, *South America: Observations and Impressions* (New York and London, 1912); Javier Bueno, *Mi viaje a América* (Paris, 1913); François Castre, *A travers l'Argentine moderne* (Paris, 1910); Mario Cattaruzza, *Buenos Aires* (Rio de Janeiro, 1906); Georges E. B. Clemenceau, *South America Today: A Study of Conditions, Social, Political, and Commercial in Argentina, Uruguay and Brazil* (New York and London, 1911); Carlo Cortellini, *Attraverso Buenos Aires* (Buenos Aires, 1913); Manuel Gil de Oto, *La Argentina que yo he visto* (Barcelona, 1914); Charles Grandpierre, *What We May Learn from the Other Americans* (New York, 1912); John A. Hammerton, *The Real Argentine* (New York, 1915); W. A. Hirst, *Argentina* (London, 1910); Jules Huret, *En Argentine* (2 vols.; Paris, 1911–13), Vol. I, *De Buenos Aires au Gran Chaco*, Vol. II, *De la Plata à la Cordillière;* William H. Koebel, *Argentina, Past and Present* (London, 1910); Manuel Manacho, *Impresiones de un viaje a Buenos Aires* (Barcelona, 1911); A. Stuart Pennington, *The Argentine Republic* (New York, 1910); Adolfo Posada, *La República Argentina* (Madrid, 1912); Santiago Rusiñol, *Un viaje al Plata* (Madrid, 1911); Wilhelm Schmidt, *Argentinien in geographischer, geschichtlicher und wirtschaftlicher Beziehung* (Hannover, 1912); Adolf N. Schuster, *Argentinien, Land, Volk, Wirtschaftsleben und Kolonisation* (2 vols.; Munich, 1913); Henri Turot, *En Amérique Latine* (Paris, 1908); Nevin O. Winter, *Argentina and Her People of Today* (Boston, 1911).

3. Exceptions were a twenty-five-block area around the War Arsenal in the northeast corner of Census District 2 and another twenty-five-block area in the northwest corner of this same district.

4. The municipal slaughterhouse at Nueva Chicago provided electric light to an area of thirty-five blocks in its immediate neighborhood.

5. Archivo General de la Nación (hereafter cited as AGN), Censo de 1869, Sección 2, tomo 6, libreta 1 de Juan Guosdenovich, recorded 190 students at the Colegio Nacional: 73 from the province of Buenos Aires, 22 from Corrientes, 14 from San Juan, 10 each from Mendoza, Santa Fe, and the Republic of Uruguay, 9 each from Entre Ríos and Salta, 8 each from San Luis and Santiago del Estero, 6 from Jujuy, 4 from Tucumán, 3 from La Rioja, and 1 each from Córdoba, the republics of Bolivia and Paraguay, and Spain.

6. AGN, Censo de 1869, Sección 2, tomo 6, libretas 1 y 2 de Pedro Rivero, libreta 2 de Juan Guosdonovich, libreta 1 de M. Gallard.

7. AGN, Censo de 1869, Sección 2, tomo 5, libreta 2 de Pedro Y. López, Moreno 20.

8. AGN, Censo de 1869, Sección 2, tomo 5, libreta 1 de Pedro Y. López.

9. AGN, Censo de 1869, Sección 2, tomo 6, libretas 1 y 2 de Marcos Levalle.

10. AGN, Censo de 1869, Sección 2, tomo 4, libreta 1 de Nero Vásquez, libretas 1 y 2 de Francisco M. Victori.

11. AGN, Censo de 1869, Sección 2, tomo 6, libreta 2 de Bernardo Folkenand.

12. Technically, *La Prensa*, located on the south sidewalk of Rivadavia, was on the edge of the parish of Catedral al Sud.

Chapter 3

1. *Censo nacional de 1869*, pp. 674–83.
2. Argentina, Cámara de Diputados, *Diario de sesiones*, 1881, III, Oct. 5, p. 85. (Hereafter congressional references are cited as Diputados, *Sesiones*, or Senadores, *Sesiones*. For debates in the provincial legislature, Buenos Aires appears before Diputados or Senadores.)
3. Particularly useful to understanding the early period of port development are Luis A. Huergo, *El puerto de Buenos Aires. Historia técnica del puerto de Buenos Aires* (Buenos Aires, 1904), written by one of the main protagonists, and Guillermo Madero, *Historia del puerto de Buenos Aires* (Buenos Aires, 1955), written by a grandson of the leader of the other faction. Unfortunately, numerous factual errors mar this latter work.
4. Senadores, *Sesiones*, 1869, Sept. 11, 14, 16, pp. 676–85, 700–754.
5. Particularly damaging were Knut Lindmarck, *Obras de puerto proyectadas para Buenos Aires* (Buenos Aires, 1872), a pamphlet by the deputy director of the National Engineering Office; Vicente F. López, "Las obras del puerto de Buenos Aires," *Revista del Río de la Plata*, IV, 1872, pp. 98–237; Antonio Somellera, *Obras del puerto de Buenos Aires. Consideraciones sobre el proyecto del Ing. Bateman* (Buenos Aires, 1872); and Luis A. Huergo, *Los intereses argentinos en el puerto de Buenos Aires* (Buenos Aires, 1873).
6. Law No. 997, Oct. 22, 1875, of the Province of Buenos Aires, and Law No. 820, Oct. 12, 1876, of the Argentine Republic. The debates appear in Buenos Aires, Senadores, *Sesiones*, 1875, Aug. 12, 17, and 24, pp. 446–47, 466–71, and 493–515; Buenos Aires, Diputados, *Sesiones*, 1875, I, Oct. 18, pp. 1123–38; Diputados, *Sesiones*, 1876, II, Aug. 21, Sept. 28, Oct. 11, pp. 37–38, 458–60, 582–86; Senadores, *Sesiones*, 1876, Oct. 10, pp. 1185–93.
7. Law No. 1273, Feb. 4, 1879, of the Province of Buenos Aires.
8. Law No. 1376, March 26, 1881, of the Province of Buenos Aires.
9. Buenos Aires, Municipalidad, *Actas del Honorable Concejo Deliberante*, 1881 (Buenos Aires, 1882), Aug. 4, pp. 125–29 (hereafter cited as *Actas*).
10. Law No. 1124, Oct. 28, 1881, of the Argentine Republic. The debates on this measure can be found in Diputados, *Sesiones*, 1881, III, Oct. 3, 4, 5, and 28, pp. 16–20, 36–80, 441–49; Senadores, *Sesiones*, 1881, II, Oct. 6, and 27, pp. 822, 1009–14.
11. Diputados, *Sesiones*, 1882, I, Aug. 23, pp. 998–99.
12. Diputados, *Sesiones*, 1881, III, Oct. 5, Nov. 2, pp. 82–95, 533–35.
13. Diputados, *Sesiones*, 1882, I, Aug. 21, 23, pp. 979–80, 990–1017. The Woodgate proposal was finally dismissed in 1885 as no longer relevant; see Diputados, *Sesiones*, 1885, I, June 15, pp. 99–100.
14. Diputados, *Sesiones*, 1882, I, July 26, p. 770.
15. Huergo, *El puerto de Buenos Aires*, p. 39, stated: "El Gobierno no cumplió esta ley imperativa [No. 1124] y no remitió cuenta de este proyecto [the plans drawn up by Huergo at the request of the Ministry of War] al Congreso en las

sesiones del año 1882. Por el contrario, algunos años después, el Autor [Huergo] lo encontró accidentalmente en la casa de Gobierno, entre papeles pertenecientes al señor Eduardo Madero."

16. Law No. 1257, Oct. 27, 1882, of the Argentine Republic. The presentation and discussion of the measure appears in Senadores, *Sesiones*, 1882, Sept. 26, 27, pp. 702-21, 724-25, 727-31; Diputados, *Sesiones*, 1882, II, Oct. 20 and 21, pp. 904-45. The Senate approved the project in general Sept. 26 and then voted on it by sections without discussion Sept. 27. Clearly a deal had been worked out, although the exact arrangements have not emerged in the documentation known to this writer.

17. *La Prensa*, Sept. 28, 1882, p. 1; two other editorials on the subject appeared immediately after the passage of this bill, Oct. 28, 29, 1882, p. 1.

18. *La Prensa*, Jan. 26, 1883, p. 1. The residents of La Boca as well as the members of the Bolsa de Comercio, or stock exchange, each awarded gold medals to Huergo to commemorate this important event.

19. The steady increase of shipping into the Riachuelo is reflected in the following figures:

Year	Total Overseas Shipping Entering Buenos Aires		Shipping Entering the Riachuelo as a Percentage of Total Buenos Aires Shipping	
	Ships	*Tonnage*	*% ships*	*% tonnage*
1879	2247	801,000	8.8	6.9
1880	2201	734,000	11.8	9.5
1881	2763	833,000	15.2	15.6
1882	2994	937,000	14.6	17.7
1883	3216	1,126,000	18.7	22.1
1884	5107	1,543,000	22.5	34.7

From Luis A. Huergo, *Memoria de la comisión administradora de las obras del Riachuelo, año 1884* (Buenos Aires, 1885), p. 24, and the annual volumes of Argentina, *Estadística del comercio exterior y de la navegación interior y exterior*, 1880-85.

20. Quoted in *La Prensa*, Feb. 17, 1883, p. 1.

21. Report signed by Guillermo White, Juan Anchorena, John Coglan, Hunter Davidson, and A. E. Rusiñol, March 21, 1883, and published in *La Prensa*, April 15, 1883, p. 1.

22. The barrage of editorials began on April 29, 1883, with "El puerto de Buenos Aires," p. 1, and continued with nearly daily, page-one articles through May 30, when the final shot was fired in "Resumen. Puerto de Buenos Aires."

23. "Las obras del puerto. Adulteraciones, verdades, antecedentes," *La Prensa*, May 1, 1883, p. 1.

24. *Ibid.*

25. *La Nación*, April 28, 1883, p. 1. Other editorials, all p. 1, appeared in the issues of April 26, May 1, 3.

26. *El Nacional* printed editorials on page 1 in its issues of May 4, 5, 8, 10, 11, 12, 15, 17, 19, 21, 1883.

27. Law No. 1385, Oct. 25, 1883, of the Argentine Republic. The national executive originally requested an appropriation of three million gold pesos, but objections in the Senate reduced the amount finally voted to 1.8 million. Senadores, *Sesiones*, 1883, Sept. 6, 13, and Oct. 6, 23, pp. 563-75, 581-83, 796-805, 1184-87; Diputados, *Sesiones*, 1883, II, Oct. 22, pp. 1226-40.

28. *La Prensa*, Oct. 4, 1883, p. 1.

29. Law No. 1577, Oct. 31, 1884, of the Argentine Republic. There was virtually no debate on this measure: Senadores, *Sesiones*, 1884, Oct. 7, pp. 709-11; Diputados, *Sesiones*, 1884, II, Oct. 30, pp. 776-77.

30. *La Prensa*, June 4, 10, 1885, p. 4, 3; Nov. 7, 1886, p. 3.

31. Luis A. Huergo, "Puerto de Buenos Aires," a lecture which appeared on page 3 of *La Prensa*, May 1, 4, 5, 6, 1886, and in *Anales de la Sociedad Científica Argentina*, No. 21, 1886, pp. 145-87. Also see letters from Luis A. Huergo published in *La Prensa* in 1886: dated March 1, in March 3, p. 3; dated March 5, in March 6, p. 3; dated March 6, in March 7, p. 3; dated March 10, in March 12, 13, 14, 16, p. 3; dated March 21, in March 23, 24, 25, p. 3; dated March 24, in March 26, 27, and 28 on pp. 3, 5-6, and 3; undated in March 31, April 1, 2, p. 3; dated April 7, in April 9, p. 3; dated April 10, in April 13, p. 3; dated May 5, in May 7, 8, 9, 12, p. 3.

32. "Expediente del Departamento Nacional de Ingenieros," published in *La Prensa*, Feb. 28, March 1, 2, 1886, p. 3.

33. "Asamblea de Ingenieros," March 30, 1886, as reported in *La Prensa*, April 4, 1886, p. 3.

34. *La Prensa*, March 12, 1886, p. 3.

35. Huergo, *El puerto de Buenos Aires*, pp. 70-72.

36. *La Prensa*, Oct. 6, 1887, p. 5, Nov. 31, 1887, p. 4.

37. *La Prensa* discussed these matters in several issues in 1888: July 3, on p. 5, and on p. 4 for July 4, 5, 6, 17 (which presented the competing bid by Carlos Lumb), and Oct. 27. Law No. 2414, Nov. 10, 1888 (briefly discussed in Senadores, *Sesiones*, 1888, Nov. 2, pp. 802-6, and Diputados, *Sesiones*, 1888, II, Nov. 6, pp. 555-57) provided for public auction of the lands. The decree of the sale appeared in *La Prensa*, Oct. 3, 1889. The first auction, held March 1, 1890, was suspended after the sale of one lot; another auction for six blocks was held on June 19, 1890; see *La Prensa*, March 4, p. 7; June 19, p. 7; June 20, 1890, p. 5.

38. This series of editorials ran on page 4 of *La Prensa*, April 12, 14, 15, 16, 17, 19, 22, 23, 24, 26, 30, May 2, 5, 1891.

39. Law No. 3315, Nov. 4, 1895, of the Argentine Republic. Senadores, *Sesiones*, 1895, Sept. 10, 17, 21, pp. 322, 379-99, 415-34; Diputados, *Sesiones*, 1895, II, Oct. 30, Nov. 2, 4, pp. 294-318, 325-71, 373-409.

40. A particularly strong parting shot appeared in Luis A. Huergo, "Los dos canales de acceso al puerto de Buenos Aires. Memoria leída en la primera sección del

Congreso Científico Latino-Americano," *Anales de la Sociedad Científica Argentina*, No. 45, 1898, pp. 237–58.

41. *La Prensa*, Feb. 3, 1889, p. 4, notes the formation of the society; in the issue of Nov. 15, 1889, it was reported that construction work had begun on Dock Sud. See also "Informe sobre las obras del Dock Sud de la Capital," *Anales de la Sociedad Científica Argentina*, No. 31, 1891, pp. 36–42.

42. Laws No. 2859, Nov. 16, 1891, No. 3539, Sept. 24, 1897, No. 3552, Sept. 29, 1897, No. 3728, Oct. 10, 1898, of the Argentine Republic.

43. *La Prensa* carried news items on the progress of construction at Dock Sud April 12, 1903, p. 3, Feb. 29, 1904, p. 4.

44. Total shipping entering and leaving the Port of Buenos Aires, 1903–12:

Year	No. Ships	Total Tonnage
1903	19,000	10,100,000
1904	21,000	10,500,000
1905	22,000	11,600,000
1906	21,800	12,600,000
1907	23,700	13,300,000
1908	25,100	15,100,000
1909	27,400	17,200,000
1910	29,400	17,900,000
1911	31,000	18,000,000
1912	30,400	19,200,000

Adapted from that reported by Alejandro Gancedo, "Puerto de la Capital y puerto argentino," *Revista de Derecho, Historia y Letras*, Vol. XVI, No. 47, Feb. 1914, p. 201.

45. Harford to Lansdowne, April 30, 1903, Great Britain, Public Record Office, Foreign Office Records, General Correspondence 6 (hereafter cited as FO 6), Vol. 482, No. 8 Consular.

46. *La Prensa*, March 12, 1903, p. 7.

47. See Huergo, *El puerto de Buenos Aires*, Map 4, and pp. 89–90.

48. *Ibid.*, pp. 94–98, with sketch of changes proposed in port.

49. Laws No. 3899, Jan. 5, 1900, No. 4515, Sept. 30, 1904, of the Argentine Republic.

50. Alejandro Gancedo, "Puerto de la Capital y puerto argentino," pp. 198–215.

51. *Caras y Caretas*, Vol. IX, No. 409, Aug. 4, 1906, unpaginated.

52. *La Prensa*, June 26, 1906, p. 4.

53. Lectures by Fernand Kinart reported in *La Prensa*, July 11, Aug. 3, 4, Sept. 6, 1906, p. 8, 7, 5, and 5; also reprinted in *Anales de la Sociedad Científica Argentina*, No. 63, 1907, pp. 5–51.

54. Law No. 5126, Sept. 10, 1907, of the Argentine Republic; also see Message from the National Executive, Diputados, *Sesiones*, 1907, I, Aug. 23, pp. 823–26.

55. Law No. 5944, Sept. 29, 1908, of the Argentine Republic.

56. Law No. 8389, Sept. 28, 1911, of the Argentine Republic. This proposal was first introduced by Alberto Méndez Casariego, Diputados, *Sesiones*, 1908, July 13, pp. 560–61.

57. Like the history of the port of Buenos Aires, the history of Argentina's railroads has yet to be written. Among the helpful guides are Alejandro Bunge, *Ferrocarriles argentinos. Contribución al estudio del patrimonio nacional* (Buenos Aires, 1918); Horacio J. Cuccorese, *Historia de los ferrocarriles en la Argentina* (Buenos Aires, 1969); Dirección de Informaciones y Publicaciones Ferroviarias, *Origen y desarrollo de los ferrocarriles argentinos* (Buenos Aires, 1938); Ricardo M. Ortiz, *El ferrocarril en la economía argentina* (2d ed.; Buenos Aires, 1958); Emilio Rebuelto, "Historia del desarrollo de los ferrocarriles argentinos," *Boletín de Obras Públicas de la República Argentina*, Vols. 5–7, 1911–13; William Rögind, *Historia del Ferrocarril Sud, 1861–1936* (Buenos Aires, 1937); Raúl Scalabrini Ortiz, *Historia de los ferrocarriles argentinos* (2d ed., Buenos Aires, 1957); Emilio Vasallo Rojas and Matus Gutiérrez, *Historia de los ferrocarriles argentinos* (Santiago de Chile, 1947); Winthrop B. Wright, "Argentine Railways and the Growth of Nationalism" (Ph.D. thesis, University of Pennsylvania, 1964); Eduardo A. Zalduendo, *Las inversiones británicas para la promoción y desarrollo de ferrocarriles en el siglo XIX: Los casos de Argentina, Brasil, Canadá, e India* (2 vols., mimeo; Buenos Aires, 1968–69), Vol. 2.

58. Zalduendo, II, pp. 152–53.

59. Law No. 5315, Sept. 30, 1907, of the Argentine Republic, provided the following regulations: all building materials needed by the railroad companies could be imported free of duty until 1947, and during that period no national, provincial, or municipal taxes would be levied on their operations; in return for these privileges the companies would pay a 3 per cent tax on net revenues (*producto líquido*) to be applied to the building of access bridges and roads around the railroad stations; when gross revenues exceeded 17 per cent of a railroad company's capital, and expenses did not exceed 60 per cent of revenues, the national government could regulate rates; the national government could expropriate companies on the basis of payment of their capital value plus 20 per cent.

60. Amusing incidents in the clash between the municipality and the railroad companies are recounted in *La Prensa*, Feb. 17, 18, 19, 1897, p. 5, 4, 5. The Buenos Aires and Rosario and the Central Argentine opened temporary facilities at Retiro, and in 1900 both companies received authorization to build new terminal stations in this same area. Two years later the Central Argentine took over these operations, and in 1915 it inaugurated the imposing brick façade and spacious interior of Retiro Station. By 1906 the Buenos Aires Pacific had established a separate station at Retiro, on the east side of the Central Argentine terminal, as the first stage of moving its main operations out of Palermo. With the completion in 1912 of a separate elevated track from Palermo to Retiro, that company also installed its headquarters at Retiro.

61. Examples of such protests appeared in *La Prensa* on p. 1 on Nov. 9, 1876, and on Feb. 17, 1878. The *Memoria de la Municipalidad de Buenos Aires*, for 1879, Vol. I, pp. 262–63, and for 1881, Vol. I, p. 201, took note of incidents of damage and injuries caused by locomotives on the downtown streets. *Actas*, 1880, pp. 84–85, also commented on the problem.

62. *Actas*, 1888, Dec. 17, pp. 526–28. The council repeated this regulation in *Actas*, 1889, April 22, p. 184, and with specific reference to the Western Railroad in *Actas*, 1890, Oct. 3, pp. 184–85.

63. *La Prensa*, May 14, 1893, p. 5. Hobart A. Spalding, Jr. (ed.), *La clase trabajadora argentina: Documentos para su historia, 1890–1912* (Buenos Aires, 1970), pp. 558–60, 609–21, provides numerous examples of the railroads' defiance of the national government from the period 1900–1912.

64. Laws Nos. 3058 and 3170, Dec. 27, 1893, Oct. 11, 1894, of the Argentine Republic.

65. *La Prensa*, Dec. 12, 1897, p. 3.

66. *La Prensa* dwelt on this incident in its numbers of Dec. 6, p. 5, and thereafter on p. 4 of Dec. 8, 10, and 27, 1897.

67. *Actas*, 1907, July 2, pp. 236–37.

68. The involved political maneuvers and intrigues that led to and finally resolved the "capital" question fall outside the scope of this study. From the enormous bibliography on this topic, readers will find the following items particularly useful: Arturo B. Carranza, *La cuestión capital de la República, 1826 a 1887* (5 vols.; Buenos Aires, 1926–32); Bartolomé Galíndez, *Historia política argentina: la revolución del 80* (Buenos Aires, 1945); Lía E. M. Sanucci, *La renovación presidencial de 1880* (La Plata, 1959).

69. Law No. 1532, Oct. 10, 1884, of the Argentine Republic. Previous legislation had made only vague references to territories, and not until 1882 had two governorships, those of La Pampa and Patagonia, been established. The 1884 legislation created nine territories and defined their limits: La Pampa, Neuquén, Río Negro, Chubut, Santa Cruz, Tierra del Fuego, Misiones, Formosa, and Chaco.

70. The intricate legislative maneuverings of these months are detailed in Carranza, V, 3–661.

71. *Actas*, 1878, July 6, pp. 250–52.

72. Particularly useful in following Alvear's programs are Adrián Beccar Varela, *Torcuato de Alvear, primer intendente municipal de la ciudad de Buenos Aires: su acción edilicia* (Buenos Aires, 1926), and Alberto B. Martínez, *Estudio topográfico e historia demográfica de la ciudad de Buenos Aires* (Buenos Aires, 1889).

73. *Actas*, 1883, Nov. 2, pp. 347–48.

74. *Actas*, 1883, Oct. 22, p. 339.

75. Beccar Varela, p. 27.

76. Plan by Felipe Senillosa, in Alberto S. J. de Paula, "Una modificación del diseño urbano porteño proyectada en 1875," *Anales del Instituto de Arte Americano e Investigaciones Estéticas*, No. 19, 1966, pp. 71–77; also see plans by José M. Lagos, 1869, and by Carlos Carranza and Daniel Soler, 1872, in Martínez, *Estudio topográfico*, pp. 49–52.

77. Congress gave its approval to a municipal bond issue to finance the construction of the Avenida de Mayo; see Law No. 1569, Oct. 31, 1884, of the Argentine Republic. The arrangement was accepted by the municipal council in *Actas*, 1885, Sept. 18, pp. 64–69. Expropriation procedures were covered in general terms

without reference to the Avenida de Mayo in Law No. 1583, Nov. 4, 1884, of the Argentine Republic. *La Prensa* published a list of donors of properties, Oct. 20, 21, 23, 26, 27, 30, 1888, p. 6, 8, 6, 6, 5, 6. *Memoria de la Municipalidad,* 1890–92, pp. 124–25, reported that a few recalcitrant owners continued to obstruct construction with demands for higher valuations on their properties.

Chapter 4

1. The Central City, composed of Districts 1 through 6 in the censuses of 1869, 1887, and 1895, was enclosed by the streets of Independencia on the south, Solís/Rodríguez Peña on the west, Córdoba on the north, and Paseo Colón/ Paseo de Julio (Leandro Alem) on the east. Beginning with the 1904 census, Districts 13 and 14 covered roughly this same area: the northern and southern boundaries remained the same; on the west the boundary moved one block farther west, to Entre Ríos/Callao; while on the east these districts now included the reclaimed but largely vacant lands of the port area. I am now developing what may prove to be a more precise definition of the downtown core, which I base on the manuscript census materials from 1869 and 1895. These materials will also permit analysis of variables such as occupation, ethnic origins, age, and education not presented in any detail in the published censuses. Although my study is subject to further revision, it now seems that this downtown core is contained within the Central City I define here and tentatively consists of ninety-three blocks, bounded on the south by Belgrano, on the west by Buen Orden (Bernardo de Irigoyen)/Artes (Carlos Pellegrini), on the north by Córdoba, and on the east by Paseo Colón/Paseo de Julio.
2. In addition to standard city guides such as *Almanaque Peuser, Anuario Kraft, Anuario Pillado, The Argentine Year Book, Handbook of the River Plate,* and the numerous maps used to locate buildings and institutions, extensive information on the first and second police districts appears in A. Galarce, *Bosquejo de Buenos Aires* (2 vols.; Buenos Aires, 1886–87).
3. Galarce, I, 522–23; II, 249.
4. See esp. *La Universidad Nacional de Buenos Aires, 1821–1910* (Buenos Aires, 1910), published by the Consejo Superior de la Universidad Nacional de Buenos Aires.
5. The description of the epidemic has been compiled from accounts in Mardoqueo Navarro, "La epidemia del año 1871," *Anuario de la Dirección General de Estadística,* 1907, II, 359–64; in *Actas,* 1871, pp. 18–163; in dispatches from Macdonell to Granville, 1871, FO 6, Vol. 302; in issues of *La Nación* and *La Prensa* for the first half of 1871; and in Besio Moreno, pp. 149–57.
6. *La Prensa,* March 18, 1871, p. 1.
7. Macdonell to Granville, April 13, 1870, FO 6, Vol. 302, No. 42, indicates that there were little more than 30,000 persons left in the city. Besio Moreno, pp. 153–57, reports that 53,000 persons left the city.
8. *La Prensa,* Aug. 11, 1871, Jan. 18, Feb. 15, 1872, p. 2.
9. Zelmira Garrigós, *Memorias de mi lejana infancia: el barrio de la Merced en*

1880 (Buenos Aires, 1964), p. 113. Accounts that suggest Flores' importance as a summer retreat also appear in *La Prensa*, Feb. 10, 1877, and Nov. 9, 1880, p. 1.

10. *Actas*, 1887, March 16, p. 69.

11. Other unsuccessful efforts to close Florida to vehicular traffic at certain hours were recorded in *Actas*, 1887, Oct. 24, p. 458; 1891, Oct. 23, p. 669; 1893, May 22, pp. 274–76; 1908, July 24, pp. 300–301.

12. *Actas*, 1909, June 15, pp. 146–47. Protests against this measure were published in the *Revista Municipal*, VI, Nos. 282, 288, July 5, Aug. 2, 1909, pp. 11–12, 14; X, No. 518, Dec. 29, 1913, p. 4; XI, No. 531, March 30, 1914, pp. 3–4. The regulation was temporarily rescinded in 1912 but reinstated in 1913.

13. *La Nación*, May 17, 1911, p. 11.

14. There are useful though scattered references to changing architectural designs affecting wealthy residential housing in Mario J. Buschiazzo, *La arquitectura en la República Argentina, 1810–1930* (Buenos Aires, 1966); Jorge O. Gazaneo and Mabel M. Scarone, *Arquitectura de la revolución industrial* (Buenos Aires, 1966); Instituto de Arte Americano, Facultad de Arquitectura y Urbanismo, *La arquitectura en Buenos Aires, 1850–1880* (Buenos Aires, 1965); José Xavier Martini and José María Peña, *La ornamentación en la arquitectura de Buenos Aires* (2 vols.; Buenos Aires, 1966–67), Vol. I, *1800–1900*, Vol. II, *1900–1940;* Carlos María Morales, "Estudio topográfico y edilicio de la ciudad de Buenos Aires," *Censo general de la ciudad de Buenos Aires, 1909*, III, 497–580; Federico F. Ortiz *et al., La arquitectura del liberalismo en la Argentina* (Buenos Aires, 1968).

15. Ortiz, *La arquitectura del liberalismo*, biographical notes and p. 137.

16. Buschiazzo, *La arquitectura*, p. 30. This edifice, which today serves as central offices for the Argentine Foreign Affairs Ministry, was designed by Alejandro Christophersen.

17. *La Prensa*, Aug. 6, 1906, p. 12. The minimum bidding price was fixed at 30,000 pesos; the house sold for 43,500 pesos.

18. *La Prensa*, Aug. 30, 1907, p. 13. The minimum bidding price was 14,000 pesos; the house was finally sold for 18,500 pesos.

19. Another characteristic dwelling appears in the recollections of Julia Bunge. Her father, a judge on the Supreme Court, father of eight children, and a man of substantial commercial wealth, rented a summer home in San Isidro and owned a house near the northern end of Callao in what was rapidly becoming known as part of Barrio Norte:

> Consta de: hall, sala, salita, escritorio, comedor grande, ante comedor, hall interno, nueve dormitorios y tres baños. . . . Una galería abierta, que da al jardín, une todos los dormitorios. La parte de servicio abajo, es muy amplia: hall, cocina muy grande, cinco dormitorios, dos baños.

[Julia V. Bunge, *Vida. Época maravillosa, 1903–1911* (Buenos Aires, 1965), p. 19.]

20. James R. Scobie, *Revolution on the Pampas; A Social History of Argentine Wheat, 1860–1910* (Austin, Tex., 1964), p. 61.

21. The data on wages has been compiled from a variety of sources: "Report on the Condition of the Industrial Classes," Phipps, attached to Macdonell to Granville, July 15, 1871, FO 6, Vol. 304, No. 79; Jacinto Oddone, *Historia del socialismo argentino* (2 vols.; Buenos Aires, 1934), I, 75–78; "Report on Immigration," July 4, 1891, Herbert, attached to Pakenham to Salisbury, July 21, 1891, FO 6, Vol. 418, No. 30; M. F. Wodon, *Les états de la Plata au point de vue de l'emigration et de la colonisation* (Paris, 1892), pp. 116–27; Adrián Patroni, *Los trabajadores en la Argentina* (Buenos Aires, 1898), pp. 113–14; William I. Buchanan, "La moneda y la vida en la República Argentina," *Revista de Derecho, Historia y Letras*, I, 2, Dec. 1898, pp. 211–13; a series of forty articles entitled "Los obreros y el trabajo," appearing in *La Prensa*, Aug. 16– Dec. 22, 1901; "Condiciones del trabajo en la ciudad de Buenos Aires," *Boletín del Departamento Nacional del Trabajo*, No. 3, 1907, pp. 319–44, 347–58; No. 4, 1908, pp. 13–50; No. 6, 1908, pp. 347–99; 1909, No. 10, pp. 326–51; No. 11, 1909, pp. 476–502; No. 12, 1910, pp. 5–22; No. 14, 1910, pp. 528–31; No. 16, 1911, pp. 5–23, 32–37; No. 17, 1911, pp. 261–63; No. 19, 1911, pp. 765–87, 788–806, 807–11; F. Stach, "Estudio sobre salarios y horas de los obreros y empleados en los diferentes trabajos en la Capital Federal y en el resto de la República Argentina," *Boletín del Museo Social Argentino*, 1913, III, 44–49, 193–200; Spalding, Jr. (ed.), *La clase trabajadora argentina*, pp. 35–43.

22. The extensive investigation needed to develop a cost-of-living index or to secure a real-wage index for the late nineteenth century has not yet been accomplished. A significant effort in that direction has been made by Roberto Cortés Conde, *El mercado de trabajo en Argentina, 1880–1913. Evolución de los salarios y condiciones de vida de los trabajadores* (Buenos Aires, 1973), published by the Instituto Torcuato di Tella.

23. "Report on the Condition of the Industrial Classes," Phipps, FO 6, Vol. 304, No. 79.

24. St. John to Granville, March 6, 1873, FO 6, Vol. 314, No. 5.

25. *La Prensa*, Sept. 10, Dec. 23, 1876, p. 1; *La Nación*, Sept. 10, 1876, p. 2.

26. *Actas*, 1874, Aug. 17, pp. 152–53, Aug. 20, p. 159; *La Prensa*, Aug. 9, 1876, April 1, 1877, p. 1.

27. *Actas*, 1880, Sept. 24, 25, pp. 174–75, 180–84; *La Prensa*, Sept. 15, 26, 1880, Jan. 14, 1881, p. 1.

28. Sandford to Petre, April 20, 1882, FO 6, Vol. 368, unnumbered, folio 154.

29. *La Prensa*, Aug. 15, 1888, p. 4.

30. *La Prensa*, Aug. 2, Sept. 26, 1891, p. 5, 6.

31. Pakenham to Salisbury, Oct. 21, 1891, FO 6, Vol. 418, No. 47 Commercial.

32. Oddone, *Historia del socialismo argentino*, II, 7–8.

33. *Caras y Caretas*, IV, No. 150, Aug. 17, 1901, V, No. 201, Aug. 9, 1902, unpaginated; *La Prensa*, Aug. 13, 19, 1901, pp. 4–5, 3; *La Nación*, Aug. 13, 1901, p. 5; *El Diario*, Aug. 11–12, 1901, p. 1.

34. The value of the paper peso fluctuated markedly until 1903, when it was finally stabilized at 2.27 to the gold peso. In 1901 it averaged 2.32. *Censo nacional de 1914*, X, 395–96.

35. *La Prensa*, Sept. 3, 28, Oct. 6, 10, 1901, p. 5, 5, 4, 4.

36. Haggard to Lansdowne, March 12, 1905, FO 6, Vol. 490, No. 12; also see his communication of June 14, 1905, No. 29.

37. *Caras y Caretas*, XI, No. 534, Dec. 26, 1908, unpaginated.

38. See Humbert S. Nelli, *The Italians in Chicago, 1880–1930; A Study in Ethnic Mobility* (New York, 1970), pp. 55–65.

39. *La Prensa*, Aug. 25, 1901, p. 4.

40. Samuel L. Baily, *Labor, Nationalism, and Politics in Argentina* (New Brunswick, N.J., 1967), pp. 9–50, discusses the start of an Argentine labor movement. An examination of the labor movement falls beyond the scope of the present study. Although much investigation remains to be done on the subject, a very promising beginning has been given by Spalding, Jr. (ed.), *Historia de la clase trabajadora argentina;* Torcuato di Tella (ed.), *Estructuras sindicales* (Buenos Aires, 1969); Hilda Iparraguirre and Ofelia Pianetto, *La organización de la clase obrera en Córdoba, 1870–1895* (Córdoba, 1968); José Panettieri, *Los trabajadores* (Buenos Aires, 1967); and Jorge N. Solomonoff, *Ideologías del movimiento obrero y conflicto social: De la organización nacional hasta la primera guerra mundial* (Buenos Aires, 1971). Also see the valuable work of Sebastián Marotta, *El movimiento sindical argentino* (3 vols.; Buenos Aires, 1960–70).

41. *Actas*, 1881, Sept. 27, Oct. 14, pp. 143–48, 172–75. The newspapers paid considerable attention to this issue; articles appeared in *La Prensa*, Sept. 29, Oct. 5, 12, p. 1, and *La Nación*, Oct. 1, 2, 4, 5, 15, p. 1.

42. Egerton to Granville, Oct. 7, 1881, FO 6, Vol. 364, No. 58.

43. *Actas*, 1883, Aug. 22, p. 238.

44. *Actas*, 1883, Sept. 7, 12, pp. 263–65, and 267–68. Once again the newspapers gave extensive coverage to the debate; articles appeared in *La Prensa*, Aug. 30, Sept. 15, Oct. 6, p. 1, and *La Nación*, Aug. 24, 25, 26, Sept. 1, 9, 16, p. 1.

45. The press covered this demonstration thoroughly, further suggesting its eminent respectability, although one of the government organs, *El Diario*, Sept. 1, 1902, p. 2, indicated that police reports had given only 800 as the number of marchers. *La Nación*, Sept. 1, 1901, p. 5, gave extensive versions of the demonstration, as did *La Prensa*, both before and after the event, Aug. 24, 30, Sept. 1, p. 4, 3, 6.

46. Particularly appropriate in this regard are articles in *La Prensa*, Jan. 17, 23, 29, 1904, p. 5, 4, 6; *La Nación*, Jan. 16, 24, p. 6, 5; *El Diario*, Jan. 9, 25, p. 5, 2.

47. Law No. 4661, Sept. 2, 1905, of the Argentine Republic. Diputados, *Sesiones*, 1904, Sept. 26, 28, 30, pp. 547–56, 569–92, 594–607; Senadores, *Sesiones*, 1905, Aug. 22, pp. 554, 615–21; Diputados, *Sesiones*, 1905, Aug. 31, pp. 568–70. The public still raised considerable objection to the law; see *La Prensa*, Oct. 20, Dec. 12, 1905, p. 5.

48. *Actas*, 1894, Sept. 17, Oct. 5, pp. 495–96, 541; the final disposition was "to send the proposal to the archives." The press carried extensive coverage of the demonstrations and the discussions: *La Nación*, Sept. 18, 22, Oct. 4, 6, 15, 1894, pp. 5, 4, 5, 6, 4; *La Prensa*, Sept. 20, 23, 27, 29, Oct. 4, 8, 15, 1894, pp. 5, 4, 6, 5, 5, 5, 4.

49. See President Roca's message to Congress in May 1904, in Heraclio Mabragaña, *Los mensajes: Historia del desenvolvimiento de la Nación Argentina redactada cronológicamente por sus gobernantes, 1810–1910* (6 vols.; Buenos Aires, 1910), VI, 74–75.

50. *La Prensa,* Jan. 24, Feb. 3, April 5, May 16, Aug. 22, Sept. 5, 28, 1904, p. 7, 6, 7, 3, 6, 3, 7.

51. Diputados, *Sesiones,* 1906, I, May 28, June 22, pp. 140–45, 345–50.

52. Law No. 5291, Sept. 30, 1907, of the Argentine Republic. Diputados, *Sesiones,* 1907, I, July 1, 3, 12, pp. 362–81, 390–414, 433–44; Senadores, *Sesiones,* 1907, Sept. 26, 30, pp. 977, 1081–84.

53. Proposals were introduced in Diputados, *Sesiones,* 1902, I, May 30, pp. 118–23; 1907, I, June 7, pp. 98–103; 1910, I, May 16, Aug. 1, pp. 77–86, 667–69; 1912, I, June 26, July 24, pp. 373–84, 724–28; 1913, I, May 26, p. 489; 1914, I, June 10, III, July 22, pp. 674–75, 181–89. Further concern was evidenced by an entire issue of the *Boletín del Departamento Nacional del Trabajo,* 1912, No. 20, devoted to the problem of employee accident insurance and the legislative precedents established in other countries.

54. The 1904 municipal census breakdown of conventillos (pp. 133–34):

No. Inhabitants	1–30	31–50	51–100	101–150	151–200	201–300	300–
% Rooms	13.8	24.7	35.8	16.4	4.8	3.4	1.1

N = 43,873 rooms.

55. *La Prensa,* Sept. 8, 1901, p. 4.

56. *La Prensa,* Feb. 27, 1871, p. 1.

57. *La Prensa,* Sept. 8, 1901, p. 4.

58. The descriptive material on the conventillo is based on a number of authoritative sources: *Boletín del Departamento Nacional del Trabajo,* 1908, No. 5, pp. 230–40; *La Prensa,* Sept. 8, 1901, p. 4; Adrián Patroni, *Los trabajadores en la Argentina,* pp. 126–33; Guillermo Rawson, "Estudio sobre las casas de inquilinato en Buenos Aires," *Escritos y discursos* (2 vols.; Buenos Aires, 1891), II, 110–14, 142–44; Samuel Gâché, *Les logements ouvriers à Buenos Ayres* (Paris, 1900).

59. *Censo de la ciudad de Buenos Aires,* 1887, II, 30.

60. *La Prensa,* May 22, 1871, p. 2.

61. *Actas,* 1871, June 5, 14, pp. 120, 125–26.

62. *Actas,* 1873, March 20, p. 110.

63. *La Prensa,* Dec. 30, 1873, p. 1.

64. *La Prensa,* Jan. 3, 1874, p. 1.

65. *Actas,* 1875, Oct. 30, pp. 442–46.

66. *La Prensa,* Nov. 28, 1879, p. 1.

67. *Memoria de la municipalidad,* 1879, I, 30–31.

68. *La Prensa,* Dec. 17, 1882, p. 1.

69. *La Prensa,* Jan. 12, Feb. 19, 1889, p. 5, 6.

70. *La Prensa,* Sept. 15, 1887, p. 5.

71. Based on 1912 calculations of an average monthly rent for a conventillo room of 30 pesos, or 14 gold pesos, that being eight to ten times that of Paris or Lon-

don rents, in Casimiro Prieto Costa, "Las viviendas en la Capital Federal," *Boletín del Museo Social Argentino*, 1920, IX, 542.

72. *Actas*, 1893, May 8, p. 236.
73. *Actas*, 1893, Nov. 8, p. 566; 1894, April 13, Aug. 3, p. 101, 308; 1899, Oct. 3, Dec. 26, p. 325, 540.
74. Domingo Silva, "La habitación higiénica para el obrero," *Revista Municipal*, I, No. 46, Dec. 5, 1904, pp. 1–3, provides an excellent assessment of the contemporary conditions in the conventillo, along with a review of changes in these dwellings since the 1870s.
75. *Boletín del Departamento Nacional del Trabajo*, 1908, No. 5, p. 231; on these crowded conditions, also see *Boletín del Museo Social Argentino*, 1919, VIII, 225.
76. Silva, "La habitación higiénica para el obrero," and *La Prensa*, May 23, 1905, p. 6.
77. *La Prensa*, Nov. 13, 1890, p. 6.
78. *La Voz de la Iglesia*, June 3, 21, 1893, Nov. 5, 1894, p. 1, cited in Hobart A. Spalding, Jr., "Cuando los inquilinos hacen huelga . . . ," *Extra*, II, No. 14, Sept. 1966, p. 34.
79. *Caras y Caretas*, X, No. 468, Sept. 21, 1907, unpaginated.
80. *La Prensa*, Oct. 5, 1907, p. 6.
81. *La Prensa*, Oct. 23, 24, 28, 1907, p. 5, 9, 7; *Caras y Caretas*, X, No. 474, Nov. 2, 1907, unpaginated.
82. *La Prensa*, Nov. 1, 6, 15, 1907, p. 8, 6, 5.
83. Spalding, Jr., "Cuando los inquilinos hacen huelga . . . ," p. 38.
84. *La Prensa*, Dec. 5, 1907, p. 9.
85. *La Prensa*, May 18, 1908, p. 7.

Chapter 5

1. See debates in Buenos Aires, Diputados, *Sesiones*, 1868, July 15, Oct. 24, pp. 224–38, 456; Senadores, *Sesiones*, 1868, Aug. 22, Oct. 17, 22, pp. 73–86, 121–22, 123–24, 126. The provincial government finally assumed this jurisdiction, to be replaced in 1880 by the national authorities.
2. Pedro Agote, *Breve reseña de la fundación de los tramways en la ciudad de Buenos Aires, año 1868* (Buenos Aires, 1916).
3. Marino Jalikis, *Historia de los medios de transporte y de su influencia en el desarrollo urbano de la ciudad de Buenos Aires* (Buenos Aires, 1925), pp. 58–59.
4. *La Prensa*, Aug. 18, 1870, p. 2.
5. *La Prensa*, March 3, 1870, p. 2.
6. *Ibid.*
7. *Actas*, 1870, March 29, pp. 79–83.
8. *Actas*, 1870, Aug. 23, p. 275.
9. *La Prensa*, Jan. 21, 1871, p. 2.
10. *La Prensa*, March 10, 1871, p. 1.

11. *La Prensa,* June 22, 1871, p. 2; the schedule was printed in an advertisement, Jan. 19, 1871, p. 3.
12. Buenos Aires, Municipalidad de, *Recopilación de leyes, ordenanzas, decretos y contratos de concesiones de tranvías* (Buenos Aires, 1908), pp. 179–459, 622–34, *passim* (hereafter cited as *Recopilación de tranvías*).
13. *Memoria de la Municipalidad,* 1872, pp. 41–42.
14. *Actas,* 1873, Aug. 7, pp. 255–56. The deposit requirement had been established by decree, Nov. 28, 1872.
15. From the Archivo de Planos de Remates, Casa Adolfo Bullrich, Buenos Aires, Oct. 16, Nov. 18, 1870, Sept. 17, 1871, April 20, 1873. I am indebted to Professor Joseph Tulchin for identifying these private archives to me.
16. *La Prensa,* June 22, 1871, p. 1. Several years later *La Prensa,* Nov. 13, 1879, p. 1, made an even more pointed comment: "¿En cuántos millones ha subido la propiedad raíz gracias a la influencia de los tranvías? Todo el mundo sabe que una propiedad vale más o menos según su proximidad con una línea tranviaria."
17. *Actas,* 1870, Aug. 31, p. 285.
18. *Memoria de la Municipalidad,* 1878, I, pp. 258–59.
19. An illustrative article entitled "Trenvías [*sic*] en Nueva York y en Buenos Aires," *La Prensa,* Sept. 27, 1876, p. 1, suggested that Buenos Aires streetcar fares were considerably higher than those of New York. Also see "Compañía de Tramways Anglo-Argentina Limitada," *Caras y Caretas,* XI, No. 483, Jan. 4, 1908, unpaginated.
20. *La Prensa,* Jan. 31, Feb. 2, 3, 1884, p. 3, 4, 4.
21. *Actas,* 1886, June 7, p. 290. During debate on this question, it was observed that most passengers used streetcars for relatively short distances of ten to fifteen blocks.
22. *La Prensa,* Nov. 24, 1882, p. 1.
23. *Recopilación de tranvías:* Concession to Carlos Gutiérrez, Oct. 12, 1887, which subsequently became the Gran Nacional, pp. 813–19; to Pedro A. Gartland, March 27, 1888, to become La Nueva, pp. 943–48; to Wenceslao Villafañe, Oct. 22, 1887, to become La Capital to Flores, pp. 995–99; and to Antonio Carrozzi and Nicolás Figueredo, Jan. 11, 1888, to become the Metropolitano, pp. 1089–93.
24. *Recopilación de tranvías,* pp. 1143–62; *Actas,* 1887, June 30, pp. 290–99.
25. *Memoria de la Municipalidad,* 1890–92, pp. 400–401.
26. Law No. 1752, Nov. 9, 1885, of the Argentine Republic. Diputados, *Sesiones,* 1885, II, Nov. 3, pp. 862–66; Senadores, *Sesiones,* Nov. 4, pp. 855–61, 863. When the new companies secured concessions in 1887–88, an 8 per cent tax was initially agreed upon, but it was lowered in 1892 to 6 per cent.
27. *La Prensa,* Feb. 26, March 30, 1876, p. 1. Between 1874 and 1876 land values fell an estimated 50 per cent; *La Prensa,* April 1, 30, June 8, Sept. 17, 1876, p. 1.
28. *La Prensa,* Aug. 22, 1886, p. 3.
29. *La Prensa,* Jan. 1, 1887, p. 17.
30. *La Prensa,* April 21, May 11, 1887, p. 3.

31. Auction notice by Luis Godoy, *La Prensa,* April 7, 1887, p. 8, and notice by Sánchez y Moreno, July 1, 1887, p. 6.

32. *Recopilación de tranvías,* p. 148. For resistance by the companies, see *La Prensa,* Aug. 9, Sept. 22, 1891, and Oct. 26, 1893, p. 5. The matter was finally resolved with the companies' acceptance of rate regulations, *Actas,* 1894, May 14, pp. 207–9.

33. *Actas,* 1895, Nov. 13, pp. 726–37. During the summer, worker cars were to run from 5:00 to 6:00 a.m. and from 7:00 to 8:00 p.m., while in the winter the schedule was 6:00 to 7:00 a.m. and 5:00 to 6:00 p.m. In discussing the regulation, it was observed that several companies had already instituted this practice on their own.

34. *La Prensa,* April 28, 1896, p. 5.

35. *Actas,* 1895, Nov. 28, 29, pp. 805–20, 826. The municipal council finally accepted an alternate route along Las Heras and Santa Fe.

36. *Revista Municipal,* III, No. 290, March 13, 1896, p. 220.

37. *Actas,* 1895, Nov. 8, p. 720.

38. *Memoria de la Municipalidad,* 1890–92, p. 210.

39. *La Prensa,* April 12, 1894, reported a suggestion for removal of streetcar tracks for a twenty-five-block area immediately around the plaza. The vicissitudes of the Lacroze authorization were recorded in *Actas,* 1899, Dec. 21, pp. 528–29, and 1901, May 21, pp. 93–4, June 28, pp. 148–49, July 5, pp. 157–58.

40. *La Prensa,* Jan. 13, 1900, p. 5.

41. *Revista Municipal,* II, No. 228, Sept. 27, 1895, pp. 2020–21.

42. One such early concession was discussed in Diputados, *Sesiones,* 1894, II, Nov. 7, pp. 461–66, and was granted to Quesada Hermanos. It was to run from the corner of Rioja and Victoria at Plaza Once to the suburbs of Caballito and Nuevos Mataderos and terminate at the town of San Justo, southwest of the Federal District. For other examples, see *La Prensa,* May 28, 1896, p. 6, and *Memoria de la Municipalidad,* 1896, pp. 53–54.

43. *Memoria de la Municipalidad,* 1897, p. 81.

44. *La Prensa,* June 14, Aug. 19, 1900, p. 5.

45. *La Prensa,* March 30, May 30, 1902, p. 2, 3.

46. *Actas,* 1899, Dec. 21, pp. 525–26. The lower speed was ordered within the area bounded by Centro América (later renamed Pueyrredón), Jujuy, and Caseros, roughly that area of twenty to thirty blocks beyond the "walking" city of 1880 that had been built up with assistance from the streetcar system.

47. *La Prensa,* Aug. 21, 1908, p. 8.

48. *La Prensa,* Oct. 21, and 24, 1903, p. 4, 7.

49. Carlos María Morales, "Las mejoras edilicias de Buenos Aires," *Anales de la Sociedad Científica Argentina,* No. 52, 1901, p. 75.

50. *La Prensa,* Feb. 23, 1903, p. 3.

51. *La Prensa,* June 30, July 27, 29, 1900, p. 5, 6, 6.

52. *Actas,* 1903, Nov. 17, p. 499; repeated 1904, June 7, pp. 175–76. Also in *Actas,* 1904, Nov. 8, pp. 590–91, the deadline for the 1903 ordinance was extended to 1905. *Actas,* 1907, Nov. 15, pp. 522–23, gave a year's extension to the Lacroze company to carry out the 1903 order.

53. *La Prensa*, March 17, 1903, p. 7.

54. *La Prensa*, Feb. 15, 1905, p. 6.

55. *La Prensa*, Dec. 13, 1906, p. 5.

56. One major effort by such a syndicate in 1906–7 seems to have failed, but the activities of representatives in Europe and in Buenos Aires fueled new rumors; see *La Prensa*, Feb. 19, March 6, April 4, 1907, p. 8, 5, 9.

57. *Actas*, 1908, May 22, pp. 170–77.

58. *La Prensa*, Oct. 10, 1908, p. 6.

59. *Actas*, 1909, July 12, pp. 187–201.

60. The *Revista Municipal* continued to point out the absence of "worker cars" after electrification and unification of the system; see VII, No. 318, Feb. 28, 1910, p. 13; VIII, No. 375, April 3, 1911, p. 13; X, No. 475, Feb. 17, 1913, p. 12; XI, No. 553, Aug. 31, 1914, pp. 13–14.

61. *Revista Municipal*, VI, No. 284, July 5, 1909, p. 14, noted that built-up areas usually extended back as far as eight blocks on each side of a streetcar line.

62. *Censo general de la ciudad de Buenos Aires de 1904*, pp. 105, 109; *Tercer censo nacional, 1914*, X, 485–95.

63. Average for lots taken from numerous auction notices from 1905 through 1909; estimate on building costs noted in *La Prensa*, Jan. 16, 1900, p. 3.

64. Manuel de Oliveira Lima, *En la Argentina; impresiones de 1918–19*, trans. by Valentín Diego (Montevideo, 1920), p. 100.

65. *Revista Municipal*, III, No. 263, Jan. 8, 1896, p. 2. The reference to *cinta negra* appears, for example, in Alcides Greca, *Problemas del urbanismo en la República Argentina* (Santa Fe, 1939), pp. 34–35, and in Rodolfo Borzone, "Peligrosidad sanitaria del suburbio," *Revista de Ciencias Jurídicas y Sociales* (Santa Fe), 1937, pp. 157–74.

66. Federico R. Cibils, "La decentralización urbana de la ciudad de Buenos Aires," *Boletín del Departamento Nacional del Trabajo*, 1911, No. 16, p. 89.

67. Gabriela L. de Coni, "El barrio de las ranas," *La Prensa*, Feb. 7, 1902, p. 3; "La quema de basuras," Feb. 8, 1902, p. 3.

68. Sale by Bollini Muro y Cía, *La Prensa*, Oct. 2, 1888, p. 7. Another sale by G. Gowland, advertised on p. 8, offered land in return for one-half in cash and the balance in four months; still another sale by Francisco Constenla required half in cash and the remainder in six months. For lands in Flores, Florencio Carreras offered terms of the first quarter in cash with the other quarters paid at four, eight, and twelve months; *La Prensa*, Oct. 12, 1888, p. 7.

69. Banco Hipotecario Nacional, *75 aniversario, 1886–1961* (Buenos Aires, 1961), p. 36. Laws Nos. 3751 and 4500, Dec. 24, 1898, and Sept. 29, 1904, of the Argentine Republic authorized emissions of cédulas; Law No. 3889, Dec. 26, 1899, of the Argentine Republic, created a Caja de Crédito Hipotecario to facilitate land mortgages in the Federal District.

70. Carlos A. Aldao, "Consideraciones sobre la justicia argentina," *Revista de Historia, Derecho y Letras*, I, No. 1, 1898, p. 361. *La Prensa*, Aug. 17, 1901, p. 4, indicated that 15 per cent interest was the general rule for mortgages. An article on usury in *La Prensa*, Jan. 10, 1904, p. 4, stated that, with closing expenses, the interest on real estate loans approximated 1.75 per cent per month.

71. *La Prensa*, Oct. 26, 1900, p. 3, quoting an article from an undated issue of *La Propiedad*.

72. On the basis of advice from legal counsel, *La Prensa*, Aug. 15, 1901, p. 3, reported that costs for a 1000-peso mortgage for two years amounted to 100 pesos; for a 10,000-peso loan for two years the cost was 200 pesos. Another case cited in *La Prensa*, Dec. 26, 1902, p. 5, involved a recent 1000-peso mortgage secured from the Banco Hipotecario Nacional on a property worth 9000 pesos. The loan was requested in Sept. 1901 and finally secured fifteen months later; legal costs took 155 pesos and the depreciation and first interest charges subtracted another 213 pesos, which left the borrower with cash of 632 pesos in return for a 1000-peso debt.

73. *La Prensa*, Jan. 10, 1904, p. 4.

74. *Revista Municipal*, I, No. 47, Dec. 12, 1904, pp. 4–5.

75. Auction of 200 lots by V. S. Lobato y Cía, *La Prensa*, Nov. 13, 1902, p. 9.

76. Auction by Guerrico y Williams, *La Prensa*, Nov. 8, 16, 1903, p. 12, 8.

77. Auction by Risso y Patrón, *La Prensa*, May 7, 1904, p. 12.

78. This last inducement, adequate to build a small two- or three-room house, was offered in an auction by Román Bravo at a sale of 460 lots of the Sociedad Fomento Urbano in Floresta; *La Prensa*, Aug. 22, 1906, p. 3.

79. *La Prensa*, Jan. 19, 1906, p. 10.

80. *La Prensa*, May 6, 1907, p. 10.

81. *La Prensa*, Dec. 3, 1905, p. 20.

82. *La Prensa*, Dec. 10, 1905, p. 12. The first sixteen to receive loans were a shoemaker, a blacksmith, a shopkeeper, a streetcar inspector, a cigarette vendor, an army enlisted man, a gilder, two mechanics, and seven employees; *La Prensa*, Jan. 17, 1906, p. 4.

83. *Actas*, 1905, Oct. 1, p. 498. This council action implemented the ordinance of July 31, 1905.

84. *La Prensa*, April 16, 1908, p. 5.

85. Adolfo Mugica noted that costs on a 1000-peso mortgage still amounted to 71 pesos in addition to whatever depreciation the mortgage bonds might suffer; Diputados, *Sesiones*, 1910, II, Sept. 16, p. 541. See also note 72 above.

86. Banco Hipotecario Nacional, *El banco en su primer cincuentenario* (Buenos Aires, 1936), p. 73.

87. *Actas*, 1874, Dec. 31, p. 306.

88. *Memoria de la Municipalidad*, 1879, I, p. 31, and, for 1880, p. 121. Owned by the Cano family and located on Corrientes between Esmeralda and Suipacha.

89. *Actas*, 1884, Dec. 31, p. 253; 1885, July 27, p. 55; 1889, March 29, April 8, pp. 147–50, 170.

90. *La Prensa*, Jan. 31, 1891, p. 5. Details of the plans are given in the *Memoria de la Municipalidad*, 1885, pp. 58–63.

91. Particularly noteworthy publicity appeared in the *Revista Municipal*, I, No. 42, Nov. 7, 1904, pp. 1–2; II, No. 73, June 12, 1905, pp. 1–2; and in *La Prensa*, May 29, June 2, 1905, p. 7, 6.

92. Law No. 4824, Oct. 10, 1905, of the Argentine Republic. Diputados, *Sesiones*,

1904, I, July 6, pp. 418–22; 1905, I, May 3, pp. 35–36; II, Sept. 18, pp. 1032–33; Senadores, *Sesiones*, 1905, I, Sept. 19, 25, 27, pp. 914, 1017, 1137–38.

93. *Revista Municipal*, II, No. 82, Aug. 14, 1905, pp. 1–3.

94. *Actas*, 1905, Sept. 19, pp. 441–42. The public competition was announced for December 1906, the two winners were selected in April 1907, and the prize money of 1500 pesos each was paid in November 1907, see *La Prensa*, Aug. 6, 1906, p. 9; *Caras y Caretas*, X, No. 445, April 13, 1907, unpaginated; *Actas*, 1907, Nov. 15, p. 526.

95. *Actas*, 1907, July 30, pp. 318–19. *La Prensa*, March 24, April 7, 1907, p. 10, 4.

96. *La Prensa*, Nov. 20, Dec. 16, 1907, p. 9, 5. This project was to be located at Avenida La Plata and Chiclana.

97. Donation from Azusena Butteler of land bounded by Avenida La Plata, Avenida Cobo, Senillosa, and Zelarrayán; see *Actas*, 1907, Nov. 12, pp. 504–5. Construction was begun on this property, as noted in *Actas*, 1908, Oct. 9, pp. 407–8.

98. *Actas*, 1909, July 28, p. 28; *Memoria de la Municipalidad*, 1910, p. xii, 1911, pp. xvi–xvii.

99. *Actas*, 1910, July 27, pp. 414–18. The municipal council did not surrender control to this society without voicing some opposition. Councilmen Delio Aguilar and Esteban Canale both observed that religious sentiments might dominate the decisions of these good ladies and that an organization more closely linked with the workers should administer the housing.

100. Law 7102, Sept. 21, 1910, of the Argentine Republic. Diputados, *Sesiones*, 1910, I, July 27, pp. 643–46; II, Sept. 14, pp. 465–78; Senadores, *Sesiones*, 1910, I, Sept. 20, pp. 676–78. Also see *Revista Municipal*, VI, No. 296, Sept. 27, 1909, pp. 14–15, for the origins of this proposal.

101. Diputados, *Sesiones*, 1913, I, June 11, pp. 960–67.

102. *Revista Municipal*, X, No. 505, Sept. 29, 1913, pp. 3–4; *Actas*, 1913, Oct. 17, pp. 558–69.

103. Law No. 9677, Oct. 5, 1915, of the Argentine Republic. Diputados, *Sesiones*, 1912, II, Aug. 14, pp. 180–86.

104. Juan A. Buschiazzo, "Memoria descriptiva del proyecto para la construcción de una gran casa de inquilinato para el Banco Constructor de la Plata," *Anales de la Sociedad Científica Argentina*, No. 26, 1886, pp. 134–44.

105. *Caras y Caretas*, VI, No. 232, March 14, 1903, unpaginated.

106. *Caras y Caretas*, X, No. 463, Aug. 17, 1907, unpaginated.

107. Carolina Muzzelli, "El Hogar Obrero," *Boletín del Museo Social Argentino*, II, 1913, pp. 209–20. For further details see Nicolás Repetto, *Mi paso por la política: De Roca a Yrigoyen* (Buenos Aires, 1956), pp. 98–101.

108. Based on total capital invested, given in lists of societies incorporated in the city of Buenos Aires for 1906, 1907, and 1908, *Anuario Estadístico de la Ciudad de Buenos Aires*.

109. *La Prensa*, Aug. 24, Sept. 27, Nov. 4, 1906, p. 8, 5, 9.

110. *La Prensa*, Oct. 4, Nov. 10, 1906, p. 9.

111. Federico Rahola y Tremols, *Sangre nueva. Impresiones de un viaje a la América*

del Sud (Barcelona, 1905), p. 89. These kinds of comments came frequently from foreign visitors to Buenos Aires after the turn of the century. Similar amazement at the degree to which Buenos Aires had spread out came from a New York City resident; see *Revista Municipal*, I, No. 2, Feb. 1, 1904, p. 2.

112. Outlying districts constituted a smaller percentage in the 1870 city. If one considers Districts 1, 2, 3, 4, 5, 6, 13, 14, and 16 as built-up zones in the 1869 census, then 30 per cent of the population (including those living in La Boca and Barracas) lived in suburbs.

113. *La Nación*, Oct. 7, 1882, p. 1. The prestigious surnames that appeared on the four-man parish committees appointed during that meeting reflected the considerable influence still associated with the city's south side: for Catedral al Sur, Marcó del Pont, Martínez de Hoz, Bullrich, and Nazar; for Concepción, Marín, Tamini, Areco, and Eizaguirre; for San Telmo, Boeri, French, Casares, and Naón; for San Cristóbal, Quesada, Gowland, Casares, and Aldao; for Monserrat, Malaver, Orr, Shaw, and Bullrich; for San Juan Evangelista or La Boca, Drysdale, Badaraco, Fernández, and Casares; and for Santa Lucía, Arditi, Pérez, Mañé, and Guerrero.

114. *La Prensa*, Oct. 8, 1882, p. 1.

115. *Actas*, 1883, June 8, Aug. 3, pp. 55, 180–81. Similar observations were made by Onésimo Leguizamón in the national Congress; Diputados, *Sesiones*, 1883, I, Aug. 1, pp. 824–25.

116. *Actas*, 1883, Aug. 6, p. 189.

117. *Actas*, 1884, March 19, pp. 48–49.

118. *Actas*, 1885, Sept. 18, Dec. 18, pp. 63, 149–50. The avenue was not named for the Intendente, but for his grandfather, Carlos María de Alvear, a leader in Argentina's independence movement.

119. *La Prensa*, April 10, 1889, p. 6.

120. Émile Daireaux, *La vie et les moeurs à la Plata* (2 vols.; Paris, 1888), II, 123.

121. *La Prensa*, Aug. 21, 1897, p. 5.

122. *Actas*, 1873, March 20, pp. 112–15; *Memoria de la Municipalidad*, 1886, pp. 75–77.

123. *La Prensa*, Feb. 9, April 9, 10, 1897, p. 5, 4, 5. The resultant regulations (*Actas*, 1900, Dec. 10, pp. 429–32) established two categories of industries—those which had to be located at least 200 yards away from all housing, and those that could be established anywhere.

124. *Revista Municipal*, III, No. 112, March 12, 1906, pp. 3–4; IV, No. 179, June 24, 1907, p. 7.

125. *Revista Municipal*, VI, No. 268, March 8, 1909, p. 11.

126. *Actas*, 1914, Nov. 17, pp. 727–34; *Revista Municipal*, XI, No. 565, Nov. 23, 1914, pp. 13–14.

127. *Censo de la ciudad de Buenos Aires de 1909*, I, 96–101.

128. Lucas Benítez, *Para la antología de los barrios porteños: "Los Olivos," Barracas al Norte, 1895–1960* (Buenos Aires, 1965), pp. 25, 35.

129. Benítez, "*Los Olivos*," pp. 93–100.

130. *La Prensa*, Aug. 27, 1907, p. 5.

Chapter 6

1. A more detailed list of occupations generally held by gente decente, compiled from the 1914 national census (IV:201–12), includes *criadores, cabañeros, estancieros, hacendados, invernadores, banqueros, capitalistas, empresarios, exportadores, gerentes, importadores, clérigos, sacerdotes, abogados, contadores públicos, escribanos, procuradores, dentistas, médicos, químicos, profesores de enseñanza secundaria y universitaria, agrimensores, agrónomos, doctores, escritores, ingenieros, matemáticos, periodistas, peritos, estudiantes secundarios y universitarios*. These occupations, or easily recognizable substitutes, appear in all the preceding censuses. In such lists, however, there are no specific enumerations of heads of government offices or owners of major industrial and commercial establishments, since there is no reliable measure from census data to establish the percentage or number of such people—as distinct from government employees, artisans, or shopkeepers in general. Several assumptions are made in justification of this omission: that the numbers of top bureaucrats and wealthy merchants, as developed from other sources such as almanacs and city directories, were small and did not amount, even in 1914, to more than 1000 persons; that inclusion of such men in lists of occupations on the borderline of gente-decente status—such as *contadores públicos, procuradores, periodistas,* and *dentistas*—balance some of those omitted in administrative and owner functions; and, most important, that, given the importance of professional titles and landed wealth in Argentina, a large proportion of the administrative-owner category will appear under headings of *banqueros, capitalistas, empresarios, abogados, escribanos, ingenieros, estancieros,* and *hacendados*, rather than under *empleados* or *comerciantes*.

2. The sub-category of blue-collar and white-collar, established from 1914 census classifications, embraces the next three strata to be discussed, since no reliable means have been devised by which the strata lumped together in occupational classifications can be divided. Those occupations in this sub-category with at least 1000 males (an asterisk denotes over 10,000) fourteen years of age and over in the 1914 census are: *agricultores, jardineros, albañiles,* aparadores, aprendices, carboneros, carniceros, carpinteros,* confiteros, constructores, curtidores, ebanistas, electricistas, encuadernadores, estibadores, foguistas, fundidores, gasistas, herreros,* hojalateros, industriales, lecheros, maquinistas, marmoleros, mecánicos,* mosaiqueros, muebleros, operarios, panaderos, peluqueros, pintores,* sastres,* sombrereros, talabarteros, tipógrafos, yeseros, zapateros,* comerciantes,* corredores, dependientes, empleados de comercio,* repartidores, vendedores ambulantes, tenedores de libros, conductores, empleados de ferrocarril, empleados de tranvía, guardas de tranvía, motormen, telegrafistas, rentistas, empleados de gobierno,* jubilados, maestros de escuela primaria, dibujantes, escultores, músicos, empleados en general.**

3. A more detailed list, consisting of the sub-category of manual laborers established from the 1914 classifications, gives occupations with at least 1000 males

(an asterisk denotes over 10,000) fourteen years of age and over as *carreros, cocheros, personal de servicio,* marinos, militares, jornaleros,* peones.**

4. Toward the end of this period, an awareness of class interests had begun to appear in certain highly unionized trades and occupations in the city of Buenos Aires, as evidenced by strike manifestoes, anarchist propaganda, Labor Department reports, Socialist party activity, and other signs of labor solidarity; see Spalding, Jr. (ed.), *La clase trabajadora argentina*, and Marotta, *El movimiento sindical argentino*.

5. The well-known sociologist Gino Germani first related occupation to social class in his pioneer work, *Estructura social de la Argentina* (Buenos Aires, 1955). His classifications came from the 1947 national census and the 1935 industrial census and are applicable to class categories (*clase alta, clase media superior, clase media inferior, clase popular*) that developed well after 1910. John J. Johnson, *Political Change in Latin America: The Emergence of the Middle Sectors* (Stanford, 1958) applied the three-class model with some misgivings and difficulties to the Latin American scene. Works such as Gino Germani, *Política y sociedad en una época de transición: De la sociedad tradicional a la sociedad de masas* (Buenos Aires, 1962), Claudio Véliz (ed.), *Obstacles to Change in Latin America* (New York, 1965), and Irving L. Horowitz (ed.), *Masses in Latin America* (New York, 1970) suggest further problems with and limitations to the application of this model to Latin America.

6. *Censo municipal, 1887*, II, 43–47, 543–44; *Censo nacional, 1914*, IV, 201–12.

7. *La Prensa*, Aug. 6, 1873, p. 1.

8. *Actas*, 1889, March 22, p. 121.

9. *La Prensa*, Aug. 12, 1902, p. 4.

10. Rahola, p. 83.

11. Comments by Antonio Piñero in Diputados, *Sesiones*, 1907, I, June 26, p. 138.

12. Comments by Felipe Guasch Leguizamón in Diputados, *Sesiones*, 1908, I, June 1, p. 150.

13. *Censo general de la ciudad de Buenos Aires, 1909*, II, 337.

14. *Censo nacional de 1914*, IX, 127.

15. Juan Balestra, while Minister of Education, also provided a clear rationale of the humanistic orientation in secondary school studies. He maintained that classical and theoretical studies best prepared individuals for the university and as members of an educated ruling class: "Tal género de estudios lleva, como pendiente de fácil ascensión, a los altos estudios y carreras universitarias. Eso es lo natural, lo lógico, lo inevitable. Si de la gramática hacéis ascender al alumno a la literatura; si de la literatura preceptiva lo pasáis a Ovidio, Virgilio, Salustio y Cicerón; si de allí lo lleváis a aprender las leyes del entendimiento y de la conciencia humanos, con la filosofía; si, al mismo tiempo, de las simples operaciones aritméticas lo lleváis a razonar sobre ellas para ascenderlo luego al álgebra; si hacéis aplicar las reglas de las ecuaciones en los problemas de óptica y de acústica; si con la trigonometría lo preparáis para demostrar la rotación de los planetas alrededor del sol, según fórmulas matemáticas, ¿ cómo podréis impedir que ese alumno aspire a ir más y más allá, e intente aprender

en la Universidad las leyes que gobiernan al mundo físico o el mundo social y político, para ejercer, por su pensamiento y su palabra, una acción superior y dirigente? Si los colegios nacionales dan origen a las aspiraciones universitarias, están, pues, en su papel; para eso sirven. . . . Esa es una tendencia indiscutiblemente benéfica, esencial, salvadora, *cuyo destino especial es la formación de la más alta clase intelectual, de la gente ilustrada, de los hombres dirigentes.*" [Italics added]. Quoted in José Bianco, "Enseñanza pública: tendencias y orientaciones nacionales," *Tercer censo nacional de 1914*, IX, 32.

16. *Censo general de la ciudad de Buenos Aires de 1909*, II, 337–38.

17. The two quotations are from *La Prensa*, Oct. 24, 1872, July 8, 1873, p. 1. Projects for university reform were introduced in Diputados, *Sesiones*, 1901, I, May 13, pp. 24–41; 1903, II, Dec. 14, pp. 184–85; 1904, May 6, 9, 20, Sept. 16, 20, I, pp. 48–52, 57–64, 210–17, II, pp. 259–85, 401–3.

18. Comments by Manuel Carlés in Diputados, *Sesiones*, 1904, II, Sept. 16, pp. 263–64.

19. Universidad Nacional de Buenos Aires, *La Universidad Nacional de Buenos Aires, 1821–1910* (Buenos Aires, 1910), p. 151.

20. Comments by Mariano Demaría in Diputados, *Sesiones*, 1882, I, July 3, p. 509. The bill was introduced by Demaría on May 22, p. 92.

21. Diputados, *Sesiones*, 1882, I, July 3, 5, 7, pp. 509–33, 537–39, 567–75; see, esp., Onésimo Leguizamón's comments on July 3, pp. 515–16. *La Prensa*, July 19, 1882, p. 1, expressed disgust at the lack of action by the Chamber of Deputies on this project.

22. Otto Krause, "Instrucción industrial. Su implantación en el país," *Anales de la Sociedad Científica Argentina*, No. 47, 1899, p. 139.

23. *La Prensa*, June 19, 1908, p. 9.

24. Diputados, *Sesiones*, 1908, I, July 31, pp. 774–75; 1911, V, Nov. 15, pp. 32–33.

25. Comments by Lucas Ayarragaray in Diputados, *Sesiones*, 1910, I, June 8, p. 137.

26. Hobart A. Spalding, Jr., "Education in Argentina, 1890–1914: The Limits of Oligarchical Reform," *Journal of Interdisciplinary History*, III, No. I (Summer 1972), pp. 31–61, points out that, despite the adoption of certain reform principles and rhetoric in Argentine education, little more than token changes took place.

27. Based on families with three or more servants in Police District 1, City of Buenos Aires, manuscript returns of 1869 and 1895 national censuses.

28. Beyond such classics of the gaucho epic as José Hernández, *Martín Fierro*, Hilario Ascasubi, *Santos Vega*, and Estanislao del Campo, *Fausto*, stretches a sizable group of popularizers headed by Eduardo Gutiérrez, *Juan Moreira*. See Madaline W. Nichols, *The Gaucho: Cattle Hunter, Cavalryman, Ideal of Romance* (Durham, N.C., 1942); Raúl A. Cortázar, *Indios ye gauchos en la literatura argentina* (Buenos Aires, 1956); Enrique Williams Alzaga, *La pampa en la novela argentina* (Buenos Aires, 1955); Justo P. Sáenz (h.), *Equitación gaucha en la pampa y mesopotamia* (4th ed., Buenos Aires, 1959); Ricardo Rodríguez Molas, *Historia social del gaucho* (Buenos Aires, 1968).

29. The legends that subsequently developed around the figure of the compadrito

emerged in Miguel D. Etchebarne, *La influencia del arrabal en la poesía argentina culta* (Buenos Aires, 1955), pp. 80-82. Also see Francisco L. Romay, *El barrio de Monserrat* (Buenos Aires, 1962), pp. 57–60, and Adolfo Batiz, *Buenos Aires, la ribera y los prostíbulos en 1880* (Buenos Aires, n.d.), p. 93.

30. *La Prensa*, Feb. 3, 1902, p. 6, noted: "No será poco el asombro de los argentinos que completan su instrucción social en las viejas capitales europeas, al ver en los más afamados salones y en los más encumbrados *chateaux* bailar en sus barbas el tango tradicional, el tango argentino, que ellos altivamente desprecian por antiestético y antisocial."

31. See Julio Mafud, *Psicología de la viveza criolla* (Buenos Aires, 1965).

32. Adolfo Posada, *La República Argentina* (Madrid, 1912), pp. 76–77.

33. Julia V. Bunge, *Vida. Época maravillosa, 1903–1911* (Buenos Aires, 1965), p. 63.

34. Bunge, pp. 215–16.

35. *La Prensa*, Aug. 14, 1906, p. 8. Also see Bunge, pp. 280–90.

36. Rahola, pp. 295–98; Ibarguren, *La historia que he vivido*, pp. 239–40; Juan Balestra, *El noventa* (3d ed.; Buenos Aires, 1959), pp. 14–15.

37. *La Prensa*, Jan. 18, 1904, p. 4.

38. *La Prensa*, Aug. 19, 1901, p. 5.

39. Daireaux, II, 122.

40. The reported insult, printed in *Los Intereses Argentinos*, Feb. 18, 1870, p. 3, under the title of "Bandidos," told of the intervention by Argentine authorities to force the return to Italy of several known criminals who had come to the Río de la Plata. It continued, editorially, "Falanges como éstas son las que nos llegan por lo regular de Italia. Después querrán decirnos que la inmigración italiana es la mejor que viene a nuestras playas! La industria que nos traen, cuando no son bandidos, es tocar el organillo, limpiar botas, vender fruta, etc. etc. ¿Y diga alguno que no es cierto? Es la verdad, pese a quien pese." See *La Prensa*, Feb. 22, 23, 24, 1870, p. 2, for accounts of disturbances, and *Los Intereses Argentinos*, Feb. 24, 1870, p. 2, for the report of a threatened attack on its offices.

41. *La Prensa*, Jan. 1, March 18, 1874, p. 1, 2; *La Nación*, March 10, 1874, p. 2.

42. Sackville West to Earl of Derby, March 2, 1875, FO 6, Vol. 326, No. 12. Also see Leandro Gutiérrez, "El incendio del Colegio del Salvador, 1875: expresión de protesta social," *Segundo seminario sobre métodos de investigación y enseñanza de la historia y literatura rioplatense y de Estados Unidos* (mimeographed; Buenos Aires, Nov. 1967), pp. 1–7.

43. *La Prensa*, April 16, 18, July 2, 1876, p. 1.

44. *La Prensa*, Sept. 9, 1873, p. 1; Sackville West to Earl of Derby, Dec. 23, 1874, FO 6, Vol. 321, No. 113.

45. *La Prensa*, March 5, 1880, p. 1.

46. *La Prensa*, Feb. 22, 1878, p. 1; also see "Gratitud a los extranjeros," *La Nación*, Feb. 27, 1878, p. 1.

47. *La Prensa*, May 1, 18, 20, 22, 1880, p. 1.

48. *La Prensa* and *La Nación*, June 27, 1882, p. 1.

49. From *El Industrial*, July 17, 1880, p. 3, commented on in *La Prensa*, July 20, 1880, p. 1.

50. Diputados, *Sesiones*, 1882, I, May 27, pp. 131–32, II, Sept. 4, 5, pp. 125–55. Émile Daireaux, in commenting on this project, noted that while most foreigners delighted in criticizing the local government, customs, and values, they invariably refused to participate in politics; see Daireaux, II, 13–15.

51. A characteristic view of the weakened influence and power of the foreign diplomatic representative, even from England, to intervene within Argentina appears in the dispatch, Sackville West to Earl of Derby, Jan. 10, 1877, FO 6, Vol. 339, No. 2 Confidential. A Mr. Davison, a British subject and a contractor for part of the city waterworks, complained to the British Minister concerning three days' illegal detention by the local police. He was immediately informed by the local authorities that he had better drop the matter or his life would be endangered. Despite inquiries from the Foreign Office, Davison chose not to press the issue.

52. Daireaux, II, 123.

53. *La Prensa*, July 16, 17, 1903, p. 4, 6.

54. Comments by Antonio de Tomaso in Diputados, *Sesiones*, 1914, III, Aug. 17, p. 732.

55. These proposals, in order of presentation, were made in: (1) Diputados, *Sesiones*, 1885, I, July 24, pp. 322–23; (2) 1895, I, July 5, p. 236; 1898, I, Aug. 17, pp. 586–88; 1904, I, May 18, pp. 200–201; 1905, II, Sept. 19, pp. 1045–47; 1908, I, July 1, pp. 477–79; (3) 1912, I, July 17, pp. 568–70; (4) 1902, I, Aug. 28, pp. 682–3; 1911, I, June 25, pp. 514–16.

56. *La Prensa*, Aug. 29, 1902, p. 3. For comments on the large numbers of foreigners employed by the national and city governments, see *La Prensa*, Feb. 1, 1904, p. 6, and *Revista Municipal*, VIII, Nos. 410 and 413, Dec. 4, 25, 1911, pp. 12–13, 12.

57. *Segundo censo nacional de 1895*, II, 19. If the denominator is changed to the total number of voting-age foreign males, eighteen and over, the percentage of naturalized citizens becomes 0.4 per cent; II, 11–12.

58. If the denominator in each case is changed to voting-age foreign males, eighteen years and over, the percentages become 2.3, 2.8, and 4.5 per cent, respectively; see *Censo de la ciudad de Buenos Aires de 1904*, pp. 23, 30–34; *Censo de la ciudad de Buenos Aires de 1909*, I, 17, 32, 47–49; *Tercer censo nacional de 1914*, II, 3, 403, III, 17–19.

59. Diputados, *Sesiones*, 1913, II, Aug. 1, p. 709.

60. *Tercer censo nacional de 1914*, I, 213–14.

61. *La Prensa*, May 8, 10, 29, June 6, 1899, p. 6.

62. The initial meeting to organize the Liga, highlighted by an inflammatory address by Estanislao Zeballos, was reported in *La Nación*, Dec. 19, 1901, p. 5. Thereafter the press carried daily reports on the extensive activities of the Liga, climaxing with its definitive organization on Jan. 16, 1902; see *La Nación*, Jan. 17, 19, 1902, p. 5, 3; *La Prensa*, Jan. 19, 1902, p. 6.

63. *Revista Municipal*, VII, No. 328, May 9, 1910, p. 6; also see *Caras y Caretas*, XIII, No. 606, May 14, 1910, unpaginated.

64. Spalding, Jr., "Education in Argentina, 1890–1914," p. 42.

65. Diputados, *Sesiones*, 1894, I, Sept. 17, pp. 811–18; 1896, I, Sept. 4, 7, 9, pp. 751–69, 771–91, 793–831.

66. Consejo Nacional de Educación, *La educación común en la República Argentina: Primer informe presentado al Ministerio de Justicia e Instrucción Pública por el Presidente del Consejo* (Buenos Aires, 1910), p. 145.

67. *Ibid.* pp. 146–47.

68. *La Prensa*, July 8, 9, 1909, p. 11, 15; *La Nación*, July 4, 9, 1909, p. 8, 9.

69. *La Prensa*, May 21, 25, 1910, p. 13, 42.

70. *La Prensa*, May 24, 25, 1911, p. 12.

71. John A. Hammerton, *The Real Argentine*, pp. 241–42; also cited in Spalding, Jr., "Education in Argentina, 1890–1914," pp. 44–45.

72. Posada, p. 222.

73. Posada, p. 224.

74. Mabragaña, *Los mensajes*, V, 353.

75. The major subject of Argentina's economic development can only be touched upon in this study by means of these examples. For more detailed understanding of the issues and areas involved one must turn to Carlos F. Díaz Alejandro, *Essays on the Economic History of the Argentine Republic* (New Haven, Conn., 1970); Guido di Tella and Manuel Zymelman, *Las estapas del desarrollo económico argentino* (Buenos Aires, 1967); Adolfo Dorfman, *Historia de la industria argentina* (2d ed.; Buenos Aires, 1971); Aldo Ferrer, *The Argentine Economy* (Berkeley, Calif., 1967); Ricardo M. Ortiz, *Historia económica de la Argentina, 1850–1930* (2 vols.; Buenos Aires, 1965); Leopoldo Portnoy, *Análisis crítico de la economía argentina* (Buenos Aires, 1961); and Vicente Vásquez-Presedo, *El caso argentino: migración de factores, comercio exterior y desarrollo, 1875–1914* (Buenos Aires, 1971).

76. Diputados, *Sesiones*, 1897, II, Jan. 3, 1898, p. 771.

77. Diputados, *Sesiones*, 1891, I, July 3, 17, 20, 22, pp. 247–56, 306–27, 328–48, 351–66.

78. Diputados, *Sesiones*, 1897, II, Dec. 21, pp. 477–502.

79. "El malestar comercial," *La Prensa*, Oct. 12, 19, 22, 1902, p. 4, 5, 3.

80. Law No. 759, Oct. 14, 1875, of the Argentine Republic. Diputados, *Sesiones*, 1875, II, Sept. 14, 15, Oct. 11, 12, pp. 1102–34, 1135–51, 1455–58, 1463–64; Senadores, *Sesiones;* evidently this law was discussed in secret session or sent directly back from the Senate subcommittee to the Chamber of Deputies, for no Senate debate on the measure appears. See pp. 1123–24 for Carlos Pellegrini's remarks. Articles that stressed the complementary aspects of certain industries to Argentina's agricultural production appeared in the leading livestock journal, *Anales de la Sociedad Rural Argentina*, under the titles "Lo que somos y lo que debemos ser" and "El pastoreo y las fábricas," V, No. 4, April 30, 1871, pp. 128–30, 130–33. To British interests concerned with free trade with Argentina even the 1875 tariff provisions for support of flour milling seemed

"ultra-protectionist." See Sackville West to Earl of Derby, Oct. 3, 1877, FO 6, Vol. 341, No. 22 Commercial.

81. Diputados, *Sesiones,* 1892, II, Nov. 7, p. 182.
82. Diputados, *Sesiones,* 1892, II, Nov. 4, pp. 152–55.
83. Law No. 2766, Oct. 18, 1890; Law No. 2923, Dec. 27, 1892; Law No. 3672, Jan. 3, 1898; Law No. 3757, Dec. 30, 1898; Law No. 3890, Jan. 4, 1900, of the Argentine Republic.
84. *Tercer censo nacional de 1914,* VII, 68.
85. Diputados, *Sesiones,* 1898, II, Nov. 4, 7, 10, pp. 121–51, 152–55, 213–30; 1899, II, Nov. 10, pp. 213–30.
86. Diputados, *Sesiones,* 1907, I, July 31, pp. 617–39.
87. *La Prensa,* Dec. 13, 1905, p. 7, assigned principal blame for this inferior record to the lack of protection or reward for inventors in Argentina.
88. Law No. 3975, Nov. 14, 1900, of the Argentine Republic. Senadores, *Sesiones,* 1900, Sept. 28, 29, Nov. 14, pp. 346, 373–92, 606; Diputados, *Sesiones,* 1900, II, Oct. 5, Nov. 14, pp. 3, 446–52.
89. Statement accompanying a project from the executive branch, Diputados, *Sesiones,* 1910, II, Aug. 24, p. 51.
90. Diputados, *Sesiones,* 1913, II, June 19, p. 181.

Chapter 7

1. The statement of the commercial-bureaucratic type of city first appeared in James R. Scobie, "Buenos Aires as a Commercial-Bureaucratic City, 1880–1910: Characteristics of a City's Orientation," *The American Historical Review,* Vol. 77, No. 4 (Oct. 1972), pp. 1035–73.
2. For a provocative explanation of the dynamics of the multiplier effect as experienced in Great Britain and the United States, see Allan R. Pred, *The Spatial Dynamics of U.S. Urban-Industrial Growth, 1800–1914: Interpretive and Theoretical Essays* (Cambridge, Mass., 1966), pp. 25, 177–79.
3. For a discussion of the effect of heavy investment in urban real estate and construction accompanied by a more temporary postponement of industrialization, see N. G. Butlin, *Investment in Australian Economic Development, 1861–1900* (Cambridge, Eng., 1964), pp. 211–14, 245–46.
4. Philip M. Hauser, in Philip M. Hauser and Leo F. Schnore (eds.), *The Study of Urbanization* (New York, 1965), p. 36, suggests that in underdeveloped nations such a single major city frequently grows excessively because of its position as entrepôt between the "colony" and the imperial country. Disruption of the imperial system often leads to some loss of the city's basic economic function. "To the extent that this has occurred, such cities must await further national economic growth adequately to support their present size."
5. One such parallel appears in the "commercial city" described by John W. McCarty, "Australian Capital Cities in the Nineteenth Century," *Australian Economic History Review,* X, No. 2 (Sept. 1970), pp. 107–37.

Selected Bibliography

A NOTE FOR FURTHER READINGS ON THE CITY OF BUENOS AIRES

For those who wish to probe more deeply into the development of Buenos Aires, I have prepared the following selective bibliography. It is divided into two sections: the first lists general works on the city, while the second provides commentary on the principal sources used in the preparation of this study. Additional detailed information can be found in the notes. I call particular attention to the specialized bibliographies listed therein: travelers' accounts published between 1906 and 1916 (Ch. 2, note 2); development of the port of Buenos Aires (Ch. 3, notes 3 and 5); railroad expansion (Ch. 3, note 57); the "capital" question (Ch. 3, note 68); the yellow fever epidemic of 1871 (Ch. 4, note 5); changing architectural styles (Ch. 4, note 14); wages and labor conditions (Ch. 4, note 21); the labor movement (Ch. 4, note 40); conditions of conventillo life (Ch. 4, notes 58 and 74); class and occupations (Ch. 6, note 5); gaucho influences (Ch. 6, note 28); the compadrito (Ch. 6, note 29); and economic development (Ch. 6, note 75).

I. GENERAL WORKS

Arrieta, Rafael A., *La ciudad y los libros* (Buenos Aires, 1955).

Beccar Varela, Adrián, *Torcuato de Alvear, primer intendente municipal de la ciudad de Buenos Aires. Su acción edilicia* (Buenos Aires, 1926).

Benítez, Lucas, "*Los Olivos.*" *Barracas al Norte, 1895–1960. Para la antología de los barrios porteños* (Buenos Aires, 1965).

Besio Moreno, Nicolás, *Buenos Aires: puerto del Río de la Plata, capital de la Argentina. Estudio crítico de su población, 1536–1936* (Buenos Aires, 1939).

Bilbao, Manuel, *Buenos Aires, desde su fundación hasta nuestros días, especialmente el período comprendido en los siglos XVIII y XIX* (Buenos Aires, 1902).

Bossio, Jorge A., *Los cafés de Buenos Aires* (Buenos Aires, 1968).

Bucich, Antonio J., *La Boca del Riachuelo en la historia* (Buenos Aires, 1971).

Bucich Escobar, Ismael, *Buenos Aires, ciudad. Reseña histórica y descriptiva de la capital argentina desde su primera fundación hasta el presente* (Buenos Aires, 1936).

Buenos Aires, Honorable Concejo Deliberante de la Ciudad, *Evolución institucional del municipio de la ciudad de Buenos Aires* (Buenos Aires, 1963).

Buenos Aires, Municipalidad de la Ciudad de, *Cuadernos de Buenos Aires.* This is a series of forty-one brief, often illustrated, studies; particularly useful items to local history are listed by author.

> Bucich, Antonio J., *Los viajeros descubren la Boca del Riachuelo,* Vol. 14 (Buenos Aires, 1961).
>
> Córdoba, Alberto O., *El barrio de Belgrano; hombres y cosas de su pasado histórico,* Vol. 27 (Buenos Aires, 1968).
>
> Corrodi, Hugo, *Guía antigua del oeste porteño,* Vol. 30 (Buenos Aires, 1969).
>
> *Evolución urbana de la ciudad de Buenos Aires; breve síntesis histórica hasta 1910,* Vol. 12 (Buenos Aires, 1960).
>
> Fernández Moreno, Baldomero, *San José de Flores,* Vol. 22 (Buenos Aires, 1963).
>
> García de Lloydi, Ludovico, *La catedral de Buenos Aires,* Vol. 36 (Buenos Aires, 1971).
>
> Lafuente Machain, Ricardo de, *El barrio de la Recoleta,* Vol. 16 (2d ed.; Buenos Aires, 1962).
>
> ———, *El barrio de Santo Domingo,* Vol. 10 (Buenos Aires, 1956).
>
> ———, *La plaza trágica,* Vol. 17 (Buenos Aires, 1962).
>
> Lanuza, José L., *Pequeña historia de la calle Florida,* Vol. 5 (Buenos Aires, 1947).
>
> Llanes, Ricardo M., *El barrio de Almagro,* Vol. 26 (Buenos Aires, 1968).
>
> ———, *El barrio de Flores,* Vol. 24 (Buenos Aires, 1964).
>
> ———, *El barrio de San Cristóbal,* Vol. 34 (Buenos Aires, 1970).
>
> ———, *Dos notas porteñas: La plaza y la manzana,* Vol. 33 (Buenos Aires, 1969).
>
> Maroni, José J., *El alto de San Pedro; Parroquias de la Concepción y de San Telmo,* Vol. 39 (Buenos Aires, 1971).

————, *Breve historia física de Buenos Aires*, Vol. 29 (Buenos Aires, 1969).

————, *El barrio de Constitución*, Vol. 6 (2d ed.; Buenos Aires, 1969).

Pino, Diego A. del, *La chacarita de los colegiales*, Vol. 38 (Buenos Aires, 1971).

————, *Historia y leyenda del Arroyo Maldonado*, Vol. 37 (Buenos Aires, 1971).

Puccia, Enrique H., *Barracas en la historia y en la tradición*, Vol. 25 (Buenos Aires, 1964).

Romay, Francisco L., *El barrio de Monserrat*, Vol. 19 (2d ed.; Buenos Aires, 1962).

Cánepa, Luis, *El Buenos Aires de antaño* (Buenos Aires, 1936).

Casadevall, Domingo F., *Buenos Aires, arrabal, sainete, tango* (Buenos Aires, 1968).

Escardó, Florencio, *Nueva geografía de Buenos Aires* (Buenos Aires, 1971).

González Arrili, Bernardo, *Buenos Aires, 1900* (Buenos Aires, 1951).

————, *Calle Corrientes entre Esmeralda y Suipacha, comienzos del siglo XX* (Buenos Aires, 1952).

Hardoy, J. Ferrari, and others, "Evolución de Buenos Aires en el tiempo y en el espacio," *Revista de Arquitectura*, Vol. 40 (1955), No. 375, pp. 25–84, and Nos. 376/77, pp. 25–125.

Iñigo Carrera, Héctor, *Belgrano: Pueblo, ciudad, capital y barrio* (Buenos Aires, 1962).

Jalikis, Marino, *Historia de los medios de transporte y de su influencia en el desarrollo urbano de la ciudad de Buenos Aires* (Buenos Aires, 1925).

Kühn, Franz, "Nuevas contribuciones al estudio de la geografía urbana de Buenos Aires," *Ibero-Amerik Rundschau*, I (1935/36), pp. 362–73.

Larroca, Jorge, *San Cristóbal, el barrio olvidado* (Buenos Aires, 1969).

Llanes, Ricardo M., *La avenida de Mayo; media centuria entre recuerdos y evocaciones* (Buenos Aires, 1955).

Martonne, H. de, "Buenos Aires. Étude de géographie urbaine," *Annales de Géographie*, Vol. 44, No. 249 (1935), pp. 281–304.

Pinasco, Eduardo H., *El puerto de Buenos Aires. Contribución al estudio de su historia, 1535–1898* (Buenos Aires, 1942).

Pintos, Juan M., *Así fue Buenos Aires: tipos y costumbres de una época, 1900–1950* (Buenos Aires, 1954).

Romay, Francisco L., *Historia de la policía federal argentina* (5 vols.; Buenos Aires, 1963–66).

Salas, Alberto, *Relación parcial de Buenos Aires* (Buenos Aires, 1965).

Sanguinetti, Manuel J., *San Telmo y su pasado histórico* (Buenos Aires, 1965).

Schiaffino, Eduardo, *Urbanización de Buenos Aires* (Buenos Aires, 1927).

Scobie, James R., "Buenos Aires as a Commercial-Bureaucratic City, 1880–1910: Characteristics of a City's Orientation," *The American Historical Review*, Vol. 77, No. 4 (Oct. 1972), pp. 1035–73.

Sebreli, Juan J., *Buenos Aires. Vida cotidiana y alienación* (Buenos Aires, 1965).

Taullard, Alfredo, *Nuestro antiguo Buenos Aires. Como era y como es desde la época colonial hasta la actualidad* (Buenos Aires, 1927).

————, *Los planos más antiguos de Buenos Aires, 1580–1880* (Buenos Aires, 1940).
Viñas, David, *Del apogeo de la oligarquía a la crisis de la ciudad liberal: Laferrère* (Buenos Aires, 1967).

II. SOURCES UTILIZED

The Notes (pp. 275–301) outline the framework on which this investigation rests. The general reader as well as the specialist, however, may find a brief discussion of the major sources useful, particularly since many of these materials never found their way into a note. As with most historical research, this study is based principally on the writings of contemporary observers and participants: newspapers and journals; almanacs, directories, travelers' accounts, and memoirs; and government publications, especially censuses, congressional debates, periodic ministerial or departmental reports, and municipal records. Photographs, maps, works of literature, and oral reminiscences added illumination to many facets of the city's growth. Because of the volume and quality of this available and largely published material, I have not relied heavily on archives, except for manuscript census returns.

The reading of forty years of *La Prensa* provided a wealth of information on the city, in large measure because that newspaper, from its establishment in 1869, spoke for reform- and civic-minded persons. I also scanned *La Nación*, founded in 1870, as well as other porteño newspapers published during this period, including *El Diario* and *El Nacional*, whenever an issue critical to the city's development came before the public. Journals added specific dimensions to the over-all narrative. Particularly helpful in this investigation were the *Anales de la Sociedad Científica Argentina*, established in 1876; *Boletín del Museo Social Argentino*, started in 1912; the popular satirical magazines, *Caras y Caretas*, from 1898, and *PBT*, from 1904; *Revista de Derecho, Historia y Letras*, from 1898; *Revista de Economía Argentina*, from 1918; and the *Revista Municipal* in two periods, from January 3, 1895, to May 28, 1896, and from January 18, 1904, through 1914.

Contemporary almanacs and city directories as well as accounts by travelers and memoirs provided added perspective. The *Handbook of the River Plate*, first appearing in 1863, was joined by a number of other guides, frequently published yearly: *Gran guía general del comercio de la República Argentina de Francisco Ruíz* (1873), *Gran guía de la ciudad de Buenos Aires de Hugo Kunz y Cía* (1886), *Anuario Kraft* (1885), *Almanaque Peuser* (1888), *Anuario Pillado* (1900), and *The Argentine Year Book* (1902). Publications by travelers to Argentina just before and after the centennial celebrations in 1910 have already been noted (Ch. 2, note 2). Other outstanding observers of the porteño scene include:

Akers, Charles E., *Argentine, Patagonian and Chilian Sketches with a few notes on Uruguay* (London, 1893).

Clark, Edwin, *Visit to South America* (London, 1878).

Clemens, Eliza J. M., *La Plata Countries of South America* (Philadelphia, 1886).

Colombo, Ezio, *La Repubblica Argentina nelle sue fasi storiche e nelle sue attuali condizioni geografiche, statistiche ed economiche* (Milan, 1905).

Daireaux, Émile, *La vie et les moeurs à la Plata* (2 vols.; Paris, 1888).

Dávila, Francisco, *La babel argentina* (Buenos Aires, 1886).

Dias, Arthur, *Do Rio a Buenos - Aires* (Rio de Janeiro, 1901).

Denis, Pierre, *The Argentine Republic, Its Development and Progress* (trans.; New York, 1922).

Dreier, Katherine S., *Five Months in the Argentine from a Woman's Point of View, 1918 to 1919* (New York, 1920).

Elliott, Lilian E., *The Argentina of Today* (London, 1926).

Gómez Carrillo, Enrique, *El encanto de Buenos Aires* (Madrid, 1914).

Graham, Robert B. Cunninghame, *El Río de la Plata* (Buenos Aires, 1938).

Greger, José, *Die Republik Argentinien. Reisehandbuch für Geschäftsleute, Fremde und Auswanderer* (Basel, 1887).

Guilaine, Louis, *La République Argentine, physique et économique* (Paris, 1889).

Hadfield, William, *Brazil and the River Plate in 1868* (London, 1869).

———, *Brazil and the River Plate, 1870–1876* (London, 1877).

Hutchinson, Thomas J., *Buenos Ayres and Argentine Gleanings* (London, 1865).

Koenig, Abraham, *Á través de la República Argentina* (Santiago, 1890).

Malaurie, Clément, *L'émigrant à la Plata* (Paris, 1883).

Martin, Percy F., *Through Five Republics* (London, 1905).

Oliveira Lima, Manuel de, *En la Argentina; impresiones de 1918–1919* (trans., Montevideo, 1920).

Rahola y Tremols, Federico, *Sangre nueva. Impresiones de un viaje a la América del Sud* (Barcelona, 1905).

Rumbold, Horace, *The Great Silver River; Notes of a Residence in Buenos Ayres in 1880 and 1881* (London, 1887).

Salaverría, José M., *Paisajes argentinos* (Barcelona, 1918).

Scardin, Francesco, *Vita italiana nell' Argentina; Impressioni e note* (Buenos Aires, 1899).

Turner, Thomas A., *Argentina and the Argentines; Notes and Impressions of a Five Years' Sojourn in the Argentine Republic, 1885–1890* (New York, 1892).

Memoirs, although almost solely written by members of the upper class, contribute information on society and contemporary attitudes. Significant items for this study include:

Battolla, Octavio, *La sociedad de antaño* (Buenos Aires, 1908).

Bilbao, Manuel, *Tradiciones y recuerdos de Buenos Aires* (Buenos Aires, 1934).

Bioy, Adolfo, *Antes del novecientos: recuerdos* (Buenos Aires, 1958).

Bucich Escobar, Ismael, *Visiones de la gran aldea. Buenos Aires hace sesenta años* (Buenos Aires, 1933).

Bunge, Julio V., *Vida. Época maravillosa, 1903–1911* (Buenos Aires, 1965).

Calzadilla, Santiago, *Las beldades de mi tiempo* (Buenos Aires, 1891).

Carranza, Adolfo P., *Argentinas* (Buenos Aires, 1913).

Carranza, Carlos A., *Recuerdos de infancia* (Buenos Aires, 1947).

Castro, Manuel, *Buenos Aires de antes* (Buenos Aires, 1949).

Ceppi, José (pseud. Aníbal Latino), *Cuadros sudamericanos y europeos* (Buenos Aires, 1888).

D'Amico, Carlos (pseud. Carlos Martínez), *Buenos Aires, sus hombres, su política* (Buenos Aires, 1952).

Delpech, Emilio, *Una vida en la gran Argentina: relatos desde 1869 hasta 1944, anécdotas y finanzas* (Buenos Aires, 1944).

Del Solar, Alberto, *Buenos Aires antiguo y su tradición social* (Buenos Aires, 1916).

Gálvez, Manuel, *La vida múltiple; vida y literatura, 1910–1916* (Buenos Aires, 1916).

Garrigós, Zelmira, *Memorias de mi lejana infancia; el barrio de la Merced en 1880* (Buenos Aires, 1964).

Ibarguren, Carlos, *La historia que he vivido* (Buenos Aires, 1955).

Lastra, Felipe A., *Recuerdos del 900* (Buenos Aires, 1965).

Lusarreta, Pilar de, *Cinco dandys porteños* (Buenos Aires, 1943).

Obligado, Pastor, *Tradiciones argentinas* (Buenos Aires, 1955).

Orgambide, Pedro, *Memorias de un hombre de bien* (Buenos Aires, 1965).

Payró, Roberto J., *Evocaciones de un porteño viejo* (Buenos Aires, 1952).

Piaggo, Juan A., *Tipos y costumbres bonaerenses* (Buenos Aires, 1889).

Quesada, Vicente (pseud. Víctor Gálvez), *Memorias de un viejo* (Buenos Aires, 1889).

Rizzuto, Francisco, *El Buenos Aires que yo ví* (Buenos Aires, 1959).

Saldías, José A., *La inolvidable bohemia porteña. Radiografía ciudadana del primer cuarto de siglo* (Buenos Aires, 1968).

Viale, César, *Cincuenta años atrás* (Buenos Aires, 1950).

Wilde, Eduardo, *Prometeo y Cía* (Buenos Aires, 1899).

Wilde, José A., *Buenos Aires desde setenta años atrás* (Buenos Aires, 1881).

Official sources and publications added substantially to the data collected. The *Actas del Honorable Concejo Deliberante* from 1870 to 1914 and the annual *Memoria de la Municipalidad* from 1872 to 1912 provided the departure point for my investigations. Additional information was gathered from the *Anuario de Estadística de la Ciudad*, from its start in 1891 to 1914; from the *Boletín de Estadística Municipal*, from 1887 to 1894; from the *Registro Estadístico de la Provincia de Buenos Aires*, from 1870 to 1880; and from the *Anuario del Departmento Nacional de Estadística*. (This title has been used since 1893. It was previously known as the *Estadística de la República Argentina; cuadro general del comerico exterior*, from 1870 to 1879, and as the *Estadística del comercio exterior y de la navegación interior y exterior*, from 1880 to 1892.) In addition, I examined the published sessions of the provincial legislature of Buenos Aires from 1868 until federalization in 1880 for discussions of matters relevant to the city's development. Debates in the national Congress from 1880 to 1914 received similar scrutiny. Because of the national government's heavy involvement in labor matters within the Federal District, the *Boletín del Departmento Nacional del Trabajo* from its start in 1907 proved extremely informative.

Three national censuses (1869, 1 vol.; 1895, 3 vols.; and 1914, 10 vols.) and three municipal censuses (1887, 2 vols.; 1904 1 vol.; and 1909, 3 vols.) afforded extensive although often not comparable data. Behind the available and processed information stand manuscript materials for the 1869 and 1895 national censuses from the Archivo General de la Nación. In this study the information from these booklets of individual census takers has been utilized selectively and as illustrative of urban processes rather than in systematic analysis of samples or populations.

Additional perspective has come from the complete and discerning reports of British ministers and consuls resident in Buenos Aires during these years, filed under General Correspondence 6, Volumes 293 (1871) to 492 (1905) in the Foreign Office Records of the British Public Record Office. Similar reports from United States representatives, listed as National Archives, Department of State, United States Ministers in Argentina, Microfilm No. 69, and United States Consuls in Argentina, Microfilm No. 70, also reviewed for this study, yielded no additional significant information.

Analysis and presentation also depend on less specific sources than those discussed above. The past has been recaptured in part by systematic collection of cartographic and photographic materials. In the excellent map files of the Archivo General de la Nación, Museo Mitre, Biblioteca Municipal, Museo de la Ciudad, Dirección de Geodesia de la Provincia de Buenos Aires, and Instituto Geográfico Militar, I found major maps that provided the basis for this book's cartography, including:

Plano catastral por Ing. Pedro Beare, several volumes, 1860–1870.

Plano topográfico de la ciudad incluyendo parte de los partidos de Belgrano, San José de Flores y Barracas al Sur por Antonio E. Malaver, 1867, 1:8,000.

Plano topográfico de la ciudad con la red de tramways por Ernst Nolte, 1882.

Plano catastral de los alrededores de la ciudad por Carlos de Chapeaurouge, 1888.

Ciudad de Buenos Aires por Pablo Ludwig, 1892, 1:35,000.

Plano topográfico de la ciudad por la Oficina de Obras Públicas de la Municipalidad, 1895, 1:20,000.

Plano de la ciudad por el Departamento de Obras Públicas de la Municipalidad, 1907, 1:10,000.

Plano de la ciudad por el Departamento de Obras Públicas, Intendencia del Dr. Arturo Gramajo, 1916, 1:20,000.

In like fashion, the illustrative material in this book has been culled from the important Archivo Gráfico de la Nación, located within the Archivo General de la Nación. This visual impression of the city has been further supplemented by photographs from the Biblioteca Municipal and the Museo de la Ciudad.

Creative literature (novels, essays, short stories, poems, and plays) that deal with the city in its transition from gran aldea to metropolis constitute another important source for ideas and atmosphere. Significant works that have colored my analysis include:

Álvarez, José S. (pseud. Fray Mocho), *Cuadros de la ciudad* (Buenos Aires, 1961).

——, *Memorias de un vigilante* (Buenos Aires, 1920).

Argerich, Antonio, *Inocentes o culpables* (Buenos Aires, 1884).

Arlt, Roberto, *Aguafuertes porteñas* (Buenos Aires, 1933).

——, *El amor brujo* (Buenos Aires, 1933).

——, *El juguete rabioso* (Buenos Aires, 1926).

——, *Los lanzallamas* (Buenos Aires, 1931).

——, *Nuevas aguafuertes porteñas* (Buenos Aires, 1960).

——, *Los siete locos* (Buenos Aires, 1929).

Arredondo, Marcos F., *Croquis bonaerenses* (Buenos Aires, 1897).

Barra, Emma de la (pseud. César Duayen), *Mecha Iturbe* (Buenos Aires, 1906).

——, *Stella* (Buenos Aires, 1905).

Barreda, Ernesto M., *Una mujer* (Buenos Aires, 1924).

——, *La garra de la quimera; tres novelas* (Buenos Aires, 1937).

Blomberg, Héctor P., *Las puertas de Babel* (Buenos Aires, 1920).

——, *Los soñadores del bajo fondo* (Buenos Aires, 1924).

Borges, Jorge L., *Evaristo Carriego* (Buenos Aires, 1955).

——, *Fervor de Buenos Aires* (Buenos Aires, 1923).

Bullrich Palenque, Silvina, *Entre mis veinte y treinta años* (Buenos Aires, 1971).

Bunge, Carlos O., *Los envenenados* (Madrid, 1926).

Cambaceres, Eugenio, *Obras completas* (Santa Fe, Arg., 1956), which includes *Silbidos de un vago, Música sentimental, Sin rumbo,* and *En la sangre.*

Cancela, Arturo, *Tres relatos porteños y tres cuentos de la ciudad* (Buenos Aires, 1944).

Cané, Miguel, *Juvenilia* (Vienna, 1884).

Cantilo, José M., *Los desorbitados* (Buenos Aires, 1916).

Carrizo, César, *El dolor de Buenos Aires* (Buenos Aires, 1920).

Cayol, Roberto, *El debut de la piba y otros sainetes* (Buenos Aires, 1966).

Delfino, Augusto M., *Fin de siglo* (Buenos Aires, 1939).

Domínguez, Silverio (pseud. Ceferino de la Calle), *Palomas y gavilanes* (Buenos Aires, 1886).

Eichelbaum, Samuel, *El gato y su selva. Un guapo del 900. Pájaro de barro. Dos brasas* (Buenos Aires, 1952).

Etchevers, Sara, *El hijo de la ciudad* (Buenos Aires, 1931).

Fernández Moreno, Baldomero, *Buenos Aires: Ciudad, pueblo, campo* (Buenos Aires, 1941).

——, *Ciudad, 1915–1949* (Buenos Aires, 1949).

Fernando, Valentín, *La calle tiene sus hijos* (Buenos Aires, 1947).

Gabriel, José, *La fonda* (Buenos Aires, 1939).

Gálvez, Manuel, *Historia del arrabal* (Buenos Aires, 1922).

——, *El mal metafísico* (Buenos Aires, 1916).

——, *Miércoles santo* (Buenos Aires, 1953).

——, *Nacha Regules* (Buenos Aires, 1919).

Ghiano, Juan C., *Narcisa Garay, mujer para llorar* (Buenos Aires, 1962).

Gilardi, Fernando, *Gramilla* (Buenos Aires, 1941).

——, *La mañana* (Buenos Aires, 1938).

——, *Silvano* (Buenos Aires, 1938).

González Tuñón, Enrique, *La calle de los sueños perdidos* (Buenos Aires, 1941).

——, *A la sombra de los barrios amados* (Buenos Aires, 1957).

Grandmontagne, Francisco, *La maldonada* (Buenos Aires, 1898).

——, *Teodoro Foronda* (2 vols., Buenos Aires, 1896).

Guibert, Fernando, *Poeta al pie de Buenos Aires* (Buenos Aires, 1953).

Kordon, Bernardo, *Cuentos de Bernardo Kordon* (Buenos Aires, 1969).

——, *Un horizonte de cemento* (Buenos Aires, 1963).

————, *La vuelta de Rocha* (Buenos Aires, 1936).

Laferrère, Gregorio de, *Jettatore* (Buenos Aires, 1904).

————, *Las de Barranco* (Buenos Aires, 1908).

Leuman, Carlos A., *Adriana Zumarán* (Buenos Aires, 1922).

Loncán, Enrique, *Aldea millonaria* (Buenos Aires, 1933).

————, *Las charlas de mi amigo* (Buenos Aires, 1921).

————, *Mirador porteño* (Buenos Aires, 1932).

————, *La reconquista de Buenos Aires* (Buenos Aires, 1936).

López, Lucio V., *La gran aldea* (Buenos Aires, 1960).

Mallea, Eduardo, *La ciudad junto al río inmóvil* (Buenos Aires, 1938).

————, *Historia de una pasión argentina* (Buenos Aires, 1944).

————, *La vida blanca* (Buenos Aires, 1960).

Marechal, Leopoldo, *Adán Buenosayres* (Buenos Aires, 1948).

Martínez, Benjamín, *Los chiflados* (Buenos Aires, 1925).

Martínez Cuitiño, Vicente, *Los Colombini* (Buenos Aires, 1912).

————, *El malón blanco* (Buenos Aires, 1912).

Martínez Estrada, Ezequiel, *La cabeza de Goliat* (Buenos Aires, 1947).

Martínez Zuviría, Gustavo (pseud. Hugo Wast), *Ciudad turbulenta, ciudad alegre* (Buenos Aires, 1919).

Miró, José (pseud. Julián Martel), *La Bolsa* (Buenos Aires, 1891).

Nalé Roxlo, Conrado (pseud. Chamico), *La medicina vista de reojo* (Buenos Aires, 1952).

Noel, Martín A., *Andanza porteña de Simón Badajo* (Buenos Aires, 1947).

Novión, Alberto, *La cantina* (Buenos Aires, 1907).

————, *Los equilibristas* (Buenos Aires, 1912).

Ocantos, Carlos M., *León Zaldívar* (Buenos Aires, 1888).

————, *Quilito* (Buenos Aires, 1891).

Olivari, Nicolás, *Mi Buenos Aires querido* (Buenos Aires, 1966).

Pacheco, Carlos M., *Los disfrazados* (Buenos Aires, 1906).

Palazzo, Juan, *La casa por dentro* (Buenos Aires, 1921).

Pascarella, Luis, *El conventillo* (Buenos Aires, 1918).

Podestá, Manuel T., *Irresponsables* (Buenos Aires, 1889).

Rojas, Ricardo, *Cosmópolis* (Buenos Aires, 1908).

Rojas Paz, Pablo, *Biografía de Buenos Aires* (Buenos Aires, 1943).

Saavedra, Osvaldo (pseud. Barón de Arriba), *Risa amarga* (Buenos Aires, 1896).

Sábato, Ernesto, *Sobre héroes y tumbas* (Buenos Aires, 1961).

Sánchez, Florencio, *Canillita. Los muertos, Nuestros hijos* (Buenos Aires, 1966).

————, *El conventillo* (Buenos Aires, 1906).

————, *El desalojo* (Buenos Aires, 1906).

————, *Moneda falsa* (Buenos Aires, 1907).

————, *Teatro completo* (Buenos Aires, 1952).

Scalabrini Ortiz, Raúl, *El hombre que está solo y espera* (Buenos Aires, 1951).

————, *La manga* (Buenos Aires, 1923).

Sicardi, Francisco, *Libro extraño* (2 vols.; Barcelona, 1910).

Soria, Ezequiel, *La bestia* (Buenos Aires, 1902).

——, *Justicia criolla* (Buenos Aires, 1897).

——, *Política casera. El deber* (Buenos Aires, 1965).

Trejo, Nemesio, *Los políticos* (Buenos Aires, 1897).

——, *Los inquilinos* (Buenos Aires, 1907).

Vacarezza, Alberto, *El conventillo de La Paloma* (Buenos Aires, 1929).

——, *Tu cuna fue un conventillo* (Buenos Aires, 1920).

Verbitsky, Bernardo, *Café de los angelitos* (Buenos Aires, 1949).

——, *Calles de tango* (Buenos Aires, 1953).

——, *Es difícil empezar a vivir* (Buenos Aires, 1941).

——, *La esquina* (Buenos Aires, 1953).

Viñas, David, *Los años despiadados* (Buenos Aires, 1956).

——, *Cayó sobre su rostro* (Buenos Aires, 1955).

——, *Los dueños de la tierra* (Buenos Aires, 1959).

Finally, a most significant influence and a principal source of inspiration and information for this work have come from the extended periods of residence in Buenos Aires that I have enjoyed since 1949, each in a different zone of the city. Combined with that physical contact with the present-day city have been the untold insights afforded me by many porteños over the years, sometimes directed specifically to their reminiscences of earlier years, but most often contributed by the expression of their own attitudes and values. To those friends I owe ideas and interpretations that cannot be fully acknowledged.

Index

accidents: railroad, 102, 281n61; compensation for, 146, 283n53; streetcar, 175

agriculture, 8, 10; basis of Argentine economy, 11, 244, 245, 254

almacén (grocery store), 204, 206; Illus. 42

Alvear, Torcuato de, 60, 109–11, 154, 195, 282n72

amusements, 27, 48–49, 207. *See also* Carnival; *fútbol;* horse racing; theaters.

architecture, 284n14; Italian and French influence, 62–63, 121, 127, 129–32; ostentation, 130–32, 134, 232–34; patio-style, 44–45, 46–47, 62, 148–49; Illus. 11, 25, 26, 27, 28, 32. *See also* chalet; *conventillo;* housing; *palacio; quinta.*

arrabales (outlying districts), 229

Avellaneda, Nicolás, 106, 108, 111, 161

Avellaneda (city, formerly Barracas al Sud), 16; port facilities, 77, 85–86; Map 1

Avenida Alvear (street, renamed Libertador General San Martín), 103, 110, 132, 172; Illus. 7; Map 2

Avenida de Mayo (street), 34, 120, 140, 145, 157, 174; construction of, 111–13; demonstrations on, 140, 144, 157, 282n77; Illus. 8, 47, 49; Map 1

Bahía Blanca (city), 70, 96, 99, 256; Map 7

Bajo de Belgrano (district), 30, 180, 182; Map 2

banks and financial institutions, 62, 115–16, 118; financed worker housing, 189–90; mortgages, 182, 186, 188; Map 5. *See also* Baring Brothers; building and loan companies; credit.

Baring Brothers, 75, 80, 82

Barracas (suburb), 19, 51, 89, 157, 163, 165, 207; industry, 16–17, 180, 199; port facilities, 67–68, 73; railroad, 40, 92; Illus. 5, 13; Maps 1, 2

Barracas al Sud. *See* Avellaneda.